PATTERNS OF SEX
The Mating Urge and our Sexual Future

PATTERNS OF SEX

The Mating Urge and our Sexual Future

BRIAN J. FORD

ST. MARTIN'S PRESS
NEW YORK

Library of Congress Cataloging in Publication Data

Ford, Brian John.
  Patterns of sex.

  Bibliography: p.
  1.   Sex.   I.   Title.
HQ12.F66   301.41   79-5329
ISBN 0-312-59811-4

LIST OF CONTENTS

PATTERNS OF SEX
The Mating Urge and our Sexual Future

INTRODUCTION

We have lived through the greatest sexual revolution in history, yet it is one which has largely failed. For – although there is an unprecedented frankness about sex, and the topic is daily aired in all the media almost to the point of boredom – there is more evidence of discontent and sexual dissatisfaction than ever before. The swinging age of sexual liberation has become the era of the sexual hang-up.

Yet in spite of the manifest failure of the liberalization movement, it is showing few signs of slowing down. I have before me, as I write, two new proposals which typify what is happening: one is an official report calling for sex education classes for eight-year-olds, the other is the appointment of a committee to report on sexism in infants' school books, so that any 'sexist' references can be extirpated as a matter of urgency.

What such activities fail to disclose is that sex remains an unfathomable mystery for sociologists as much as for the detached realities of biological theory; and instead of the open and easy-going society we ought to have created we find ourselves in the middle of uncertainty and confusion.

The aim of this book is to act as a discussion document, and it analyzes sexual behaviour in a way that produces some unexpected conclusions – some of which will turn established orthodoxy on its head.

For example, I do not believe, as do some commentators, that sex education in our schools is going to produce a generation of sex-crazed, free-loving teenagers; in my view the trend will dampen down sexuality and impede the development of sexual freedom – to a great extent it is already doing so for the young of today. What I seek is a true broadening of sexual understanding in its emotional context, and a potentiation of mankind's sexual energies.

It is an old myth that the purpose of sex is to procreate. That is certainly the result of a minority of sexual encounters, but is far from being the 'purpose' experienced at a personal level. No, the purpose of sex is to enjoy oneself or to express a relationship, homosexual or heterosexual, in tactile, bodily terms. It is a matter of sensual communication and sexual

7

satisfaction. The old argument about the anatomical site of the orgasm in women is in this light pointless: orgasms are neither centred on the clitoris, nor on the vagina, but in the brain. If we understood the importance of the cerebral orgasm, and tried to recognize our desire for sexuality without any suggestion of a desire to reproduce ourselves, then we could aspire to a new level of sexuality that surpasses the remote, animal orthodoxy of the teachers who proclaim that sex is intercourse, and only that.

The number of youngsters in the early teens who want to be taught about copulation is tiny, compared with those who seek an explanation of emotions so powerful they can leave the victim breathless. It is the emotional turmoil of sexual relationships that provoke day-to-day problems, not the bare facts of intercourse.

Today's widespread 'do you or don't you?' approach short-circuits man's overwhelming desire for courtship and is stultifying our sexuality in consequence. And it is not only our attitudes towards the sex act that are misplaced: the idea that we have to defeat sexism is equally erroneous. Images of boys and girls in children's books emphasize real sex differences more often than they distort them. The much-attacked gender differentiation we see in our societies is actually a mainstay of civilization and a necessary consequence of the constraints exerted by our evolution. There are clear factors which really do make men the more aggressive sex, for instance; and one can even interpret the upheavals of adolescence in similar chemical terms rather than always resorting to high-flown psychological explanations.

In some cases the sexual liberation movement has had clear political purposes and an economic motive: thus it is far more acceptable to describe the need of women to work as 'the freedom to carry on their own careers' rather than expressing it in more truthful terms, such as 'women being driven out to the monotony of work because of rising prices'.

I find it distasteful that so much of the women's movement has been directed to making women more like men, rather than vice versa. The moves in fashion, even nomenclature ('Ms', for instance) have been making the women copy the men. One campaigner in the United States (no doubt carried along by the momentum of the trend away from natural breast-feeding) has even proposed that in future women's breasts should be amputated to make it easier for them to run! This does not point towards a freer and liberated society at all, but towards a de-sexed future.

One important aspect I have to consider is the concept of sexual normality. No-one is going to draw hard and fast lines, though it is clear that heterosexual lovemaking is on the 'normal' side of the line, whereas lust murder is not. But by mirroring human sexuality in the lives of other species, and by linking our sexual development to the demands of evolution, we can begin to make some sense of mankind's many deviations, from sadism to displays such as flashing in the park.

In this context, the questions that arise are fascinating. How often does a sexual sadist become the office tyrant, genuinely persecuting unhappy underlings for the sake of the pleasure it gives? How do sexual factors influence the timing of examinations so that a student gets the best results? We will examine Britain's widely documented case of 'virgin birth' and its surprising conclusion; sex change and what it means; the reported pregnancy in a boy; and the use of transvestites in espionage. Yet I am not merely going to reiterate the view so often vulgarized as 'man's behaviour is controlled by his sex life'. My view is that the converse is often the case: that our sex life is regulated by codes of behaviour laid down at genetic level, and which exert sanctions against us if we do not act in accordance with our evolutionary destiny. These broad-based strictures I call biological imperatives, and I think that homosexuality may be one example of this idea in operation. Our lowered sexuality and the falling birth-rates, mirrored in a growing tendency to see child-rearing as a 'burden', may be a similar imperative exerted to limit our rates of reproduction in an age when our behaviour is conflicting with what nature expects of us. No-one doubts that one essential function of sexual reproduction is the passing on of selected items of genetic information from one generation to the next. However, I wish to introduce a parallel notion that explains how we inherit behaviour. Part of this is teaching by older people of the young (an activity which I am sure the menopause, by lifting the reproductive burden from the fittest and longer-living female members of society, was meant to facilitate) and it is certain that many traditions – like the ritual driving to an out-of-town hilltop on Whit Sunday, for instance – are an example of behaviour that dates back centuries or even thousands of years. The way we shake hands, decorate our homes for festivals, and so on, are all examples of what you could call cognitive archaeology and that in itself would be a rewarding study.

But quite apart from this, astonishing as it seems, I propose that there must be innate mechanisms at work that select and pass on from one generation to the next behavioural norms that are compatible with continued evolutionary progress and with the maintenance of viable communities. I am increasingly sure that a vast and unrecognized range of codes of criteria is programmed into us at some sort of genetic level, which allows us to respond and to behave in a manner that equips us for our civilized life. A new-born baby is equipped with just such a code that enables it to recognize a nipple and to respond by sucking so that it can be nourished from the start. It is often assumed that this is as far as our innate instincts go, and that all the rest is taught.

The error in this line of argument in my view is this: the response to the nipple was inborn right enough, but the nipple itself had to be learned.

Babies that get used to a rubber teat, for instance, may take a long time to become accustomed to a nipple – the child's criteria have been trained to identify the artificial substitute.

Young animals can become imprinted with unexpected objects instead of with their mothers (the way that Lorenz was followed round by such 'imprinted' geese is one example of that) and here, too, we see an inborn code of criteria being applied to the recognition of the wrong object – ie, the codes are intact, but the learning opportunity is misdirected.

What I propose is that parallel opportunities exist in our own species. Thus there is an age at which a person is going to learn sexual rightness and wrongness, and if we supply the wrong impulse to the learning process we can misdirect the innate criteria until an undesirable factor becomes identified as wholly acceptable from that moment on. We can experience the tug of this innateness in our instinctive liking for stimuli that accord with sexuality: there is an inbuilt code of criteria which directs our learning in ways we do not consciously appreciate but which accord with our evolutionary past. This is how sexual symbolism originates; the way that a hot-dog sausage slides into its roll is comforting and mildly pleasurable, as is the 'ejaculation' of sauce into it afterwards. At the seaside you can buy elephant cakes, made to look like an elephant in bed with its trunk and ears expressively moulded in marzipan almond paste. A second glance reveals that the object is in fact a set of male genitals; the trunk is a penis, the ears are testicles (and indeed the whole thing is always fashioned in that most un-elephantine colour, flesh pink). Similarly, the throbbing pulsation of pop music mimics the frequency of pumping pelvic thrusts in copulation, and is no sort of incitement to lewdness but is more like the tuning of our subconscious to something which those inborn codes of criteria make it necessary for us to recognize.

It is well known that the development of an individual repeats, more or less, its entire evolutionary history. Thus the human embryo goes through a stage where it has gill slits, like our fish ancestors, and a tail; shortly before birth we were – like our ape-like antecedents – covered with fur. This principle (usually taught as 'ontogeny recapitulates phylogeny': the development of an individual mirrors that of the race) helps make sense of anatomy. The eustachian tube that joins the throat to the ear, for instance, is a vestigial gill-silt; the coccyx at the base of the spine is the remains of our tail.

What I now wish to suggest is that something similar takes place as our behaviour develops. If I am right, and codes of criteria do exist with us in an encoded form that we learn to exploit as we mature, then these may appear in a pre-programmed sequence too. This thesis would explain that a child at the age of asking 'why?' a thousand times a day is passing through the phase in which he has to acquire a vocabulary of causality. If the answers are not supplied, then it may be that part of the intellectual capacity concerned with cause-and-effect is not allowed its full rein and never quite makes up the deficiency.

If the mental unravelling of childhood does somehow repeat the intellectual development of our species in unrecorded times past, the building of dens in childhood could easily be explained and so could other games, like hide-and-seek (foraging and trapping) and even making models.

In a similar way, it may well be that the learning of gender roles in childhood, through playing mothers and fathers to cite one instance, is necessary if a fully expressed adulthood is to follow. Skills of inter- and intra-sexual communication have to be learned and if they are not then some kind of stunting must surely result. The fact that we are surrounded by such overwhelming obstacles to conversation, openness and direct relationships with each other at a time when we are surrounded by media of communication as never before (in contradistinction to the patterns of communal relationships which often pertain in societal systems we in the West would regard as 'primitive') shows to my mind how easily we neglect up-bringing, and fail to instil comradeship and human feelings into our children.

Our past is so clearly mirrored in our present development that we must try to ensure that our future life-styles are compatible with the dictates of that evolutionary legacy. We cannot merely launch a trendy campaign against, say, breast-feeding without considering whether the change would prove harmful to our species in the long term. Put at its simplest, if we evolved for a certain way of life in the past (and have therefore been selected because of those constraints) we cannot hope to adapt easily into something totally alien, without some far-reaching consequences.

Exactly what these results might be I have touched on in the past (for instance, the effect of too profoundly altering our dietary intake from the kind of food we evolved with) but it now seems clear that there may be more fundamental controls at work, through the imposition of biological imperatives. There are at the moment some indications that there may be an increase in reports of effeminacy in men, and of hirsute masculinization in women, who are being subjected to the wholly unnatural pressures of sexual equality groups.

What I would like to do is, firstly, recognize as unhealthy our obsession with the orgasm and the teaching to the very young of the isolated mechanisms of copulation, and replace that with a new and relevant appreciation of sensuality and the pair-bonding instinct. Secondly we have to dispel the sexual myth we have elaborated (the doctrine of the gasping virgin and the endless one-night-stand) which means that everyone with a normal and fulfilling sex life – since they are not getting the same as the hero in the sex film on TV – is still encouraged to feel frustrated or a mite envious. And third on my list is the matching up of our present and future with the constraints of our past, since nature will undoubtedly weigh in against our profligacy if we do not. Standards of child up-bringing need re-thinking, for a start.

Finally, we must stand back from the argument about nature and nurture and grasp the importance of our inbuilt codes of criteria that our development must set out to satisfy. It is a return to relevance and realism I am after, not a new age of chastity as some have dubbed it, but an era of openness and honesty: one which will make the idiocies of trans-sexual women's fashions and the gross arbitrariness of the male chauvinist's unthinking arrogance seem self-evidently ludicrous, and which will transform the power of passion and the loving pair-bond drive into objects of sane and serious scientific study. People often pretend it doesn't exist; yet they still die from it, cross continents because of it, and starve for it.

In my view it is not primarily important to argue whether nature or nurture come out at the top of the list. What matters is human care, and scientific objectivity; and what must concern us tomorrow is the nurture of nature.

CHAPTER ONE

A PURPOSE FOR SEX?

Little wonder that the well-loved British broadcaster Jack de Manio said recently, in a celebrated *faux pas*, 'now the Professor has succeeded in perfecting a new type of microscopic orgasm . . . I'm sorry, I think that should have been organism.' Sex is on everyone's mind these days; how we teach it, how we do it, and whether we are getting enough. A lot of people were said to have been shocked by de Manio's little slip of the tongue, but it is one any of us could have made.

Yes, sex is with us right enough. It is what life is all about, what keeps the world spinning, what everyone gets up to when they think nobody's looking, from the birds and the bees, to people, pets and protozoa. And it comes as no surprise to anyone that a male and a female cell uniting in some mysterious time-honoured fashion is at the centre of it all. It certainly comes as no surprise to our children, either, who get this message unsubtly hammered into them from the age of eight or nine.

Tumescent and rigid phalluses being 'inserted' into moist and receptive vaginas are a familiar sight to any child, straight out of the coloured diagrams in those sex-education films; sperms are as commonplace as tadpoles, and egg-cells from film-strips as familiar as hen's eggs from the store.

What we skate round, in a manner as marked for its coyness as our emphasis on the clinical details of copulation is famed for its overtness, is that the greatest mystery of sex still remains – and that is, why it should exist at all. I am not suggesting we should be in the least surprised by the business with those sex cells, for that is self-evident. It provides an opportunity for the genetic material of any species to be re-shuffled once a generation, and that is all good for evolutionary progress, giving new combinations of genes a whirl.

But if that was all sexual activity entailed, if it was simply a matter of sperm-meets-ovum, then it would be the simplest matter in the world to arrange things so that each species featured automatic gamete transfer as easily as the way people shake hands and as uncomplicated as the manner in which pollen from a grass flower blows free in the wind to find, by accident or chance, its sexual partner and mate. All that would happen in human society is that sperm would be caught, like a germ. They would spread in the manner of an infection and simply implant those re-sorted genes in the right place by simple, predestined, mechanical means.

In fact, of course, no matter what teenaged mothers-to-be have tried to impress upon their parents over the years, pregnancy does not get 'caught' on a lavatory seat, or passed by chance through some juxtaposition of jostling bodies on a crowded dance-floor. Before a man can pass over one of those sperm cells he has to undergo nothing so simple as a casual donation of one cell to another individual. The transfer of that ultimate in microdots, a sperm cell, takes place at the end of a lengthy and detailed series of predestined actions that operate at cognitive, conceptual, instinctive and psychological levels and even in its most simplified and rudimentary form, human sexuality involves the development of motivation through a lengthy and complex process: the positioning, the looks and gestures, the movements and responses; all these are necessary before orgasm occurs. It is all a far cry from the insertion of turgid penises and the depositing of seminal fluid, like squirting jam in a doughnut. Even that outline applies only to a situation where we are assuming there to be a desire for what you might call 'instant consummation'; in the ordinary way, the sex act rarely occurs under such circumstances. It is predicated instead upon endless complex factors involving personality, mood and the environment. The senses of aesthetics from the visual to the olfactory receive coordinated stimulation of the right kind and at the right time in a carefully choreographed sequence that culminates in the heady sweetness of physical union.

The essence of courtship is delay – titillation. It revolves around the ability of two people to successively show want and wantonness, with reservation and romantic coyness, a many-layered sensuous confection that applies as much to homosexual gratification as to heterosexual intercourse, so deeply rooted is it in the subconscious of our kind.

You may incline to the view that this comes from being human, and is an expression of togetherness at a civilized, conscious level – a manifestation of mankind's ability to relate. A moment's reflection demonstrates the loopholes in that idea. The animal world is replete with familiar examples of courtship rituals that are as elaborate and as far-fetched as human sexual relationships, and which can involve just as much adornment, sexual foreplay, courtesy and present-giving as any of us might aspire to. Courtship is an essential part of animal mating, and the gender identity it establishes is as deep-rooted in man as it is in any other species.

Our own refinement of sex pairing is important at a cultural level in societies the world over, and the strictures imposed by sexual conduct and its refinement into codes of criteria that dictate social behaviour and protocol have had a profound effect on the evolution of civilization and, what is more, they exert a powerful personal control on many of our individually-experienced needs, desires and means of fulfillment.

Mankind, through an understanding of this sexual potential, exploits a leaning towards erotic or pornographic display, and commercial exploitation of items from cosmetics, clothes and deodorants to tastefully decorated boxes of confectionary shows how well we use sexual pleasure and its anticipation as an important means of occupying our time and our fantasies, and in directing our leisure activities.

The foreplay that leads up to courtship and the possibility of intercourse is an important means of occupying time and establishing our identity in civilized societies – take away this sexual emphasis and there is little left to do but watch television (and even then the number of programmes would be vanishingly small if sexual motivation were to be eliminated altogether.)

Even if sexual pleasure in its broadest sense *serves* to heighten our senses and to occupy our time, that cannot be the *reason* for it all. We may agree on these obvious roles for sexual activity in the intricacies of societal conventions in human society, but how do we then explain the place of courtship in the lives of lower animals? Here we run into a brick wall across the earlier line of discussion. Is a flatworm, which is ordinarily content to glide about its pond-world, grubbing out fragments of food, looking for spiritual or sensual fulfillment when it becomes romantic towards its partner, and enters a mating phase? Is a bird which expends huge amounts of time and energy displaying, strutting about in a provocative fashion, asserting its rights and its gender individuality, simply looking for a means of acquiring higher levels of intellectual or physical development?

The anthropomorphic explanations we can put forward for the social uses of sexuality do not apply so convincingly to lowly creatures who do not, as it were, feel the pressure of time on their hands. A flatworm would do better for itself by devoting all its time to food-gathering, rather than wasting precious time in the rituals of conjugation – it is certainly not looking for something to fill the day.

The essential biological purpose of courtship is to identify a mate. Once identified, the mate has to be tested and approved, so that the breeding cycle will stand a better chance of success. More important, the courtship selects a series of propensities that define the mate's ability to perform sex-dependent tasks that identify the individual as a capable parent. There are innumerable examples in the animal world of procedures that ensure well-matched pairing or which eliminate unsuccessful individuals from the race. This has no short-term 'antisocial' purpose, of course; there is no chauvinism here. What is happening is that the good of the germ line is being protected: the passing of sound genetic information from one generation to the next, for the benefit of the species rather than the individual, is ensured.

The genetic material is not only manifest in terms of inborn physical characteristics, either; it also emerges in a strictly behavioural sense. Many species possess what we call innate behaviour patterns; an unsatisfactory term in that no-one is quite certain what 'innate' really means. I do not believe that the behaviour itself is actually coded for, so much as a series of selection mechanisms or criteria that fit a species to recognize propitious behaviour and select it from a given range of options.

We have heard much in recent years of the forms of sexist teaching and indoctrination that are imposed on young people . The argument has been that the bias in this orthodoxy has encouraged us to consciously teach girls to have specific skills (such as playing with dolls) and to teach boys quite different ones (like building models). Now, if we are talking about the way in which we tend to instruct young girls in such a way as to incline them away from, say, careers in science or politics, or which could stunt the development of their personal integrity or their confidence, then I will applaud, support, and give every encouragement to any movement which aims to remove such discrimination.

But – and this is the central question – if we are going to argue that the play patterns that fit girls for motherhood are to be extirpated, or that boys should be diverted away from playing boisterous games that emphasize evolutionary purposes of 'manliness', then I am going to refute it. It is perfectly true that much of our upbringing is 'sexist', in that it emphasizes gender roles and sexual identity. And often we do consciously set children up for sexually determined role-fulfillment in society. But – though there may be some aspects which in the future civilization might well abandon, and recognize as artificial and harmful – there are others that are as essential a part of upbringing and development as being taught to feed, walk, or communicate. And if by accident we extirpate those too, in a wave of fashionable band-waggonry, then we will simply produce a generation of deficient and half-formed people who have been deprived of a part of their experiential diet, and will grow up as mentally undernourished and stunted as any victim of scurvy, rickets or beri-beri.

The prolonged courtship rituals throughout the animal kingdom have a fundamental role to play in evolution. This is really what sex is *for*, and it does not cease to astonish me that we study the fact so little, and – even more – that we don't do more to explain it to children. Sex education in schools and on TV says little about sex that matters. It emphasizes such topics as the structure of the fallopian tubes, the microscopical appearance of sperm, and the way that the tip of the penis nestles beneath the cervix of the womb; topics distinguished by their total and bewildering irrelevance to any child of nine or ten.

But what does it say about love, affection, courtship, bond formation, lust, desire or passion – the topics about which everyone facing their teens needs a little advance information? Almost nothing. The stereotyped cardboard phalluses, inserted into those unresponsive artwork vaginas of the film strip, have no relevance at all to unravelling the emotional tangles of teenage.

Many people suffer a peculiar kind of sickness which impels them to display images of sex organs to others, and when it takes the form of crusty precentors showing to choirboys what they've got in their trousers, or lonely men drawing lurid and unlifelike genitals on the walls of down-town lavatories, we recognize it immediately as a psychological disorder. How odd it is, then, that we mistake the same activity exactly as educational and wholesome, when the medium is a sixteen millimetre sound film and the perpetrator of the exhibitionistic act a 'qualified' educator.

The televised images say so little to give children useful insight. It would be good to do some original research into the actual results, for the occasions when I have talked about sex education to young children have not filled me with any confidence that the message gets across. Many children, after a sex education film, go out into the playground arguing about how much of it was actually true. Those that do take the message to heart seem to acquire a delightfully simplistic notion of what sex is all about, like the boy who said that his friends were all invited to watch him and his girlfriend stuff his largely unresponsive penis into her genitals as far as it would go – 'that's what love really *is*,' he told them all. One teacher I know was deterred from the whole business at the first attempt. She had just explained to her class that the sperm is to small to be seen with the naked eye, when one of the girls in the class raised her hand, 'It's not true that you can't see the sperm,' she told the startled gathering, 'because my boyfriend done his down the front of my skirt and I could see that okay!'

The sensations of sexuality that most children find through manual exploration and masturbation are regularly confused by them with something else, whether it is a strange but fascinating pain, a religious seizure, or a form of punishment for self-abuse. 'Orgasm is like a kind of big sneeze,' says one instruction manual. Like thunder is a kind of loud 'pop' or an earthquake is like exaggerated hiccups, I suppose.

The sex that people do experience, and which few bother to explain, to analyse, to discuss or even to anticipate, is the sense of drive and attraction. This introduces what is to me the most intriguing biological lesson of sex. Many creatures that you would rightly think of as 'lowly' – like slugs and snails – engage in prolonged pairing, dancing, caressing and a complex ritual of physical union that looks every bit as 'loving', for a snail, as sexual union appears to be for humans.

Even at the single-celled level, when we are faced with microbes swimming together, rolling around to 'face' each other, and undergoing a delicately coordinated form of physical fusion, we see a form of copulation (Latin *copulare* – fasten together). At first sight there is nothing remarkable about that, except for one thing – what is the motivation that impels them towards the sexual act? These are uncomplicated forms of life that you would not expect to have much in the way of perception. This is particularly true of the single-celled protozoa, since they cannot – by definition – possess a brain. Brains are networks of cells, and an organism that is only one cell itself cannot be said to have a brain at all.

Yet even at this level of organization, the animals can recognize each other, move towards each other, orientate themselves in exactly the right position, undergo cellular fusion (the process is usually called *conjugation*) and have sex with each other. What does this indicate? That even if they have no brain, they still have innate codes of criteria that enable them to undertake tasks of recognition, acceptance and response in a manner which imitates perception and intelligence. It is a startling idea, but a very important one.

Here we have, at the beginning of life's journey towards sophistication, evidence that microbes themselves can undertake perception and participation – they can choose to have sex (since they are not inclined to attempt it with the wrong partner) and they must have, therefore, a sexual drive.

Consider what this means. That term, sex drive, to a human involves a whole range of activities operating at a conscious and subconscious level, some deliberate (like 'playing hard to get' as an aphrodisiac) and others – most – accidental (like falling in love with the last person you'd expect to). It involves dress, make-up, and even a special way of talking. It is all sophisticated stuff, this; part and parcel of being such a highly-evolved and all-wise species. Or so we like to think . . .

What balderdash! Worms, slugs, snails, even protozoa and, yes, right down to the bacteria . . . they all have sex too, they elect to do it, they usually choose the time to do it, they develop 'penis'-like organs and organelles to do it with, and clearly they are driven to do it by a sex drive or the phenomenon would never happen at all.

We like to imagine that our brain cells send simple signals to each other like the 'on-off' or 'go or no-go' components of a computer – either an impulse *is* sent, or it isn't. Yet here we have single-celled animals undertaking recognition and manoeuvring procedures in the space of a single cell, and experiencing sex drive in addition to it all. The truth of the matter is that none of our orthodoxies matches the complexity of these systems. We are ignorant of so much in this field that our depth of understanding is derisory. And if we know so little about microbes that we have not even tumbled to the conclusion that they have sexual impulses analagous to our own, little wonder we have grasped such a minute part of our own sexuality, and come to grips with it.

SEX IN THE MICROBE WORLD

It is somewhat surprising to discover that sexual reproduction occurs at all in something as diminutive as a single-celled microbe. Yet even bacteria, most minute of all the groups of microbe life, indulge in sexual union of a kind that anyone of us would at once recognize. The process is not merely some mechanical means of exchanging chromosomes that you would not take for sex at all, unless told; the two cells come to lie close together, the 'male' cell puts out a fine, tube-like projection towards the 'female', and passes to her a vital consignment of genetic material.

This type of conjugation has obvious parallels with sex in humans: it performs a similar function in genetic terms, and it even looks much the same as those diagrams of copulating people that litter the sex-education tracts. The phenomenon was first observed in that laboratory bacterium which everyone in bacteriology studies at one time or another, the geneticist's favourite experimental subject, *E. coli* – the organism that lives harmlessly enough in our intestines. In 1946 it was realized that some genetic characteristics could clearly be passed from one strain of the bacteria to the others, and it later transpired that physical union of the cells occurred during the exchange.

Later on, the high magnifications of the electron microscope were used to obtain pictures of the bacteria in conjugation, and the astonishing fact emerged that even at this level of minuteness, a kind of 'penis' was specifically extended to bring the cells into union. This protrusion became known as a *fimbria* or *sex pilus*. Small and delicate protrusions from the cells of *E. coli* often occur without any sexual purpose being behind it, but the sex pili have a recognizably distinct structure, with a rounded projection at the far end not unlike the glans on the end of a mammalian penis. The analogy is not a good one, since the structure is there to help the penetration of the 'female' cell wall but in many ways the human penis and the sex pilus of *E. coli* have much in common.

It is here that we meet the first instance of sex drive. It is not quite the same phenomenon that makes a man into a lustful lover, maybe, but it is similar. It is tempting to say that the cells fuse by accident, that they just 'fit together' by chance, and that the conjugation is no more 'driven' than a strip of tape sticking to a parcel, or a nail hanging onto a magnet. But that is the point – the cells unite only with each other, and only when the time is in some way ripe for conjugation to take place. These cells have the ability to recognize each other and to conjugate. Without some innate 'drive' they would simply not do it.

The existence of the drive becomes even more apparent when we look at the protozoa, the single-celled animals that are so common in fresh-water and so familiar to students of biology. Many of them, to quote the literature, 'apply themselves' to each other in 'congress'. Some of the ciliates (the protozoa which swim by means of fine, beating hair-like structures) fuse together in pairs and undergo conjugation. Even at school, we learn how they swim alongside each other, turning so that their oral grooves are facing each other (the oral groove is the 'mouth' of the cell), and then come closer and fuse. The cell membrane dissolves away at the site of contact so that the contents of the two cells can come into intimate contact, and they can then exchange genetic material. That is very good as far as it goes, but look at all the questions that such an explanation leaves unasked. The cells swim alongside each other. Why? What drives them to leave the purposeful grazing they normally carry out so that they begin instead to swim in formation? How do they detect the presence of each other at a distance, and make the distinction between a wanted and an unwanted partner? What navigational aids do they employ to keep station? And all this business of fusion and uniting of their cell contents . . . The areas of ignorance in this field are vast and impenetrable. These ciliates are performing tasks that we can understand well enough as human behaviour, if we put anthropomorphic interpretations on the microbes' instincts, but how can they use innate codes of criteria to make such complex decisions – and they are decisions and actions that no computer could go one-millionth of the way towards imitating – when they are nothing more than a single-celled species?

The task of perception is a big enough puzzle for us to grapple with when we begin to come to terms with these organisms, and it is a marvellously complex system which our routine explanations over-simplify to an absurd extent. We have a well-developed faculty, we people, for outlining systems of behaviour and imagining that we have explained them in the process. It is only when you begin to ask questions about each phase of the system that the flimsy and superficial level of our understanding becomes apparent, and there can be no better example than the way we explain away conjugation in the protozoa. *How* they approach each other; *how* do they swim facing each other; *how* do they conjugate . . .? The answer is that we have virtually no idea whatever.

But it is clear, by definition, that if the organisms do carry out sex then they must have a drive that impels them to do it.

One of the most interesting examples of sexual congress in these single celled organisms is the process known as syngamy [Greek *sun* (= syn), together; and *gameté*, wife; *gametés*, husband] – that is, the actual fusing of two sex cells. Many single-celled organisms undergo complete sexual union; the two cells, male and female, meet, join, and become one. After the genetic reshuffling that the process was developed for, the newly formed cell, or zygote [Greek *zugoó*, yoke *(zygon)*] acts as a new, single cell and begins to divide anew. Does that outline have a turgid, scientific sound to it, reminiscent of schoolbooks and educational TV? If so you must allow me to apologize. But this is not as remote a process as it may seem.

Picture a minute male-strain cell swimming along, propelled by a whip-like flagellum which thrusts it through the water at a speed that would shame any human swimmer. It is hunting for its mate. When it finds her it heads straight towards her – and she is a larger rounded cell, dwarfing the minuscule, pearshaped male partner; rich with nutriment which will nourish the daughter-cells which will soon appear, she lies glistening, unmoving. Not just one male cell is heading towards her, either; a massive wriggling community of male cells is swimming desperately in her direction, knowing exactly where they are supposed to be going. Amongst them all is her destined mate.

The cells that arrive first find their way barred by a group of protective cells that cluster round the female; bit by bit they erode this layer, struggling to get through, until eventually one single male cell manages it – he penetrates the outer cell wall of the female which in an instant closes, hardens, and prevents any others from getting in. The nuclei of the two cells join into one, and the new zygote begins to divide.

In general terms that could apply to a host of microbes, but this isn't in fact a description of anything more unfamiliar than – you. Microbes discovered, if that's the word, how to undertake sexual fusion, and the pattern has continued right up to mankind. Our own sexuality is designed to do nothing else than ensure that the process goes on. And we return to the microbe state each generation, as we pass on to the next-born a single female cell and a single male cell, bequeathed to posterity by an adult, many-celled human being who will perish whilst the immortality of mankind goes on, enshrined in a microscopic pair of cells that are nothing more than microbes, joining together like any other form of protozoan.

The biological realities of microscopic life seem remote from a society like ours, which is not brought up to think in those terms. But it is how we all began, and is a pointed reminder of our very real links with the ancient lineage of microbes. We revert to that state, ourselves, to breed.

Higher animals need to ensure that a further aspect of sexual differentiation is brought into the equation; the question of care and protection of the offspring. We, for instance, have to know that our own needs will be met by our partner – needs that range from caring and selflessness to understanding, sympathy and support, quite apart from the mundane questions of providing food, shelter and the physical accoutrements of existence – and we are subconsciously prepared to select a mate not for any consciously-experienced, quantifiable reasons, but for the intuitive response which some people think of as vibrations (they are really nothing of the sort, as far as one can tell, but the implications of that term are fair enough) and which give you that gut reaction of love, tolerance, or dislike. It is on such factors that human sexuality and sexual discrimination depend.

But there is a behavioural aspect, too. We all know how mammals and birds, the two great groups of warm-blooded creatures, undergo courtship of the kind that enables them to try out their partners, and select them on some sort of innate basis of sexual priority. This is not true of all species to the same extent, but some form of positive motivation has to be there for sexual union to eventuate, and copulation is almost always preceded by a courtship that builds up sexual pleasure for the mates themselves, and which allows some selection to take place according to the codes of criteria built in for evolutionary expediency and the safeguarding of each species' precious genetic blueprint. The idea is that the wayfarer falls by the way, and I do not doubt that our own propensity to confer homosexuality on a minority of our members is an exactly parallel safeguard.

But the criteria do not only enable us to select a mate, and engage in courtship. And our innateness is not a property designed to express pre-formed behavioural traits, as though we had a programmed system of behaviour ready to be switched on automatically. Much of the burden of inheritance is not passed on by purely genetic blueprinting at all, but by subtler means. The information moves from generation to generation by teaching. The parent(s) instruct the offspring in the ways of behaviour that are necessary for survival and for the maintainance of the race. Birds teach their young how to feed, to fly, and to avoid predators; and in mankind there are many means of passing on cultural information from one generation to the next so that the young grow up with the requisite behavioural norms that will fit them for adulthood and – more important – will fit their offspring for survival.

The great question which we have to ask ourselves is which of the orthodoxies we are now trying to overthrow are actually a part of this evolutionary background, and are needed by our young for them to develop properly. For instance, if you encourage a girl to think in terms of having as much of a professional career as she can, you are very likely freeing her from a burden of social deprivation which has unnecessarily restricted her sex for years past, and which will give her a chance of greater freedom than she would have had otherwise.

But if you discourage her from playing with dolls and in exploring ways of developing her own sense of femininity because you find yourself caught up in some overwhelming wave of conformity to a passing trend, you might well be taking away her opportunities to develop into total womanhood. It is essential that we begin to look for ways of understanding the vital importance of learned behaviour in our development, and see how these codes of criteria that have developed in the framework of being taught by one generation to the next fit us for our adulthood, and are as much a part of our acquired behavioural equipment as the predestined codes that derive from our genes allow us to stand upright and walk.

It is interesting to observe how other species train and educate their young, and how fertility rates drop off when a stressed community (perhaps through overcrowding) supervenes. Nature has not allowed us to evolve without a complex series of controls and strictures and other mammals tend to lose their ability to breed and to lose out on the behavioural front if the community is subjected to severe pressures. When the safe rearing of young ceases to be reliably practicable, those unfathomed deep-seated defence mechanisms take over and apply what could be called innate population restriction until things improve.

This is certainly what will happen to us if we cross the boundaries set up by our evolutionary past. And if we are too quick to leap onto an ill-thought-out bandwaggon of temporary faddishness then we may take from our children some of the mental attributes they need to be given to develop, and produce instead an inter-sexed race with a faulty sense of identity and a lowered ability to breed. There are some who would hail such a prospect as the ultimate contraceptive mechanism – which indeed it is – but the prospect of stunting the mental growth of our young fills me with distaste. Man did not evolve on the whim of some casual genetic gesture, but within the strict framework of evolutionary expediency. Take away our primitive lifestyle, for which we evolved, and replace it with a cushioned and air-conditioned well-fed regime and you have upset the system . . . and though there is a certain salutariness in understanding that nature will certainly limit our growth if we do not attend to the matter ourselves, it would be an appalling prospect if we had to become a part-developed, hesitant, ill-identified group of mammals before our transgression became apparent.

Exactly which of the traits we teach to our young are vital for their well-being no-one knows, and I would hesitate to guess as to what they might really be. I am certain that the vague insistence on ridding men and women from their own sexual distinctness is muddle-headed and malignant, and I am perfectly sure that one can demonstrate why in a host of cases. The tendency of men to be the more aggressive gender has been much discussed in recent years, and we have been told that this can be a result of childhood training, and ought to be extirpated. Well, a lowering of mankind's threshold of aggression is something I would welcome without a scrap of hesitation. But that does not mean that aggression itself is so easily discarded. It may be that aggression-training is a part of childhood's orthodoxy, and performed the biological necessity of fitting a man to guard and protect a young mother who was preoccupied with nursing her young, that most creative of all tasks. It may be that ridding our society of that potential produces an impaired version of mankind – in which the man is not merely a less aggressive gender but actually a *less developed* one. Aggression is in fact coded for in some way by the male Y–chromosome. The male sex-hormone testosterone potentiates aggression in men (and in women too).

Learning to control aggression is one thing. But trying to pretend that it should never have arisen, that it is just an artificiality, or something that women ought to manage to do as well as men, and what's more that it has no physiological origin or social purpose is erroneous. It would not have arisen at all without a purpose, and trying to build a society in which aggression becomes less necessary will not hold back the tide of innate behaviour that millions of years of behaviour have built up, and billions of years of evolution have dictated.

If sexism was not necessary, there would be no sexes. If gender roles were so easily blurred, nature would not have imposed them. And if courtship, love, passion and that old idea of 'animal attraction' were not a vital part of role fulfilment and gender identity we would not have courtship and intercourse at all. You would simply produce a wafted cloud of pollen that blew free like dust and settled where it fell by chance. All the allure, all the lust, and every scrap of heart-rending sexual intrigue would vanish in an instant, and a penis would function like a catkin instead.

Our sexuality is there for a purpose. I believe it is time we recognized that, and began to discover exactly what that purpose truly is.

CHAPTER TWO

THE ANIMALS' WAY

The least-sophisticated animals that we describe as having a true penis are the flatworms. Quite how valid the terminology is, it is hard to say; some of the lowlier types (like the bacteria I referred to in the previous chapter) possess organs of sexual contact which you might think warranted the term, but the point about the penis of the flatworms is that it is a protrusible structure which is always present - i.e. it does not disappear between mating, as happens in the case of some lower forms - and it is capable of becoming enlarged at the time of copulation. The flatworms are a remarkable phylum; if they are starved (which happens in nature often enough for them to need a defence against it) they simply reduce their body size, using their own tissues as a food reserve until matters improve and they are able to feed once more. First the yolk-producing organs disappear, then the male and female organs; after them the gut and the body wall muscles go too, until all that is left is a shrunken and thin flatworm with a disproportionately large head end where the animal's brain resides. They can shrink from 17 mm in length to 2 mm; and from 2.5 mm breadth to 0.3 mm, which by anybody's standards is a remarkable change. It takes only a matter of a week or two to regain their former size if food comes along again.

Even this little worm can surely appreciate sexual pleasure, yet it is difficult to see how - it has a brain that is no more than a few hundred cells and even the most far-fetched interpretation would find it difficult to see how a flatworm could develop such a highly aware sense of the pleasures of life that it deliberately sets out to fancy whatever eligible, unattached little maiden flatworm happens along (I use the term 'maiden' here only in a literary sense: not only could the term as easily be transposed, but in flatworm terms it would have to be, anyway - flatworms are bisexual).

Take a look at the flatworm's sexual organs. There are rounded testes in which the sperm appear. That sounds familiar enough, but the testes are usually not confined to a single pair - typical flatworms have scores of them. From the testes run ducts which join up to form the *vas deferens*, and there are usually two of these, one each for the sperm produced by the testes on each side of the flatworm's body. The ends of the ducts are usually expanded to form a storage sac for the mature sperm cells, which is known as a seminal vesicle; and then they unite, forming a single tube that runs into a muscular structure with extensible walls, the penis.

The female organs are similarly familiar. There is an ovary, which produces the ova, and an associated extra structure not found in mammals (but familiar enough in our cousins the birds) which supplies the nutritive yolk for the eggs and also a hardened egg-covering. The ovaries liberate their egg cells into an oviduct, and this leads to a structure called the genital atrium, in which the sperm of the mate can be received. This structure is the flatworm's vagina.

The unfamiliar aspect of the flatworm anatomy is that both sets of sex organs occur in the same individual. That seems like the perfect recipe for a life of narcissistic hedonism, but the flatworm is developed so that it cannot fertilize itself. When two of them mate, they approach each other in a state of sexual preparedness and lie together with their genital openings in contact. (The texts usually say that they 'are applied together' as though some powerful outside agency had done this . . . but in fact the agency at work is the sex drive. It has to be). The penis normally blocks the entrance to the oviduct, preventing sperm from its own testes from getting up. But when it mates, the penis is enlarged and extruded, and the opening to the oviducts becomes dilated as the penis thrusts out into its partner's genital atrium or 'vagina'.

Thus paired, the two worms can inseminate each other, but not themselves. The sperm pass into that vagina, then up the oviducts to where they fertilize the ova (an arrangement parallelled in mankind – the sperm travel to the top of the fallopian tube, which is the human version of an oviduct, where they fertilize the ova before the new zygote travels back down the tube towards the uterus). After the zygotes have formed, they travel back the way the sperm came up, through the oviduct, descending once more to the genital atrium. On the way they are given a portion of nutritive yolk to sustain the embryo, and then a tough egg-case, before they are laid on pond-weed ready to hatch.

The simple flatworm is so primitive that if you cut it into thirds, the rear portion grows a head, the front portion a tail, and the middle one of each thus giving rise to three separate new worms; yet this worm illustrates the pattern of sexual behaviour in most higher animals. The fact it is a hermaphrodite clouds the picture somewhat, since most species like to keep their sexes separate, but the outline of the sexual anatomy, and of the copulation procedure, is typical of what we find in most corners of the animal world. And the clear-cut drive towards copulation and breeding is an example of sex drive that parallels our own in a startling fashion.

There are some parasitic relatives of the flatworms which indulge in modified versions of their cousin's sexual habits. One of them which lives attached to the gills of minnows is *Diplozoon*. As a rule these live as partly-matured larvae, drawing nourishment from the blood-stream of the host. When two larvae meet they become permanently attached to each other and then go on to sexual maturity, with the penis of each firmly fixed into the vagina of the partner. Thus they live in a condition of permanent copulation. A similar condition is found in one of mankind's most damaging parasites *Schistosoma* (*Bilharzia*). Here (and this is an exceptional circumstance for these organisms) the male and female live as separate sexes inside the bloodvessels of the human host. But once they meet up, the male clasps the female in a permanent embrace and she remains lodged in a fold that runs the length of his body. Permanent copulation is the rule here too.

Schistosoma lives part of its life in man, and part in water-snails. Many of the worms in this group have similarly complicated life-stories and pass from one species to another as their various stages unravel. The liver fluke which is perhaps more familiar to Western man lives in snails and sheep as well as mankind. One enterprising species (*Distomum macrostomum*) even shares its life between a thrush and a garden snail. The adult is a parasite in the unfortunate thrush's intestines, where it produces eggs which are liberated in the bird's droppings. The eggs, when they are eaten by the unsuspecting snail, develop into the next stage of the life-cycle and make their way into one of the snail's eye tentacles. As the parasite matures it produces bands of bright colours in the snail's eye, coloured green and red, which will act as an attractant to the thrush.

Then, the presence of the parasite prevents the snail from drawing this infected eye-stalk in again, so the conspicuous coloured eye is available to catch the attention of any passing thrush. When that happens, the bird eats the snail, discarding its shell but in the process liberating the waiting *Distomum* into the new host's intestines. From then on the cycle is repeated endlessly.

The tapeworms are in the same group, and they typically develop into a long ribbon of more-or-less separate rectangular 'wormettes' joined end to end. The smaller and younger ones near the hook-bearing head which is fixed into the intestine of the host are male; as they mature (and pass along the tapeworm itself) they gradually lose their male organs and become female, and male 'segments' actually mate with these mature female ones as the tapeworm loops around in the gut.

In the end, the female 'segments' are discarded in the faeces, each one filled with ripe tapeworm eggs that are ready to be taken in by the intermediate host (a pig, in the case of mankind's most widely-studied tapeworm) so that the cycle can continue.

The demands of a tapeworm are such that the host loses weight, and tapeworm infestations have been deliberately produced in some over-weight Americans as a means of helping them to slim. At the end of the treatment (if I have the right term) the worm is expelled with drugs and the patient discharged. It is still thought by some, by the way, that a tapeworm can be expelled by holding a piece of juicy and well-blooded steak in front of the sufferer's mouth. It is said that the worm scents the meat and jumps out to bite it. If the meat is secured to a length of string, the 'bait' and the worm can be hauled safely out. If you have been told that don't believe it – it's a halfwitted rumour. The head of a tapeworm remains embedded in the gut wall of the host and anyway it has no organs of sense, nor of motility, which could ever cause it to undertake such an athletic and perceptive response.

The higher worms which we know as ragworms from the beach and earthworms from our gardens have a lifestyle which reveals many unexpected reproductive patterns. Notable is the palolo worm of the South Pacific, *Leodice viridis*. This creature lives in large numbers in the structures of the coral reefs. The head is buried in the reef itself, whilst the hind end bears the organs of reproduction in which eggs and sperm are produced. The reproductive phase itself is remarkable, more so because of its almost split-second timing.

On the day in which the October/November moon enters its last quarter, each palolo worm snaps off the rear half of its body, which swims to the surface of the sea like a miniature serpent. The timing is accurate to within a single day in the Spring, and after shedding their tails the adult worms retreat into their burrows and commence growing a new rear end with a fresh supply of gametes. That takes a year, however. Meanwhile on the days after spawning, the surface of the coral reef seas is covered with a writhing mass of palolo-tails, and soon the water is milky with the masses of gametes – sperm and ova – that have been shed. The empty tail portions meanwhile fall to the bottom of the sea.

There is a relative of the palolo which lives in the West Indies seas, and which has a similar breeding pattern. This happens a little later in the season: whereas *Leodice viridis* liberates its sexual rear end during the South Pacific Spring, in the West Indian *L. fucata* it happens in Summer, on the day of the last quarter of the moon in June/July. But for both the timing is critical – even a couple of days before the lunar quarter it is impossible to induce the phenomenon to occur.

In some other marine worms there are equally surprising sexual patterns. Ragworms only discharge sperm when stimulated by the secretions (the 'scent') of a mature female, and both usually die after liberating their load of gametes. The syllid worms, *Odontosyllis*, exchange light signals with each other as a cue to start mating, whilst some bristleworms use visual signals of a different kind – the males congregate together and dance before their prospective mates, their gyrations acting as the stimulus which causes the females to drop their ova.

The common earthworm copulates on the surface of the ground during the early morning. Two worms lie in the *soixante-neuf* position, and become joined together by a pair of elastic bands secreted for the purpose. The worms are hermaphrodite, and exchange sperm during this unusual form of copulation. Then they separate, each has one of the bands around its body where it now acts as a cocoon; it is gradually wriggled off the earthworm by a series of rippling movements of the body, collecting first the sperm from the mate and then the ova from its own ovarian apparatus, before the worm wriggles out of the cocoon altogether. It is then left as a brood chamber for the new generation of earthworms to develop inside.

Brood chambers become more specialized when we progress towards the higher-evolved crustaceans. In the water-fleas *Simocephalus* and *Daphnia*, for example, there is a brood pouch that develops inside the mother's outer case. The fertilized eggs can develop inside this protective chamber until they are ready to hatch out into the outside world. It is a distinctly anthropomorphic phenomenon, this, and looks at first sight like childbirth. It isn't of course, since there was no feeding contact between mother and young in the brood-pouch (the offspring were developing from fertile eggs without any further metabolic support from either parent). The simplicity of each of the eggs is revealed by the fact that they can be dried completely or frozen in liquid nitrogen without losing viability.

Sacculina is a crustacean parasite of crabs, and its life history is remarkable in that it interferes with the sexual identity of the host. The young of *Sacculina* are normal larvae of what is called the nauplius type, with three pairs of legs, looking very similar to the larva of any other water-flea. It then develops into a part-formed adult known as a cypris, since it looks just like the two-shelled *Cypris* that is commonly found at the bottom of muddy ponds and lakes.

But this is where things become unexpected, for the cypris clings to the leg of a crab and after a period of further development it produces a sharp dart which it stabs through the crab's joint and into its body cavity. The parasite then shrinks, so that a minute collection of cells which are by now all that remain of it, migrate through the dart and into the host crab's body. It is swept up by the bloodstream and becomes fixed underneath the intestine. It then begins to grow like a kind of fungus, sending out rootlets (that is what they are termed, for all the fact that this is an animal we are discussing) which spread through the crab's tissues, right through to the extremities of its claws. At the centre of this peculiar massive growth there forms a knob of tissue in which you can find primitive sex organs and a small collection of nerve cells corresponding to a 'brain', and this presses on the outside of the crab. At the next moult, the crab is unable to produce any new hard shell at this site and the parasitic nodule is left projecting outside the host, ready to shed its reproductive products into the surrounding water. Meanwhile, through a series of complex mechanisms that are poorly understood, the unfortunate crab begins to develop into a strange inter-sexed type. Males develop feminine appendages and a broader, more feminine outline. The females lose their distinctive sexual characteristics, and show many of the signs of immaturity. In either event, the host crab is effectively castrated by some mechanism induced by the parasite (it has been reported that crabs have been found in which the parasite has died out and a hermaphrodite sex-organ has subsequently re-grown). In time, all the sexual apparatus of an infected crab is lost so that the sexual life of the parasite can have full reign – though why it should be necessary remains a mystery.

As an example, there is a similar parasite of crabs known as *Thompsonia* which has an even more pronounced fungus-like appearance. It too produces buds on the host's body from which it liberates its sex cells, but produces none of the signs of physiological castration seen in *Sacculina* infections. In passing, it is noteworthy that a crustacean like this can become reduced to something that looks like a fungus in the process of evolving for a parasitic life-style. It would be tempting to fit this into the general plan that parasites usually seem to develop backwards towards a more primitive type – but crustaceans never were fungi! But what intriguing speculation one could introduce about the idea that fungi and crustacea do have similar origins, no matter how disparate their form and function in our own era. The tough, plastic material chitin (pronounced as kie-tin) is what the exoskeleton of the water-fleas is composed of, and the body of the *Sacculina* and *Thompsonia* larvae are made of chitin in the normal way. But the walls of some fungi contain chitin too, a form known as fungus chitin, true, but none the less it is much the same material. So perhaps water-fleas and fungi might have more in common than meets the eye: they may have shared a common ancestor, maybe fungi are a much-reduced form of animal life, perhaps the whole of the arthropod world from crustaceans to insects has in its genes the seeds sown by a fungus-like ancestry . . . the possibilities are endless, of course; but it is always interesting to recognize that the strict boundaries between plant and animal life which we like to erect in science are not always as clear-cut from the viewpoint of the species themselves. I have simplified the question here, but it remains a fascinating puzzle that some crustaceans can develop into what anyone would take to be a kind of fungus.

It is in the insect world that we find the highest level of development in the whole of the joint-limbed invertebrates that are lumped together as arthropods (covering everything from midges and mites to lobsters, butterflies and woodlice). The insects represent the culmination of this line of evolutionary specialization, and they reveal many of the earlier traits that evolved as part of the patterns of sex, but in a more sophisticated form.

For example, the worms (p. 28) include some species that use light signals as a means of attracting a mate, and the various phosphorescent insects like glow-worms and fireflies use the same principle, signalling in a fashion that their mates will instinctively recognize. Here is another example of the effects of an innate set of criteria embodied in a species' genetic make-up which subconsciously selects a given, vital signal as a cue for some specific response. Some of the insects have capitalized on the trait, though; the females of some firefly species recognize the light signals of the males of different species, and instead of emitting their own 'code' light they mimic a different call-sign and attract down some unrelated males whom they then proceed to eat (male fireflies are much smaller than the females). In this case a sexual recognition factor is applied to the devious purpose of cross-species cannibalism and, since there are few impulses stronger than the desire to respond to a sex cue, it is an irresistible force, and provides for the cannibalistic female a useful dietary supplement.

It is also in the insect world that we can see a host of mechanisms by which mates are selected for strength, stamina or whatever, in the best interests of survival of the fittest. The most frequently observed phenomenon is when winged insects take to the air in pursuit of a distant mate and it becomes a question of 'may the best male win'. Bees undertake a form of marriage flight, where the queen bee rises high in the air, pursued by a swarm of drones (males) all driven towards her by the powerful sex urge. The first to reach her (the fittest) wins the prize and pumps her receptive body as full of sperm as possible. As a rule he pays for this with his life since, as the two separate, the male's visceral organs are dragged from his body as his copulatory organ remains grasped firmly in the queen's.

It is often supposed that flying ants are a species of ant which appears only in summertime, but their occurence is the ant's version of the same phenomenon. There are almost 20,000 species of ant; but the marriage flight is a vital landmark in the life of all colonies (as well as being a periodic annoyance to mankind). Some ant species have wingless queens, in which case the fertilization ceremony occurs at ground level; others have flying queens but wingless males, in which case the queen takes to the air only *after* being fertilized. In some instances the males do not fertilize a queen from their own colony at all, but fly away to find a different community of the same species, there to mate with one of the new virgin queen ants.

The usual pattern, however, is that during the afternoon of a hot and sultry summer day a mass of winged ants appear running from a subterranean colony, spilling across the ground and climbing up nearby vegetation, looking for a place from which to take off into the air. It is then

31

that local newspapers publish their accounts of masses of flying ants swarming across picnic areas or parks and upsetting the calm routine of the suburbs.

The story really begins several days before the swarming itself takes place. The first change is produced by the maturation of the queen ants and the emergence of huge numbers of males. The winged ants are larger than the myriad workers, and cannot move through the normal channels of the nest. So the workers begin to prepare the way, removing débris and enlarging the tunnels that lead to the surface of the ground. The workers also provide the first clue to the outside world that swarming is imminent, as they show greatly increased activity, scurrying around as though checking out the entire surroundings and ensuring that the area is safe for the massive exodus that is to come.

Eventually the passages are ready. This is no small task, either; in one ant, *Carebara*, the volume of the queen is 7,000 times that of the workers, and though that is an exception there are many major modifications to the layout of the tunnels that have to be made in anticipation of the swarming itself. Most important is the need to protect the queen's wings as she moves from her brood chamber to the outside world for the first time.

The males are as a rule somewhat smaller than the queen, though much bigger than the workers. In the Doryline army ants the males are an inch long and look as fearsome as wasps, whilst the queens are wingless and grotesque. These marauding insects march in considerable numbers and are found throughout the tropics, and in India, Africa and South America they have long been feared for their fabled ability to clean a tethered goat in their path down to the bones. (On the other hand if they do happen to march through a homestead they are said to rid it entirely of vermin.) The march of the army ants is a sexual phenomenon, it is set off by the emergence of a new brood.

The familiar ants of our gardens, however, emerge into the light and immediately prepare for take-off, the workers group around them, pulling them this way and that, and apparently holding them down whilst they test the power of their wings. The little yellow lawn ant, *Acanthomyops mixtus*, which always stays in the darkness underground, emerges into sunlight on just this one day, as the queens and males leave the nest. At the same time, the workers are keeping the males away from the virgin queen ants; and you will find that the same state of energetic excitement is being enacted in all nests of the same species throughout the area. What are they detecting – humidity, temperature, light intensity? We do not know for sure, but there is a code of innate criteria carrying out the selection of the right conditions and this will determine the success of the marriage flight itself.

Within minutes of emerging, the first of the virgin queens opens her wings and, perhaps after a few false starts, flies up into the air, spiralling ever higher until she is scores of feet above the nest. She is joined by other ants, queens and workers, from her own nest and from others, and they form black misty spiral clouds in the air. The males seek out the queens, mate with them if they can, and then the queens, laden with their sperm load, drop lazily towards the ground and, with a sudden shrug of the shoulders, they shed their wings. Another remarkable process is the way in which the workers of the colony refuse to allow any fully-fledged queen back inside the nest from which she so recently emerged.

In time she finds a safe place where she can begin to establish a new ants' nest. She does not feed much during the laying of the many eggs from which her workers will hatch, and so she relies on stored body fat and also uses up the massive wing muscles she developed for her nuptial flight and which are now unnecessary. In time the new brood hatches, workers begin to care for the queen, fetching food for her and grooming her, and the cycle continues anew.

There is one important conclusion that we can carry away from this brief look at the patterns of sex in ant communities, and that is the complex systems of behaviour which are innate in each ant, which it needs to survive, which it cannot learn or be taught, and which its predestiny has decreed for it. Detailed procedures are carried out on the basis of this inborn instinct, and the extent to which our own lives are predicated upon this innateness has still to be discovered.

Many insects utilize olfaction, the sense of smell, to attract and locate a partner. The capacity of some male moths to detect odour chemicals released by a receptive female is remarkable, and exceeds the capacity of modern analytical equipment. Some of the moths can detect just a few molecules several miles down-wind. The male bumble bee (more correctly known as a humble bee) leaves chemical scent markers in a long trail across leaves and branches. When a female finds one she will wait by it until the male comes round on a second lap of the circuit. The two will then mate, and the male usually dies very shortly afterwards.

Once a male butterfly has scented a female, he will soon track her down. But she does not immediately succumb to his courtship advances; instead the female will flutter away perhaps in rejection, possibly in enticement. If she does decide to accept the male, she settles onto a leaf or twig and the male then executes a series of graceful, looping manoeuvres around her as a kind of courtship dance. He settles down alongside her then, often clasping the tips of her club-like antennae between his wings and signalling his nature to her in the process (he secretes pheromones, or scent stimulants, and this action transmits them powerfully to his partner.) Eventually the two mate: the male mounts his partner and fertilizes her supply of eggs. But the dance, the flight patterns, the chase and the courtship all precede the sex act itself.

Courtship displays immediately remind one of the flourishing of brightly-coloured plumage in the mating of birds. But dancing displays occur elsewhere in the animal kingdom. The fiddler crabs also use this courtship option to attract a mate. When the males are at rest they are a brownish colour, like the females. But in the heat of the sun on a beach at low tide, during the mating periods, the males acquire more garish colours as a sexual attractant. These crabs get their name from their habit of moving the large right claw about in a waving motion like the bowing arm of a violinist, and this coloured 'flag' is a signal to receptive females.

Should a female respond, she will head towards the male fiddler and become attentive; this serves to excite him further, his colours heighten still more, and he dances in front of her on the sand. In groups of fiddler crabs it is frequent for a female to dance with one male after another, the sexual drive heightening until at length she selects one mate and pairs off with him. He leads her away to his sand burrow and enters; the female follows him and, after he has 'closed the door' with a ball of mud, the two mate.

Dancing rituals of a sort are even found in the familiar Roman snail of our gardens. Snails are hermaphrodite, but even so go to great lengths to acquire a suitably fecund mate. Breeding begins at night, when snails begin to pair off. The partners face each other and climb upwards a little, clasping together with the base of their body 'foot', and moving from side to side in a rocking kind of dance. The sexual urge is heightened as this dancing movement continues, until one of the snails triggers his so-called love dart, a sharp spike that is used to hold the two snails together. As it pierces the partner's body it seems to cause a momentary flinching, but the response is the same stabbing with the mate's dart, and the two snails remain locked together clearly in a state of great arousal. If the snails are of different sizes then the larger will fire the dart first, and the effect is usually to cause the smaller partner to withdraw from the embrace.

Once locked together the snail partners each produce a muscular penis which seeks out the genital opening of the partner and injects the seminal secretions. Snails are not unduly complex creatures nor are they highly evolved, but no-one witnessing copulation will deny that the snails are not only possessed of a strong sexual urge, but the orgasm phase itself clearly causes a high degree of sense stimulation and physical arousal.

Many species of fish use dancing-type swimming movements to attract a mate, and in the interesting case of the bitterling, *Rhodeus amarus*, the display fulfills important functions that continue after mating has taken place. Male bitterlings find a mussel shell and attract a willing female to it by characteristic courtship displays. The male signals to the female, inducing her to lay her eggs through a two-inch tube-like ovipositor inside the cavity of the mussel, so that the eggs will lie harmlessly inside the shell, protected and provided with a continuous flow of fresh water by the mussel's filter-feeding activities. A whole range of fin-flickering and chafing movements have been shown to help the bitterling groom himself, he adopts a jerking movement of the body as a threatening gesture in the face of intervention by an unwanted outsider – and all of these are extensions of courtship display.

Birds often use ritualized displays as a means of exhibiting their territoriality, and it is well known that male birds will protect the territory selected by themselves and their mate even at the risk of losing their lives – the aggressive robin is an interesting example, since the fearsome way it will protect its home territory seems incongruous in such a small and attractive bird.

Some display dances are used for less obvious purposes. Thus some sandpipers like the dunlin *Calidris* run about when a nest is threatened, mimicking the appearance of a wounded rodent in the grass to distract a predator's attention from the nest; or will fly in low swooping circles, trailing a wing as though wounded, to coax a predator away from the young.

Sometimes behaviour is used as part of mimickry, a good example being in the false cleaner fish *Aspidontus taeniatus* which looks like the cleaner, *Labroides*, but when it weaves in and out, swimming closer to its large host fish, instead of helping to clean, as *Labroides* does, *Aspidontus* nips in and takes a piece out of the host's side, before swimming off at speed to digest its stolen morsel in safety. The graceful swimming displays of the cleaner fish are perfectly copied by this underhand species.

The cleaner fish themselves have an unusual form of sexual behaviour, in that they take turns to be males. A dominant male rules a harem of four or five females, and they all behave in a strict hierarchical system paying attention to the order of seniority. When the male dies or is killed, the next most senior female begins to change into a male, and within two or three days will be beginning male courtship behaviour. Sperm are ready to be liberated two weeks later, by which time the new male has been completely accepted by the harem as the new leader, and so the process continues, each female taking over as head male in turn.

This points us towards the ways in which our stereotyped ideas of gender are upset by nature. Indeed in some species the behaviour of one sex is copied by the other in a clear case of homosexuality – but occasions when the boundaries of orthodoxy are transgressed enter the discussion later on.

Before we consider the sexual behaviour of the mammals, including ourselves, it would be worthwhile to introduce one or two of the creatures who have carried the ritual of courtship and mating to some unusual extremes. The grouse family include many species which construct mating arenas, or leks, in which displays and mating take place, for all the world like an avian sex night-club set apart for exactly that purpose and no other.

The sage-grouse, which is perhaps the most remarkable of them all, shows how different the two sexes appear to be – the male is covered with grandly coloured feathers, has a spiked tail, pure white breast plumage and large yellow air-sacs which he can blow up and deflate with a characteristic popping sound, which greatly excites the females.

The males show a marked dominance, with one of them being accepted as leader; and when mating takes place after a prolonged display, it is this male which carries out most copulation, as many as a hundred sex acts in one mating session. The lesser males are lucky to mate even once. Much the same seems to be true of the females, too, which move from lek to lek, looking over the available males. Here we have a clear selection against 'unfit' or diminutive would-be parents in favour of the sexiest and most active pairs.

But if the setting aside of arenas for mating in this way seems surprising, consider the bowerbirds. They have an extraordinary devotion to attracting the right partner, and the males erect love-nests for the purpose only of courtship into which they try to entice their choice. The bowerbirds are members of the bird of paradise family and are without doubt the most innovative architects and interior decorators in the entire world of birds.

The bower that the male constructs is made of twigs, branches and leaves. It may be a simple structure – just a latticework – or a complex and roomy bower with several separate compartments. Each of the little bowers may be surrounded with coloured vegetation, shells or pebbles, and inside the decoration consists of flowers, petals, coloured seeds and there may even be a 'floor' of neatly arranged stones.

The satin bowerbird of Australia is probably the most adventurous of all, for he constructs a bower with two parallel walls about one foot high and two inches thick, and then lines them with a mixture of charcoal and saliva. The charcoal may come from some distance away, where there was a eucalyptus forest fire. (Such conflagrations sometimes occur spontaneously, and some species of eucalyptus produce seeds that have to be seared by flame before they will germinate, proof of the regularity of naturally-caused forest fires.) The bird uses a wad of bark as a brush to apply the 'paint'.

Then he adds man-made scraps, like broken pieces of glass or tinfoil, together with parrot feathers, berries and seeds and flowers. The effect sets off his magnificently glossy blue-back plumage. When a female comes near he – like all other bowerbird males – flashes his wings and emits a characteristic mating call (in his case a curious series of croaks). A female who is attracted will inspect the bower, and she may even enter it. She is quite likely to re-arrange the accoutrements with her beak before she finds it to her satisfaction.

She may move on, of course, to consider a more suitable mate. But if she does settle in and decide to stay, the male will join her in the bower after a few minutes, and they will then mate.

The bower serves no other purpose than as a shelter for courtship and mating. The female flies away after the mating is over, builds her own nest and there she lays the eggs and rears the young. It is a remarkable story, perhaps the most intricate pattern of sexual behaviour in all the birds, and one which is heavily imbued with a sensuous sensitivity of the kind humans can readily understand. There is not only a sex drive here, but a fully developed awareness of colour and beauty in the way the bowers are made.

Mankind is not the only species to make such essentially aesthetic judgements, then. In the bird kingdom, even at this level of evolution, many of the habits and attitudes that we have tried to perfect have already been tried and tested. In that single lesson of the bowerbird there lies an important level of understanding which helps us put our own sexuality more firmly into its biological context.

Mammals other than man fall in love, and undertake the preliminaries with as much tenderness as we aspire to. The elephant is perhaps a classic example. The period of gestation (pregnancy) is as long as 22 months, and a female elephant will mate only twice every ten years or so. Elephant adults take time choosing a mate, and will share short friendships of a sort time and time again until a permanent pair-bond becomes established. Once they have settled down together the female shows all the coy behaviour you associate with romantic love in humans. She will make little darting runs away from him, though not too far; they will stroke each other's bodies with their trunks, nuzzle close together and insert their trunk-tip inside the partner's mouth in a kiss, often followed by inter-linking their trunks above their heads in a 'hand-holding' gesture.

They sleep together, feed together, forage together, all the while displaying as much tenderness and care for the partner as you would associate with human love. The sexual foreplay involves caressing, mutual stroking of the genitals by means of the sensitive tip of the trunk followed by mutual masturbation. The elephants do not reach orgasm during all this; it is merely their way of increasing their degree of sexual arousal and stimulation and also in showing their love for and reliance on each other.

When copulation is due, the elephants leave the herd and seek out a glade. It is here the male mounts his bride from the rear, and the two become sexually fulfilled at last. And, fear not, the female is not unduly disturbed by the massive weight of her empassioned partner. Most of his weight is supported on his own hind legs, and he does not indulge in normal pelvic thrusting. Instead his penis thrashes sturdily in and out of the vagina, powered by its own internal muscles.

Elephant courtship is close to what we see in our own species and it involves much of the romantic behaviour and consideration that we do not ordinarily associate with 'mere' animals.

It is well known that birds train their young to fly and to feed, and in some animals a community structure may become established to control the behaviour of the young which is organized and even ritualistic to an extent, but which does not strictly result from the courtship behaviour of the parents. One such phenomenon occurs in the red deer. The species breeds in a harem system. As soon as the rutting season approaches, male deer, stags, begin to round up groups of eligible-looking females and herd them into groups. Throughout this autumnal event the stags display to the females, but more so to the other males, using their antlers as a gesture of defiance and a sign of maturity (the complexity of antler structure being related to age). It has long been taught that the antlers are used as a physical weapon of sorts, but it seems to me more likely that they are used for brandishment, and function more at the visual than the physical level.

The strongest and more mature males acquire the largest harems; individuals with less impressive antlers do not do as well. It has been shown that artificially de-horned or polled deer fail to attract as many females – or perhaps it is because they cannot outmatch or frighten off competing stags – and they therefore stand a much reduced chance of breeding. So far this behaviour is related to the patterns of sex that we see in other species. But after the rut is over the deer sexes separate, the red stags moving out for a comparatively solitary, roaming existence whilst the does congregate in communities and exist in harmony based on a strict order of seniority. Like most mammals, if the young get out of line their elders are likely to 'smack' them on the forefeet as a warning. It is not usual for them to have to do this; but when they do, the warning is heeded.

Here we have an interesting example of a species which exhibits a well-developed community pattern of behaviour aimed in the first instance at the sexual fulfilment of the adult deer, but which persists in a modified form that gives the young a sound grounding in adult ways and behaviour. It is an instance of community cooperation in the interests of the young.

Some species go further, with elaborate behavioural conventions that involve cooperation with entirely unrelated forms of life. In the case of the mallee fowl of southern Australia the cooperation is between the birds and microbes which, in a way, takes us full circle. What happens is that the birds pair off after sizing each other up, and remain permanently bonded to each other in a 'marriage' as durable as mankind's usually seems to be. After the mating rituals, the birds combine to excavate a pit in the soil which is two to three feet deep and as much as 10 feet in diameter. They then collect a blend of leaves and bark, which they lay down in a special bed structure held open and aerated by strategically placed twigs.

After a fall of rain has fully moistened the vegetation in their incubator the birds cover it with a layer of sand and soil. Microbes in the decaying leaves now take over, and their own reproduction gives rise to a lot of metabolic energy which is trapped in the pile as heat. The reproduction of the microbes and their life processes create an incubator in the pit. From time to time the male mallee fowl probes into the mass with his beak, sensing its temperature, and when this reaches 91 °F (33 °C) he signals to the female that the incubator is ready for the eggs.

She does not lay them inside the mass, though. Instead she produces a single egg which the male moves into position, opening the layers carefully and putting the egg in a place at the right temperature before covering it over again. Each egg incubates for 50 days, so that since the hen lays one egg per week there are usually half a dozen eggs or so in the incubator at any one time in a regular developmental sequence.

For six months this cycle continues, a rare example of devotion for birds which rewards them with a single month of rest at the end of each season before the whole thing starts up again. Other organisms also cooperate with microbes (some ants, for example, build fungus colonies in their nests which provide them with warmth in a similar fashion). But the male mallee fowl has developed a system of control for their incubators which is well adapted to the metabolic needs of the chicks, and the microbes too. In the spring the warmer days encourage the microbe colony in the incubator to grow at a high rate, generating surplus heat energy, which the male mallee fowl controls by opening the top of the chamber for a few hours each morning.

In summer, when the sun would dry the mound out and interfere with the microbes by over-heating them, the bird adds layers of soil to the top to insulate the contents from the sun's rays. And in the autumn, if the microbes have pretty near exhausted their food supply, he will open the nest each morning to catch the sun's rays and allow a little extra warmth into the nest.

The birds' devotion to their young, however, is not as great as their ceaseless work to keep their microbe community growing well. At the end of the incubation period the hatchlings have to burrow upwards through the layers in order to get to the fresh air. It may take more than ten hours for them to escape from the incubator, and at the end of that time they are totally ignored by their parents. The young have to make their own way to cover, and they can fly within 24 hours of leaving the nest.

All animal species that engage in sexual reproduction must have, by definition, a sex drive that compels them to leave their normal food-gathering activities to search for a mate and take time out for sex. Clearly, no matter what is the level of sophistication of the animal concerned, there must be some gratification through all this. In many organisms the active movements and embraces of sexual union show a clear parallel to what we know as humans – the love dance of the paired garden snails is an example

– and as we go higher up the evolutionary scale we find creatures that betray increasingly complex patterns of sexual behaviour involving many of the actions we carry out ourselves – right down to the niceties of cooperative home-building, the decoration of bowers with pretty colours and the lengths some species will go to to visually or verbally impress.

And there is an endless array of cooperative patterns that show how communities of animals join forces in the common good, and even (like the beaver harnessing water or the mallee fowl putting microbe life to work) cooperating with the forces of nature as part of their breeding career. The way is clear for higher-evolved species to carry this still further, and erect well-organized communities – but they are going to be founded on innate impulses, on inborn behavioural patterns, and on codes of criteria that enable their members to make instinctive discriminations and selection decisions at appropriate times.

But it is clear that a species like ours cannot suddenly abandon evolutionary orthodoxies without running the risk of abandoning part of our birthright and perhaps an essential aspect of our adult constitution. Only a knowledge of what goes on in our own minds can provide answers to that unasked question. But the likelihood that much of our social organization is descended from our evolutionary past, and is essential for our full and free expression of our own personalities, should make us more cautious about throwing our destiny to the winds.

Until we have stopped to examine the possible consequences, we are in no position to arbitrarily decree that *this* aspect of our traditions ought to be discarded, or *that* question abandoned; we may be throwing away, unwittingly, a vital ingredient of a human adult's total personality development at the same time.

CHAPTER THREE

THE HUMAN SEX MACHINE

The sex drive in animals is strong; in some it is overwhelming. Yet, although the nature of its expression varies so much from species to species, in the end we are left with the same hidden function: the bringing together of a sperm and an egg to start off new life. In fact the only reason for being an animal at all is to provide those primitive little cells with a suitable medium in which to perform. The possession of sense organs is to perceive ways of getting food and drink, and means of surviving; the purpose of being able to move at all is to find a mate and to obtain sustenance; and the origin of thought itself is founded on these basic requirements of life and reproduction.

For all mankind's complexity, we still return to that simple microbe form when we are going to start off the next generation. Our reproductive cells live on from generation to generation; in that sense, we are truly immortal. My theme here is that man is really a microbe – a sperm, or an egg – and all the complex human being that we become is nothing more than a kind of fruiting body created for the purpose of maintaining these microbial cells in a suitable environment, and in maintaining the *germ line*, as it is called (from the same root as *germination*, Latin *germen*). You and I matter for little, compared to the need for our sex cells to grow safe and warm in their watery fluid medium.

The concept of the cell as being, as it were, the true state of mankind (with the multicellular body itself just a colony designed to keep the individual cells alive and well) is one which I believe helps us to understand more clearly why we evolved, and what are the pressures on us to conform to our evolutionary heritage. I first wrote on 'man as microbe' in a book on microbiology and food back in 1970, and the concept has since been taken to a further extreme where the genes that control the cell's inheritance have been proposed as the real 'master'.

My own view is that this 'selfish gene' idea is carrying the proposition too far. The genes exist only to serve the nature of the cell, not the other way round; and genes are included or rejected because of what the cell experiences in its daily life, rather than the converse. The idea that the minute entities of which we are composed are in a way more important than we are ourselves, because we are evolved to ensure their survival even if we do not survive ourselves, is very workable and intriguing; but there seems no good reason to extend that idea of mine back one stage further from the single cell to the gene.

No, the real vision of mankind that we need to cultivate is of single cells undergoing reproduction just as microbes have for thousands of millions of years. Some of them form fungi to produce the next generation, others produce people; and the clever thing about the human germ line is that it is able to fly from one continent to another, travel at 60 miles an hour without any great effort, survive in the cold and in the oppressive heat of the tropics, spend long periods beneath the oceans or above the atmosphere, and yet at the end of it all the many-celled body that houses them is able to bring the two vital cells together at just the right moment for the process to continue anew.

What is particularly intriguing is that whenever a societal problem occurs that prevents those humanoid fruiting bodies from being as settled and secure as they should be, nature exerts immediate controls on reproduction. It is as though biological sanctions are exerted to prevent us from carrying on along a dangerous or retrogressive pathway. Stress always causes a lowering of sex drive, of libido; and I now believe this is nature's way of cutting down the chances of us producing children who will be the victims of an unhappy or unbalanced up-bringing.

The importance of learned behaviour is often underestimated, and sometimes we assume too quickly that because something is clearly taught to our children (female role behaviour is a current hot topic) it is therefore arbitrary and wrong. It *may* be arbitrary and wrong, and dangerous too; but we would do well to look at our mammal cousins and at ourselves more closely before we *automatically* make such an assumption. Such teaching may be a mainstay of our species' normal development.

Much of the behaviour we see in connection with the reproduction of our kind is certainly not learned, but innate; that is to say it takes place without any specific triggering effect from the environment, and is not acquired in response to any outside agency. One unarguable example of that is the way that the human foetus moves inside the womb. The first of these spontaneous movements occurs when the foetus has been developing for only eight weeks (that is, a fortnight after the mother's second missed period) and takes the form of head movements caused by the flexure of the muscle bands in the neck. That may strike you as surprisingly early; but in other animals the embryo develops the ability to move far earlier – a chick in its egg can begin to make slight movements only $3\frac{1}{2}$ days after fertilization.

The innateness of these movements is best argued in comparison with other animals in which they have been observed. Some sharks are known to show muscular flexing before any nerve connections have developed to the muscles – they are obviously doing it on their own. Or you can treat the muscle with a blocking agent like curare, which prevents the transmission of impulses through nerves which might not have been noticed by the observer, and you will still see that the movements persist.

Sharks rely on what you could think of as automatic muscular movement (which is not controlled from the brain) more than do mammals, however; and these spontaneous myogenic movements are not known to occur in any of the warm-blooded animals. In chicks and mammals you find that the nerve connections to the muscles seem to *coordinate* the movements, as much as initiate them. Though embryos can be shown to respond to external stimuli it seems likely that these movements are a kind of flexing of the new muscles ready for use. The embryo later shows sucking movements in a similarly spontaneous fashion, and these are clearly carried on into early infancy when they are the principal means of feeding. No-one assumes that those actions are 'taught', either.

But some responses of the new-born offspring are most certainly learned. It has long been known, even before Konrad Lorenz first pointed to the phenomenon in a series of painstaking and eloquently reported experiments in the 1930's, that young birds and some other animals are born with an innate desire to recognize a mother. The occurrence of that phenomenon has been known for centuries, of course, and when we say that:

> 'Mary had a little lamb
> Its fleece was white as snow.
> And everywhere that Mary went,
> The lamb was sure to go.'

we are reiterating one historic example of this occurrence. Lorenz called the effect *imprinting*, and the relationship between that form of learning and other forms has been discussed ever since. The point about imprinting is that – as in that children's rhyme – the object of the learning process need not be the actual mother at all. In young birds the mother can be replaced with a different species, the wrong sex, a model, or even a most un-bird-like cushion quite apart from the experimenter, if he presents himself to the young bird at the height of its imprinting desire!

This is not innate behaviour in the sense that the young know what 'mother' is. I think the most convincing way to look at the phenomenon is to assume that the young have an inborn code of criteria that they have to satisfy, and if a model duck made of plastic satisfies the selection process of those criteria, then a duckling will accept the model as its mother without hesitation.

We use criteria ourselves to make all the decisions of our adult lives. Analyzing decisions in terms of the criteria that are utilized to reach them is of great value when we try to understand how a given conclusion is reached. And the concept does away with many of the absurd so-called anomalies that people sometimes like to celebrate. Optical illusions are one example; if you provide a drawing which satisfies two opposing sets of criteria then clearly you have an 'illusion' – but there is no mystery about it, and what is more, no 'illusion'. The recognition of the code of criteria which is involved, and the manner in which it is being ambiguously satisfied, takes all the supposed incongruity out of the situation.

There are many ways in which you could study the criteria; and in fields from the recognition of handwriting and the drawing of political cartoons that are instantly recognizable, to the artificial enhancement of taste and the interpretation of sexual stimuli, the experimental situations are as varied and as endless as mankind's circle of experience itself. For example, how would you recognize a church minister? You might use as your selection criterion 'the man who preaches in the church'; only to find that this is an invited university don instead. You might then say, 'the man with the white dog-collar', only to find that this criterion lets you down as well. This man in a clerical collar is a confidence trickster collecting money for non-existent charities.

Very well, you choose another criterion in the hope of getting the right man, and select as your minister the man who is not only leading the service (a corrected version of criterion 1), but who is wearing full clerical robes (a completed version of criterion 2), and what is more possesses certified documentation that proves he really is a qualified cleric, and not an imposter. You have now three sound criteria, all tested, considered, and watertight. Does that allow you to select the man? On this occasion, no: the real minister is off sick and this is his stand-in for the day.

Now, we can recognize when a set of criteria is deficient (or at least, we can sometimes) and if we do know that they are letting us down we can change them or think of an additional selection mechanism. But a newly hatched chick has nothing so refined; he is stuck with the code of criteria that he has been innately provided with for the purpose of basic survival. He needs to form an instant attachment to his mother if he is to be provided with food, shelter, protection and training. The criterion he has been given is something simple, like 'the nearest chunky living thing' or failing that perhaps 'the nearest chunky object, even if not apparently moving at the moment', so if a person is nearby, they will do; if a male of the species, or even another species, that will suffice too; and failing either alternative, then the nearest vaguely friendly-looking cushion or model will be accepted instead.

What is interesting is that the process is only detectable during a relatively limited period after the young bird has hatched (about 10–20 hours); once established, the code of identification criteria are unchangeable – the mother or mother-substitute represents an ineradicable memory – and the individual, to quote Lorenz, 'from whom the stimuli are issuing, does not necessarily function as an object of this reaction'. In other words, acceptance of a cushion as a mother-figure does not imply that the cushion has to act as a mother. In terms of my criterion concept, all it had to do is satisfy whatever are the basic and innate criteria operating at the time.

There is one fascinating observation which throws light on the relationship between the innate capacity to act in a specific manner, and innate codes of criteria. This concerns the exchanging of eggs between nests of migratory and non-migratory species of gulls, which was carried out by M. P. Harris in the late 1960's. He exchanged eggs between the herring gull and the lesser black-backed gull in colonies on islands off the west coast of Wales. The herring gull does not migrate, whereas the lesser black-backed gull migrates to Spain, Portugal and North Africa. What he observed was that the two sets of hatchlings, as predicted, recognized each other's species as their parents, and were reared by them in the normal way.

However as autumn came on, the lesser black-backed chicks began to prepare for migration and although they had not been brought up by their own species (and therefore had not been able to learn anything from their previous generation) they were able to leave their home territory and fly south as normal. This complex and still unresolved phenomenon of innateness was shown up beautifully by this simple and convincing experiment.

But what happened to the herring gulls reared by the lesser black-backed gull? They flew south too, for the first time, and *became* migratory. There were no reliable records of herring gulls being seen anywhere in Spain or Portugal, yet there they were, migrating as though it was the most natural thing in the world. Discussions of this work have agreed how remarkable it is that it is harder to suppress the migratory restlessness of lesser blackbacks than to entice herring gulls 'to migrate through social pressures'. My own interpretation is that it is not a matter of 'social pressure', whatever that precisely means in this context. It is in my view more likely that here we have positive identification of a phase in the life of a young animal when it is 'available for imprinting'. It has reached a phase in life where it is seeking out behavioural responses from its parents that it can learn. Its criteria code has come to the fore again, ready to be 'educated'; and if a herring gull is in a state where this has happened it will inevitably learn from its parents. If they happen to be foster parents and

45

teach it how to migrate, then that is what it will do.

The black-backed gulls reared by herring gulls have no such pressure to force them to do anything. They have learned to fend for themselves, to feed, or whatever from their own foster parents in the normal way; but when migration time comes along their innate behaviour forces them to abandon that daily routine and take part in a migration that their background has bred into them. In short, innate behaviour is ineradicable; and innate codes of criteria just have to be satisfied. Behaviour will modify such criterion-based decisions, of course; but let no-one underestimate the potency of the latter.

UPBRINGING

I am inclined to suggest that periods when codes of criteria surface in the mind of a developing child result in phased learning which has an inevitable quality about it. For example, suppose that a child of five, say, is at that age satisfying a series of criterion options that govern the child's view of sharing (to take a single imaginary example). If that were to happen, then the child will learn whatever pattern of sharing behaviour he or she is being taught at that time. The parent who teaches the child about sharing will help the child to build up a series of criteria which select normal sharing behaviour as correct.

But suppose you have a parent who argues that he will not teach the child, but will leave it to find out for itself. If that occurs the criteria may well be set up to select a range of selfish, or quarrelsome, or possessive options instead. The criteria have to be satisfied, then; and if there is any flaw in the *laissez faire* approach it is that the assumption is made that a child will learn for himself. He most certainly will; but whether he will learn a socially satisfactory code of behaviour is another matter altogether. Letting a child to his own devices in the matter of learning, when his innate characteristics are demanding that he has his criteria satisfied, can do nothing but stunt his intellectual maturation if we have (as a species) developed in a way that *depends* on being provided with information at pre-determined periods.

It is in this phenomenon that I think we will find a pointer to many of the difficulties that seem to be suddenly facing us as we wrestle with the various demands of civilization on one hand, versus our innate sexual imperatives on the other. Many of the facets of development which we observe in children are not just the tiring, irritating, personal problems that they seem. They represent a choreographed and perfectly-timed sequence of developmental opportunities, if you like, that appear at pre-ordained intervals. The phase when children say 'why?' to everything is simply the age at which they have to acquire codes of behaviour predicated upon a knowledge of causality. The age of asking 'how?' is not just a device for annoying mother or father when they would rather be doing something else; it is the symptom that a child is now tuning up his mechanism-diagnosing facilities. Similarly, a child feeling the twinges of growing sexuality or sexualism needs to have these impulses satisfied. The adolescent needs opportunities to distinguish sex, love, lust and passion in a growing sequence; and needs to learn sex roles too.

If we present a child with a host of artificial and unrealistic notions based on mechanistic intercourse, when the child-mind is actually searching for explanations of togetherness, pairing, closeness and warmth, then these codes of innate criteria will select the wrong behavioural pattern. If you see a child trying to stand and to balance, then it is natural to help it up, to support it, to warn it if it is going too far or is likely to fall. This is instinctive, of course; and everyone will agree that this is part of the parental function – to supply information necessary for development. Similarly, if a child is trying to communicate verbally then it seems the most natural thing in the world to talk back, to correct wrong words, to encourage the development of language.

But suddenly – when it involves *sexual* development – we too often withdraw our support. We rely instead on the sophisticated and arbitrary inventions of sex-educationalists, and the longing for a discovery of loving, tender, caring relationships in adolescence is 'satisfied' instead by an artificial and unreal emphasis on copulation, as an act, like picking your nose.

If parents, finding it tiresome or embarrassing to spend time helping a child to stand or to walk, put their offspring instead into a room without handy supports, and did not provide help at the time when the child needed it, then society would quickly condemn that as inhuman and, at best, unhelpful. Yet the teaching that children demand at such times has to be provided by conscious giving from the parent(s) and it is in that sense perfectly possible to argue that you needn't provide it, if you don't want to. Such a proposition is self-evidently wrong and muddle-headed – and that is just how it seems to me, when I see parents who refuse (and it is an act of refusal) to pass on to children other behavioural norms that they want to acquire as they get older.

Mammals regularly use signals of approval or disapproval to pass on to their offspring a knowledge of what is right or wrong, and the signalling process usually includes a quick cuff from a loving parent as a means of associating short, sharp signals of disapproval with unsocial or destructive actions on the part of the offspring. Western man does not like to do this any more, but I am not certain that our insistence that it is civilized and morally right to refuse to occasionally smack a child is biologically sound, any more than pragmatically worthwhile.

Many studies have shown that smacking is more widespread amongst lower-educated social groups, whilst middle-class families rely more on subterfuge training (appeals to reason, banning TV, associations with guilt or shame, and so on) which allows one to infer that the withholding of this form of instinctive corporal punishment has its origins in reason and culture, rather than in impulse and innateness.

It may be the distinction is a bad one, and that many of the ways in which modern families correct their offspring, like the withdrawal of privileges and drawn-out reasoning, are probably far more traumatic and counterproductive than the slap which we probably evolved with. Here too, I am very far from suggesting that we ought to reintroduce corporal punishment on a Dickensian scale for the supposed moral good of our children! But it is arguable that in the right circumstances a smack is far more telling, and far less wounding, than dissertations or recriminations that are administered verbally, as an insult to the child's security, and often at a time when the 'naughtiness' of the act has entirely vanished from the child's mind.

It is all very well for us to feel smugly civilized and in some ways apart from, and above, all other animals. In a host of ways, we are. But we remain mammals for all that, and the mere possession of a level of intellect is no guarantee that the arbitrary way in which we decide to make some facets of our behaviour unfashionable, and introduce others on the flimsiest of trendy evidence, will in any way benefit ourselves or our children. I have long believed that in so many areas (from our diet and our need for exercise, to our love-lives and the way we deal with stressful situations) we need to try to strike a balance between the ways in which we live, and the manner in which our species evolved.

In no area is this more important than in sex, and in the way we bring sexual awareness to the attention of our children. Taking away the natural sequence of sexual development and supplanting it instead with an arbitrary and traumatic display of the sex organs, isolated and caricatured, is as absurd as suddenly refusing to help a baby to walk. And the stumbling manner in which our new generations fumble towards the free expression of their sexuality is as destructive as the prospect of a generation of adolescents crawling around on all-fours. As every fully-sexed adult will agree, the most important task to undertake when refining your sexuality into its adult form is to *unlearn* the nonsense one was taught at school. Our misbegotten approach to sex education is traumatizing children to such an extent that I fear for their ability to revel in sex, to relax in love, and often the stultifying orientation towards intercourse and orgasm attainment does more to wreck a marriage than the previous generation's equally absurd ignorance and refusal-to-talk can ever have achieved.

My own belief is that our modern insistence on sex education in its present form is blinding the young to the fullest expression of their sexual energies, and is a contributory factor to what I see as the desexualization of society.

It is easy to demonstrate its irrelevance. If we take the generally accepted duration of intercourse in Western societies at a little over five minutes and the rate of copulation at a little less than 2.5 times per week, then on that simplistic basis alone we can calculate that a couple spend some 15 minutes per week actually copulating, which would amount to 99.9% of their time doing something else – and if you up-rate the performance to a twice-nightly half-hour session the percentage of time spent in non-copulatory activities still does not fall below 95%! Teaching about intercourse, then, is on that basis alone superfluous when the gamut of non-copulatory feelings and desires are ignored with such consistency.

Secondly, I can cite the research carried out into what factors influence attraction of the sexes for each other. One survey, based on the characteristics listed in order of preference by individuals going to a dating service, was carried out by Karl Miles Wallace and Eve Odell who showed that men and women both put 'character and personality' as top of their lists. 'Physical type' and 'love and companionship' came close to the top, with women looking for 'economic stability' in their prospective spouse, and men for 'physical type' in theirs. 'Sexuality' was reportedly way down the list (indeed it came bottom of the scores for women, and only one above that for men). The . percentage of men citing 'sexuality' on their questionnaires was 10; for women the figure was 4%.

Finally, what evidence is there that sex education as normally practised is of no value in the arena of social experience? Michael Scholfield, whose book on *The Sexual Behaviour of Young People* was published in 1965, followed this up with a report entitled *The Sexual Behaviour of Young Adults* in 1973, and he considered the question of behaviour-modification by sex education. The findings showed how useless it is. Of the people in Scholfield's (second) sample who first had intercourse with their spouse, 54% had received no sex education, 56% of those who had premarital intercourse with their spouse had had no sex education either, and nor had 63% of those who first copulated with a steady girl- or boy-friend. It is clear that sex education had negligible effect on early sex experiences. Furthermore, data revealed that sex education had no effect either on the tendency for people to be faithful or promiscuous once married. Most scandalous of all (and of greatest weight in supporting my contention that today's sex education is a valueless exercise) 68% of the whole group said they had had no sex education, whereas 62% of the men who found themselves responsible for a premarital pregnancy came into that category.

That survey as a whole suggested that sex education had no effect on peoples' views about sex before marriage, did not prepare them for their first sexual experience, had no effect on allaying or reinforcing sexual problems, nor did it make an individual more or less tolerant of the sexual behaviour of others.

My enquiries of children who had been shown sex-education programmes revealed a majority who found the concept of intercourse *per se* 'revolting'. In the words of a representative ten-year-old girl from New Jersey, who clearly described the insertion of a turgid penis into a vagina and the ejaculation of millions of tiny spermatozoa, 'you wouldn't find *me* doing any such thing'. What surprised me more was that many children come out of these sessions wondering how much of what they have been shown is true! In either event, the portrayal of intercourse out of its emotional and physiological context is absurd and harmful. Many decades ago our schools coyly avoided the very mention of sexual functioning, teaching everything about the functioning of the body's organs with the sole exception of the sexual apparatus. The wheel has now turned full circle, and we are now instructing children in the details only of that, and ignoring many of the essentials of what used to be called a balanced education. My greatest fear is that, far from encouraging experimentation and sexual excess, sex education is going to degrade sexual ecstasy, lower sexual excitement, and reduce a future generation's capacity to enjoy the extravagant and all-embracing heights of sexual liberation.

Man's pair-bonding instincts are emphasized by the extremes to which falling in love can go. It is nothing to do with automatically turgid phalluses emptying themselves into a cylindrical vagina, but with overwhelming and inexplicable urges to be with, care for, stay near a single person. Copulation as a source of relief pales into withering insignificance alongside the passionate extremes of love and passion, and the irrational 'infatuation' felt by every normal adolescent for an older person.

Young children experience sexual sensations; girls can find their clitoris and pull it excitedly as a means of obtaining comfort or relief, little boys will tug at the sensitive tip of the foreskin, and children sometimes rock against a toy, a cushion, or an adult's knee or leg in subconscious sexuality. Not that this is associated with inevitable precocity – indeed, many children who recall such activities never associated them with 'sex' at all. I have spoken to one girl who spent several years in a frankly sexual liaison with an uncle, with whom she regularly had intercourse (he even attempted sodomy). She had learned about sex in school, and done all the lessons on copulation, without once associating what she was learning about with what she was doing in the weekend sex sessions with her relative.

It has been overlooked that the criteria by which we judge such actions to be good or bad; acceptable or unacceptable; are predicated to a great extent on the manner in which the phenomenon is communicated – the reaction of the teacher, parent, or spectator – rather than on the act itself. Sexual acts against youngsters are far less traumatic than the reaction of aggrieved parents in the face of disclosure. Furthermore, I have no doubt that many of the experiences which we regard as being essentially traumatic (like the supposed aberrant behaviour of orphans or foster-children) are not brought about by the event which we regard as causing the trauma, but by reactions on the part of those involved in it. If a child commits some naughty or wilful act, it is tempting to react differently depending upon what you know of its background. If it is just your child, and that's all, onlookers say: 'Oh well, kids of that age are like that, aren't they?' and nothing more is read into the situation. But admit that the child is a foster-child (the usual expression is 'only' a foster-child, a gratuitous piece of received propaganda in the same condescending and untruthful category as being 'stuck' at home with the children, 'tied' to a home or 'just' a housewife and mother) and a difference at once appears. 'Ah, it is in the child's background; after what happened there, I'm not surprised' is the response. Onlookers signal to the child that they look at him in a different – a subtly different – way to normal children, and the innate codes of criteria coupled with the learned experiences that are inevitable in anyone who has been alive for more than a couple of years, mean that the child picks up those cues, and at once interprets them as signals to do more of the same.

The result is a child who acts as our preconceptions or simplified child-psychology lead us to anticipate; and who acts thus because of the spectator's attitudes, and not because of the child's own 'traumas' at all.

It is in this way that we fail to recognize the need for objective, unbiased and constructive teaching in the whole field of adult/child relationships. This may be a symptom of a society which is already past its developmental peak, and which is now unravelling a complex code of inborn safety controls which are destined to reduce our fertility, and to control our rate of reproduction, until mankind becomes less of a threat to his world; that is my own reading of our predicament. It may be a cumulative burden of conscious acquisition of arbitrary fashions that make us designate certain actions as good or bad, until these codes of criteria begin to let us down, and impose controls of their own. Or it may be any other related cause – for the nature of the impulse that starts off the process is somewhat academic alongside the immense practical significance of the results.

Whatever the reason, we are now entering a phase where sex is being degraded and sexuality debased; where children are seen as somehow undesirable and as an interference with the processes of money-grabbing self-sufficiency, and love an out-dated anachronism; in short, where we are giving our children a tawdry and unexciting version of orgasm-consciousness at the expense of the many aspects of sexuality that go with it. It is societal castration of a virulent and destructive kind.

Perhaps the most insidious particular result is the emphasis on sex for the sake of short-term, or immediate, gratification. For the sexual novice, or the frustrated abstinent, it performs a certain function of relief; perhaps it is this form of experience which encouraged that sex educator to describe orgasm to children as being 'like a sneeze'. But all too often, instant sex of this kind does not work. It needs to follow a pre-ordained ritual of loving behaviour, of togetherness and accumulating desire so that the sex act becomes a culmination of many hours of exploration in the psychological as well as the purely anatomical sense, and is a means of expression for deep-felt and passionately experienced feelings and desires. On this level, sexuality is long-lasting and steadily deepening. In its non-loving context, it is all too often an unmemorable, forgettable and regrettable episode so transient, so fleeting, as to signify nothing more than momentary selfish relief. 'I have enjoyed a good shit more', are the words that several separate individuals have used to describe that.

The primitive sexual feelings that some children experience are derived from stimulation that is related to the sexual innervation of areas like the clitoris and the penis, and such masturbatory stimulation is often accidental. Riding a horse may initiate it; sitting on a cushion, rubbing or leaning on the corner of a vibrating washing machine or carpet cleaner, even playing ride-a-cock-horse (as the name of the game implies) may trigger the response. Even in children who do not engage in frank masturbation there are mild sensations of comfort or low-grade satisfaction in exploring the genitals.

But it is in early adolescence that matters take a more significant turn. Dreams of a sexy nature begin to appear in more recognizable terms. A young child will dream about 'sexy' scenes, which often turn out to be nothing more than naked figures on a beach, the genitals not actually perceived in the dream at all. This dream is 'sexy' because the criteria that have been acquired associate nudity with naughtiness/sexiness; to the child such an association – once the criteria codes exist – is natural and definitive, even though it seems almost absurd to an adult with the benefit of hindsight. The dreams of adolescence centre on copulation, and in girls often on being raped. Boys dream of genital stimulation and even in heterosexual boys the gender of the stimulator seems to be irrelevant.

Games with sexual connotations take on a new guise too. The twelve-year-old girl playing Postman's Knock will find the game exciting and uniquely enjoyable; and when she is a woman she will look back with amusement to realize that at that tender age she had noticed her knickers becoming wet as the game went on – and had thought she was wetting herself with excitement. The woman looking back recalls that it was not urine which left its mark at all, but increased vaginal secretions that she later learned were part of the preparation for intercourse.

Erections become more frequent in boys during the same age-group. Sometimes they occur in bed, and the boy will have a sexy dream that results in a satisfying orgasm. Girls occasionally say they had dreams of an orgasmic nature too, but whether it is quite the same at that age for them is debatable. There is a physical reason for the boy's climax; he is accumulating small amounts of seminal fluid until this needs to be expelled, and the sexy dream that brings this about is a natural release. Semen is lost in the process, which is why the phenomenon is known in childhood slang as a wet dream. Boys also discover that moving the penis around whilst it is erect produces pleasurable sensations; they may form a pseudo-vagina with the fingers, and move them up and down; they may grasp the shaft of the penis, and masturbate that way; some engage in frotteurism against the bedclothes-whilst others hold the glans and rotate the penis in a circle, or roll it back and forth between the palms of the hands.

Girls masturbate by thrusting against a pillow or the handle of a hair-brush, by lying face-down and repeatedly contracting the thighs, by inserting objects into the vagina, playing with the breasts, and sometimes by resting the pubis against school spin-dryers during domestic science lessons . . . there are many options (and at least one popular variant in both sexes centres on the use of the neck of a 'coke' bottle).

In girls the orgasm that results is a thrilling, vibrating sensation that brings out the body in goose-bumps and causes the breath to catch; in boys the sense is of a pulsating thrusting sensation within the penis and the loins, often with spasmodic movements of the legs as the muscles of the penis seek to expel semen. Until the sexual organs are mature, no semen appears; just a milky bead of fluid may be expelled. When the organs are ready and have been stimulated by the pituitary gland in the base of the brain, according to the individual's maturation programme which is inbuilt, then the amount suddenly increases and it is emitted from the penis in short spurts which may fly some distance away. A boy before this stage will say, in child language, that he cannot yet 'come'; in children, 'coming' is associated with seminal ejaculation; in adolescents it is used to mean the sensation of orgasm itself.

There are many differences in sexuality between the sexes even at this stage. The girl does not ejaculate; she does not produce an orgasmic flow of fluid even though she will secrete vaginal juices during sexual excitement. How this is done is largely mysterious, incidentally; there are no glands in the vagina that can secrete anything, and there should be no secretion at all, in theory! The girl's orgasm is not related to the expulsion of sexual cells, whilst the boy's is. The boy needs to have his penis erect to reach a normal climax, but the girl does not need to have an erect clitoris for this to occur.

There is much confusion over the existence of erectile tissue in both sexes, and I have known many males assume that their sexual partner does not enjoy love-making if her erectile tissue in the clitoris and nipples is not turgid. This is a fundamental error. A girl's nipples, like a man's, often erect because of cold as much as anything. But female erectile tissue is often soft, pliant and relaxed during caresses or sucking and is in this state greatly arousable. The clitoris is analogous to the penis in some ways, but does not in any way function like it.

This is not a book of sexual technique in the anatomical sense. I do not want to be bogged down in lengthy descriptions of the positions and techniques of love-making, partly because an emphasis on these mechanistic methods is for many couples counter-productive. But even in the basic outline of adolescent sexual maturation which we have considered here, we can see one important principle emerging: it is that the nature of sexuality, of the sexual response, and of the manner in which mankind's anatomy is designed for the performance of sex, varies fundamentally in principle and practice from female to male. The notion that sexuality should not be reflected in sexism is in this sense alone unrealistic.

To cite just one example, no photograph of a woman can reveal whether she is actually in a state of sexual excitement or not. A glance at a full-frontal male nude shows that in an instant. No picture of a woman can demonstrate that she is in the throes of orgasm; a man can be seen to be doing that at once. Man can rape a woman, or another man; but woman cannot rape a man, though she can rape a woman by genital contact. A woman who is not sexually aroused can undertake intercourse with a man, whilst a man who is unaroused could not do so . . .

None of this can be taken to suggest that one sex has the edge over the other, or is better at sex; but it does make us realize that the tendency to encourage the illusion that sexuality is much the same for men as for women is fatuous. If sexism means the treating of the sexes differently because of the fact that they *are* different, then the defeat of sexism would not only be the defeat of our very human essence, it would also destroy much of the capacity for physical pleasure and emotional fulfilment for which we have evolved. Sexism is not an out-dated cliché which has to be extirpated at all costs; it is a fundamental part of our being, and a symptom of being a full and complete human.

It has become increasingly popular to denigrate the state of childhood, seeing it as an arbitrary anachronism and, in the words of one authority, 'nothing more than a Victorian invention'. But it is not childhood at all which is the invention. Childhood is simply that phase of living when naïvety is at its highest; but childhood (in the sense of an enjoyable, happy time of exploration and learning) is the true state of mankind. It is adulthood which is the sophistication, the unnecessary invention which distorts our lives, in contradiction to the widespread view of our age. The concept of settling down to get married, of mellowing in one's twenties and becoming quieter, far less lively, or of conforming to the workaday traditions and joining the ranks of telly-watching, hard-working parents 'stuck' with the kids and household chores . . . the whole 'why don't you settle down and become an adult?' philosophy typifies our conviction that we must consciously copy what is presumed to be stereotyped adult behaviour without stopping to consider whether that is good or bad, whether it is real or arbitrary.

One source of substantiation of my view on this matter is that adulthood is a relatively recent invention, or at least, that adolescence – as a preparatory phase for adulthood – has only recently appeared. Many of the initiation ceremonies that have been reported in primitive peoples centre on the single event of sexual maturation, or rather the onset of it; and it is interesting to note that in earlier ages and in more unsophisticated peoples this transformation is seen as occurring around the age of seven or so, rather than 21 or 18. This suggestion was supported by a most elegant and intriguing piece of work carried out in the late 1950's by Philippe Ariès (and published in his book *Centuries of Childhood*, Knopf, New York, 1962). He carried out prolonged analyses of the personal diaries and also the paintings of mediaeval Europe and showed that it was usual then – and for some time afterwards – particularly amongst the lower social classes, to regard the ending of childhood at the age of seven or thereabouts.

Societal conventions have now placed a marked emphasis on the concept of adolescence and adulthood. The growing strictures of 'grown-up' behaviour have made the ritual of acting like an adult assume greater importance as time goes by, and the weight placed on adolescence doubtless derives from the development of formal education. This is all comparatively recent, and what is more it is unrealistic. The whole idea of keeping a group of children of the same age incarcerated in a room with a person who may well be less intelligent than many of them and who is very likely three or four times their age is in accordance with no biological precedent of any kind; and the emphasis on names, dates, formulae and artificial knowledge-acquisition is an insult to the ancient lineage of instruction which one sees in less sophisticated, and more natural, societies.

As it is, children know that in school they learn about matters which are of little relevance to the outside world. Ideally, I would start each school day discussing the newspapers, sport and the pop charts, would teach pupils about their own favourite books and comics, about supermarkets and property prices, about leisure and hobbies from fishing to urban farming, about train timetables and methods of obtaining cheap travel, about creativity and freedom, about the political machine, about medicine, the organization of state power, and about how they *matter* in society. Above all I would do away with the sterile lessons on anatomical copulation and explain something of emotions, feelings and relationships – the whole based on an understanding of the role of criteria-based decisions in human existence.

One would also hope to prevent anyone from rushing headlong into the artificialities of assumed adulthood. Why shouldn't adults build dams on the beach if they feel so inclined, without receiving uncertain glances from others more interested in perpetrating the adult mystique? Why should informal meetings and discussions and a general feeling of living in the fullest and freest sense seem to be the prerogative of 'the young', to be consciously forsaken by fashion-conscious people over the age of, say, 25? Indeed, why should anyone assume that to marry, or to have children, or even to sustain a career, one has to 'settle down' – a turgid and strictured prospect.

Animals show no such division into childhood, adolescence and adulthood. A mature dog or cat that plays is regarded by its owner as healthier and happier than one that does not; it is (or rather, should be) exactly the same for the human species. The recent faddishness for adolescence has crept up on us more subtly than we usually realize, for our parents (and certainly our grandparents) had no concept of 'teenage' as an age of significance at all.

The conflict between adulthood in the societal sense and adolescence in its legally-interpreted context shows most graphically where a person defined according to one code of criteria is seen as 'adult' whilst in another as 'child'. There is the case of the young fighter pilot in World War II who on his spells of leave at home was unable even to drive his father's car because he was too young to hold a license. A marriage in California during the 1950's was curtailed because of juvenile curfew laws (the new bride was under age to stay out, legally, at night); and in Illinois there was the case of the father who was not permitted to visit the maternity hospital to see his young bride with their new-born baby; he was still fifteen, and regulations denied access to the wards for any visitor under sixteen years of age.

It is usual to point to such discrepancies as examples of the unease that teenagers experience; and – if these anecdotal examples are perhaps extreme – it is generally conceded that an uncertainty about personality identification and feelings of conflict generated by parental hostility are the root cause of the 'difficult teenager' syndrome which so bedevils contemporary family life.

It is almost self-evident that a child with good looks, a good figure and an ostentatiously free and unfettered existence where casual and intense relationships occur in an enviably easy-going sequence, may be regarded with hostility and jealousy by a parent who is past it. That form of conflict predicament is hardly conducive to harmony and familial closeness, and nobody can doubt that in that kind of situation can be found the roots of much disappointment and frank inter-generation warfare.

But this view does not account for all the truth, even if it may satisfactorily explain some of it. There are two reasons for this. First is the fact that adolescence as a condition of mankind is not as enviable as it seems. Those fleeting sequential relationships are often most unsatisfactory, even if they can be instructional. The good figure is of no consequence to a teenager who bemoans under-arm hair, acne, irregular teeth, or some fictionalized idea of what their weight should be, but isn't. Teenagers have the same uncertainties as any other person, intensified by the overlying stratum of naïvety which characterizes that stage, and from these swings of personal misidentification arise endless inward conflicts and levels of uncertainty, some of which end in death, ranging from the overdose of drugs in a boy who is confused about cognitive reality or the plastic-bag suffocation by a youth whose parents have rejected him, to the girl who starves herself to death in *anorexia nervosa* triggered by the acquisition of immutable criteria which make excess weight, and soon any weight at all, undesirable.

The 'free' life of teenagers is very far from 'free' in a host of ways, from the rigid strictures of the uniform that has to be worn at all costs (like Levi jeans) and what has to be avoided – a necktie, for example – to the stifling trap of received orthodoxies that govern which pop groups and which personalities are fashionable and which views are not.

THE CHEMISTRY OF ADOLESCENCE

Adolescence is a condition of uncertainty for many young people, like the uncertainties that dog the heels of adults, and parental suspicions that kids are wafting from bed to bar and back again in an unending sequence of sensuous satisfaction serve only to reinforce the widespread adult feeling that, 'not only am I having a rough time in trying to conform to the ideals of my teens, but everyone else is clearly having a better time than I am.' The adult faced with this predicament may rightly sense that an adolescent son or daughter is still untainted by what I have described as the unnecessary and restricting conventions of adult society (a reaction that we would abolish overnight if we could understand that this strictured notion of adulthood is entirely unnecessary), but in most respects he is envying the unenviable and wishing for something that does not exist.

Secondly, there are powerful forces at work which account for unrest, moodiness and conflict in physiological terms and not in any high-falutin and esoteric psychological sense at all. I believe that much of the turmoil of teenagers is caused by hormone surges and by the states of imbalance that inevitably occur as a body adjusts to new chemical situations and the mind responds in turn. We are well aware of the emotional problems of the menopause, when the hormone cycle of a woman's monthly menstrual pattern dies away. One can be reasonably certain that these problems are hormonal, for parallel conditions do not pertain in men (male hormone levels very gradually decline from the early twenties onwards) and in this manner men provide for women a form of direct comparison.

Psychological difficulties associated with the realization of unfulfilled ambitions, a now-reared family, and so forth, are found in both sexes; but in women alone we find intense moodiness, irritability, cyclical personality changes and hot flushes. So it is sensible to associate those signs with the hormonal changes that accompany the menopause. What interests me particularly is that these symptoms are identical to many of those of adolescence! Are we wrong in ascribing to psychological causes these phases of aberrant behaviour seen in teenagers? We surely are – if the lowering of hormone levels in middle-aged women can so radically distort their emotional lives, then the sudden rise in levels that occurs in the teens can assuredly do the same for the adolescent.

When Byron wrote, in *Don Juan*, that 'her climacteric teased her like her teens' he was recording an observation that everyone makes at some stage during life. The common chemical causation of both syndromes accounts for the upheaval of adolescence in a manner that may remove some of the grief and perplexity felt by the many parents who have truly tried to accommodate their teenaged children with the best will, and perhaps in the best way, available yet have experienced violent and inexplicable changes in behaviour. That this may have a chemical cause may comfort some teenagers who are equally bewildered by their own fluctuations of mood.

Hormones are chemical substances which act like powerful drugs; they are secreted by glands in the body which act differently to most ordinary glandular structures since (whereas a conventional gland, like a sweat-gland, produces a secretion which it passes through a duct) their hormone product diffuses or seeps straight from the cells which produce it into the bloodstream. The hormone-producing glands are for this reason known collectively as the ductless glands, and although we now know a great deal about the body's main hormones it is true that we must remain ignorant about the majority, and as yet the extent to which we can utilize hormones to predictably change our bodies is surprisingly limited. But the power of hormones is well enough known, even by those who have no contact with medical research – selective weedkillers show us the power of hormones and hormone-like substances to drastically interfere with normal growth behaviour, and the use of anabolic steroids as muscle-building agents is often mentioned in sports reports. The effects of the oral contraceptive are another example; the amount of hormone-like substance that is involved is minute (so much so, that the weight of steroid in a contraceptive pill would be perfectly safe to swallow if pure cyanide were substituted for it) and the sex hormones in mammals exert profound effects in dosages that may be less than one millionth of an ounce.

It is popular, but erroneous, to imagine that there is some magical hormone which confers sexual maturity on a person; but our present level of knowledge (even though it is certainly far from complete) suggests that many different processes happen – some of them independently of each other – and the net result of *all* this activity is maturation. The ductless gland on which much of this depends is the pituitary, a small zone in the base of the brain which holds many vital keys to human development. The region of the pituitary involved is known as the hypothalamus and it begins to alter its activity around the age of 10 in children.

Firstly, it begins to secrete hormones in larger amounts than before. It seems as though the hypothalamus is always potentially able to do this, but is held in check by the other regions of the brain – we know this because, if the connections between the brain and the hypothalamus are damaged, it begins secreting these stimulating hormones at once.

Secondly, the hypothalamus becomes altered in the way it responds to hormone levels already circulating in the blood. Before this time, some of its activities were held in check by feedback from the steroid hormones present in the bloodstream, but as the sexual maturation process switches on the cells of the hypothalamus change their ability to respond and no longer heed the signal. In animals (though perhaps not in mankind) the ovaries also need to be at the right age for maturity to ensue before they will respond to stimulation by artificially-administered hormones – if these gonadotrophins are administered after puberty has commenced, the result is a profound stimulation of the ovaries but if the administration is made too early there is no response.

So there is no easy means of understanding how the onset of maturation takes place or how its mechanisms are initiated. It is, though, clear why people vary so much in their individual reports of how they matured: some women menstruate early and take a long time to develop physically, others develop body hair early on and take years before menstruation appears. Some boys become bearded and yet not highly-sexed early in the teens, others may suddenly report genital development and ejaculation many years before facial hair has become noticeable. The old ideas that are so profound, and which like to generalize about hairy legs, the size of the feet, the spacing of periods or whatever and other sexual attributes are simply not reliable. The tale is told of the hospital matron who was attracted into a

59

noisy lecture theatre and asked the lecturer what had caused the interruption. 'They were laughing about an interesting relationship which I mentioned,' said the doctor. 'Oh yes,' retorted the matron in a loud and confident manner, 'and *what* relationship was *that* exactly?'

'Only that in women the size of the mouth is directly proportional to that of the opening of the vagina,' replied the doctor. There was a pause; and then the matron quietly lisped 'is that tho, doctor?' through tightly pursed lips.

She need not have worried – this old tale, and its fellows, are quite without meaning. Some normal women do not begin menstruating until well into their twenties (the age of 25 was noted by Kinsey); and in contrast some girls claim to have completed growing to their adult height by the age of nine. It is certainly invalid to regard menstruation as the first sign of adolescence, since physical growth spurts some time before that, and so does the development of pubic hair (most women develop pubic hair before they menstruate). Parallel observations can be made about boys.

It is in the male that the development into a sexually mature adult is easier to qualify. The male sex hormone, testosterone, increases greatly over the period of a few years some time around the mid or early teens, and ejaculation appears then too. From that time onwards it takes a very short while for sexual potency to reach its height, and from then on in quantifiable terms there is a general and slow decline. In women the position is complicated by the many sex hormones that are already known to be involved, by the cyclical nature of menstruation and ovulation, and by the undeniable fact that fertility becomes established more gradually in a woman, and dies away during the menopause. A woman reaches the peak of her sexual prowess around the age of 30, whereas a man is at his physiological sexual peak ten years earlier. This does not mean that the *expression* of sexuality is founded upon the same time-scale, of course; most men take until well into their thirties to find the most efficacious means of sexual expression and sexual fulfilment remains immensely satisfying to men and women in love well after middle age.

Most girls have begun breast development by the age of 14, though some commence around the age of 10. The average age for this phenomenon is the same as the age at which pubic hair first appears, about $12\frac{1}{2}$ years. Menstruation, on average, follows about nine months or so later. The development of the body and the cessation of physical growth does not finish, on average, for three years after that; though some girls are fully grown by the time of their tenth birthday and a few others delay physical maturity until well into their early twenties.

Boys tend to develop sexual maturity around a year later; thus the mean age at which pubic hair appears in adolescent males is $13\frac{1}{2}$ compared with $12\frac{1}{2}$ for females. But ejaculation in boys appears on average around the age of 13½ or 14, whereas the age at which 50% of girls have experienced orgasm is as late as 21. Why it should take longer for the manifestations of sexual competence to appear in boys than in girls (since the pituitary changes that are involved with the triggering mechanism seem to happen at about the same age in both sexes) is unknown.

It is quite clear that sexual maturity has been appearing at an earlier age than used to be the case. The appearance of body hair (which is referred to as 'menarche' in many texts and is what the term 'puberty' directly describes) has occurred at steadily earlier ages for many centuries. In the middle 1800's, for instance, the average age of menarche in young people was around 17. The change in recent history (over the past couple of centuries) has been a steady advance of one year younger every 30 years – a year per generation, you might say – until we have now got to 12 or 13 years of age. The usual explanation of this is better feeding in more advanced countries, but although this age in Western societies is a couple of years earlier than the age of menarche in some undeveloped nations, it is exactly the same as the age in, for instance, Hong Kong where social conditions are very different. The mature height of a developed individual has increased over the years, too, so that a given height has been reached a year earlier, on average, for every 40 years of passing time. Today's youth is at his full height by the average age of 17, whereas his father's grandfather would have continued growing until his middle, or even late, twenties. Today's mature youth is some three inches taller than was his great-grandfather.

Today's vitamin-enriched super-nourishing diet is not the entire answer. Firstly, the now-early age of the menarche in Western countries is the same as that in some of the less well-fed nations (e.g. Hong Kong), and, of course – although it is popular to believe that we are now far taller than we were centuries ago – *Homo sapiens* was pretty much the same height hundreds of thousands of years ago.

One factor that might be involved is the increasing mobility of the past centuries, which might have reversed a tendency to regional inbreeding that was causing a loss of stature and a weakening of the genetic line. It has been shown that animals given longer exposures to artificial light tend to mature earlier, so that could be involved in mankind's development. Perhaps the greater social activity and sexual awareness of recent generations has triggered a tendency towards sexual precocity. For instance, a century ago a Christian community which took biblical teachings on the 'love of man' to cover sexual promiscuity – the so-called Oneida Community – introduced young girls to intercourse with mature men when the girls were still pre-adolescent. Many of them showed an earlier menarche in consequence.

In some way, lifestyle (which obviously includes dietary considerations) plays a crucial role in the age at which puberty appears. Clear evidence of this is the fact that in any given community with common racial and climatic characteristics, the children of higher social groups mature somewhat earlier than the poorer economic classes. But an understanding of exactly what the factors are, and how they are interrelated, remains beyond our grasp.

One question that has often been raised by those teachers who have – in the space of a couple of generations – become used to seeing pubertal girls in junior school level (i.e. pre-11) is whether the trend towards precocity is going to continue, until we see adolescence emerging in the near-infant. The answer to this question is no; all the evidence currently available shows that the steady advance is now slowed down to a fraction of its earlier rate. We have witnessed the reaching of our innate sexual threshold, and if those data are to be believed, future generations will see little to match the continuous advancement of maturity towards childhood which we have seen ourselves.

The sex hormones that initiate these changes towards maturation are powerful substances (in familiar terms, as we have seen, a millionth part of an ounce per day is enough for many of them to exert wide-ranging effects), and the simplistic idea that it is the male testosterone and the female oestrogen and progesterone which are solely responsible for maturity is only a small part of the complete picture. A whole range of growth and developmental substances are involved somewhere along the line, and the eventual network of interrelated hormones which we will one day discover is surely going to make today's approach seem fragmentary by comparison.

But there are these important distinctions between the sexes – distinctions which show how fundamentally the hormones influence, not just the existence of maleness and femaleness, but also the very nature of the two sexes. The first is that testosterone triggers aggression. Here we have another example of a chemically-caused behavioural pattern; and it is one which has clear societal purposes. Men have always needed to be aggressive under the conditions through which our species evolved, firstly to capture and obtain food in competition with other predators (both human and animal); and secondly to provide a stimulus when the family needed to be protected from outside attack. It is this innate potential which has given men many of their sex-specific functions in organized societies, and which has always caused men to follow aggressive sports (like football or boxing) which the majority of their women-folk do not instinctively care for as much, and which women often find attracts them to their mate. The feeling of being harboured and protected is one which it is normal and widespread for women to experience, and it derives from this chemically-induced nature of the male of the species.

THE ACHIEVEMENT OF MENOPAUSE

In women the later years are marked by the cessation of sex-hormone production in amounts compatible with the maintenance of fertility. In middle-age the menopause occurs, a condition which produces a range of physical and psychological manifestations. Many of these are controllable, though we know far less about the management of the menopause than we should. I know how popular it has been to ascribe this to a kind of maliciousness on the part of men, as though they were all determined to allow women to suffer out of masculine bias, but this explanation will not do.

Firstly, a great many women specialists have been involved in clinical research at levels where they could have initiated research over past decades, yet they did not bring about the insights they might have done. And secondly, there are so many other areas of medical management which affect both sexes equally and which we continue to ignore. There has only been such a discipline as 'intensive care' for the past couple of decades, for instance; the post-operative patient was until our era left to suffer at his own devices for much of the time. That was not directed against women more than men; and – now that we have intensive care wards everywhere in our Western hospitals – it seems ludicrous that we waited so long before so much as thinking of the discipline.

I find myself equally non-plussed by our contemporary attitudes towards the old, who are only now coming in for the kind of attention they deserve; and I can still remember the difficulties encountered in the early 1970's when I attempted to mount some public airing of issues involving the elderly. Even then, so very recently, it was somehow accepted that there was nothing *to* be done in spite of the overwhelming evidence to the contrary that beset us on all sides.

A contemporary area which is ignored by almost everyone is the management of death. It is assumed that death in some way 'has' to be natural; and if the naturalness involves endless suffering in life (for the suffering of the terminally ill never does end as long as there is a person alive to suffer it) then we seem to consider it a part of the plan that old and feeble folk should end their existence in agony. A colleague with whom I was discussing this said to me that her mother died peacefully, 'with only about four hours of real pain at the end'. With our knowledge of pain-killing treatments there is no reason why we should not have nurses trained specifically to aid the dying; no-one should have to suffer any pain for which there is a medical or surgical solution.

We know next to nothing about what pain is, and very much less than it is usual to admit about how pain-killing works; but we can do far more than we do to ease the lot of the dying and I hope we will look back in a decade or two with disbelief at the callous manner we ignored those unfortunate enough to die around 1980, and before.

It would be foolish to interpret these large areas of ignorance as a conspiracy by the young against the old, or a plot against the dying by the quick, and there is no great point in making the lack of research into the menopause seem like an act of sexual warfare waged by men against women. Further evidence of my contention that this is nothing more than an example of what I have named 'fashionism' in research is the fact that women are not the only gender who suffer from menopausal symptoms – no, I am not referring to the so-called male menopause, but the degree to which any husband suffers from the change in his menopausal wife. The switches in mood and character and the feelings of ill-health that may be involved are distressing to any loving spouse, and (even on the selfish level) an irritation for the most feckless and uncaring husband. This alone makes it unwarrantable to suggest that male attitudes have in some way deliberately diverted attention away from the study of menopausal symptoms. Now that doctors are beginning to search for ways to treat these distressing signs in their middle-aged women patients, we are witnessing the gradual unfolding of a new branch of medicine. In my view, this is nothing more than the turning of attention to a new fashion which has been brought about by ceaseless campaigning on the part of a few lone voices – male and female – and it is not the collapse of male dominance which some individuals have claimed.

We are still faced with the question *why* human females – almost uniquely amongst all species – exhibit this phenomenon. I believe that it has an important biological function. Unlike men, who have the role of support and care for the family unit as a whole, the woman is placed at risk each time she becomes pregnant. Though her mate's function admittedly involves the arduous tasks of obtaining food, shelter and safety for the family itself, he is not at any biological risk through childbirth. (Of course, males are denied that ultimate creative experience – the production of a new body, a new living thing, through the birth process. Might it even be that the greater number of males, rather than females, who have succeeded in the arts and in a host of creative fields is not merely due to the stifling effects that society has had on women, but is also due to the need to find some kind of creative outlet which women can satisfy through the production of a unique living being?)

The hazard from childbirth is not overwhelming; but it certainly increases with advancing age, and I believe that the purpose of menopause has its roots in the tremendous advantage to any human community that an older woman alone can bring. In primitive societies, if she survived to (say) 50 she would have a unique insight into the demands of life, and a rare degree of experience. It would have been likely that she owed her survival to her own abilities in motherhood – a less fit woman, or a mother less able to master the demands of pregnancy and parturition, would very likely die before she reached an advanced age. Our evolutionary history has laid great emphasis on cultural, learned behaviour being passed from one generation to the next, and it was the wise and intelligent woman – the mother who survived – who clearly offered most to the community as a teacher and adviser of up-and-coming generations.

It is for this reason, I believe, that the menopause evolved. It was an immunity from further burden granted to the most able women, the survivors, so that they could pass on their wisdom to their youngers. There is no comparable hazard to men, so no sudden withdrawal of fertility occurs at this pre-ordained time.

It is frequently taught that the menopause is essentially a disease caused by a deficiency of the sex hormones. The argument goes: 'In primitive times, most women would have been dead before the menopause occurred, and so it was never the subject of evolutionary selection which would otherwise have tended to remove it.' Other people claim that the phenomenon marks the 'end of a woman's womanliness', and add that in modern society a woman is needed to provide help, support, teaching and encouragement for younger people. My own view is very different.

I see the menopause as potentially the beginning of trouble-free womanhood, with all worries about pregnancy or contraception removed. The menopause, in this light, is seen as a positive evolutionary advantage to the survivors even in those 'primitive societies'; and I do not imagine that the supportive and educational role of a mature woman is of such recent development. There can be no doubt that it was always so – and the removal of the menstrual burden and the attendant risks of pregnancy is nature's recognition and reward.

But we must balance up the ideal with the reality. It is a most regrettable fact that changes in hormone balance trigger many unpleasant side-effects which may only be mild, but which can show themselves in a distressingly severe manner in all too many cases (I have already referred to the psychological and physical changes associated with the onset of hormone change at puberty). On the medical front we find headaches, dizziness, palpitations and fatigue together with the celebrated (and often under-rated) 'hot flush'; in the psychological realm, depression, irritability, mood fluctuation and even character change are reported.

There has been much talk of the 'ease' with which such things can be treated by hormone replacement at the menopause. It is tempting to imagine that the whole matter is tied up and finalized – but this is in fact far from the truth. It is a shocking fact to disclose, but we know nothing of note about the cause of any of these symptoms and very little about their treatment. Some of them, in some women, can be treated by the use of artificially administered sex hormones or their analogues, and there are

65

many women on record who have found relief in this form of medication. The difficulty others have experienced in obtaining hormone replacement therapy is reprehensible; many doctors have felt uncertain about the proven merits of this form of treatment, they have been ruled by the possibility of side-effects resulting from the therapy, and seemed to feel that there was more to the menopause than the simple 'hormone deficiency' explanation. In this last case I am sure they were right. No-one would regard childhood as a condition of sex-hormone deficiency, since rarely is the body so glowing with health and vigour as it is in those early years.

The onset of menopause manifests itself in many ways, one of which is a sudden decrease in oestrogen production, but you would be wrong to assume that an outside interference with those levels is going to cure all the problems: a match may cause a massive conflagration, but you would not hope to extinguish the blaze by merely removing the match.

But it is abundantly clear that medicine has seriously underestimated the extent and severity of the menopausal syndrome. For many women it causes intense misery, and this reflects on husbands and children too. The sooner we recognize the value of therapy in alleviating many of these symptoms the better: but we must bear in mind two other vital points.

The first is that many women do find that the menopause heralds a time of unique and unprecedented freedom and release, a phase when old worries about conception disappear and a new era of sexual liberation appears. They do not fear the change of life at all, but regard it as the ultimate freedom. And of course the ending of menstrual loss and the cyclical changes of the monthly cycle is an obvious gain. Secondly, we cannot allow ourselves to be tricked into imagining a few injections or pills will somehow take the menopause away. The hormone preparations we do have can help, in many cases they can help most wonderfully; but the menopause is a major shut-down of the reproductive system that works at a host of different levels, and our meddling does little to change that. It is surely as well that we cannot interfere; some women (certainly a minority) regard menstruation as a sign of femininity above all else, and welcome perpetual withdrawal bleeding (which can be induced by therapy) as a substitute for natural menstrual bleeding, right into old age.

Now, if that is the way that some learned code of criteria makes anyone feel, so be it. There are plenty of sexual manifestations in both sexes that individuals come to associate with their potency as functioning, fully-fledged people, and menstruation could certainly be construed in the mind of a woman as her touchstone of femininity.

But in my view, sexuality has nothing in the world to do with the menstrual cycle and reproduction. Sexuality is pre-programmed into us in order that we pair off and enjoy each other and ourselves, and provides us with means of selecting mates who will rear our families with us. But people

66

do not have sex in order to procreate. They have sex in order to have a good time and enjoy themselves. A woman's fertile years are, then, a burden in biological terms; a phase when she has to be prepared to consider getting pregnant because of her sexual desires. So the menopause, which signals the ending of this phase, is actually the lifting of a burden and the restoration of unfettered sexuality. Most women seem to regard the idea of continuing to have artificially induced periods until way past middle age with distaste and even revulsion; and that view fits far closer to my own interpretation of the purpose of sexuality. Medication to help maintain a supple skin, good nutrition, a healthy vagina or whatever, is vitally necessary for anyone who needs it, in any way that it can help. But my own view remains that the attitude towards the menopause is wrong, and this very likely makes the signs and symptoms of entering into it a greater burden than they might otherwise be.

Let no-one underestimate the extent of the care that may be sought. Women may develop osteoporosis (a softening of the bones) as a result of the menopause, and the level of risk for coronaries rises from the normally low level for fertile women up to the level normal for men in the same age group. In most cases we could now offer treatment on a far wider scale than we have witnessed in the past, and it is scandalously neglectful of medical orthodoxy that it has taken so long for this really elementary lesson to be learned. But such palliative treatment should not be regarded as a postponement of the menopause, when it is really an aid to its accomplishment.

Nature's firm purpose in lifting that cyclical burden from middle-aged women is clear; for example, only a minute fraction of the egg cells present in a woman's ovaries are ever released during the fertile decades. At puberty there are roughly 35,000 immature egg-cells (oocytes) present in normal ovaries. Each time a woman is due to become fertile, and this occurs over a period of only a couple of days each month, around ten or so of these oocytes become nearly mature. One of those is released (as a rule) and the other nine break down and are reabsorbed. So in a normal lifetime of full fertility, a woman might produce 400 mature egg cells, and a total of 4,000 *nearly* mature ones form in the process. This means that in excess of 30,000 oocytes are never accounted for. Where do they go? The answer is that they disappear. Around the age of 45 or so, they have all vanished. How they go is a mystery, and where they go is only partly understood (they seem to re-enter the ovaries' structure and perhaps contribute their protoplasmic contents to the general bodily circulation, small contribution though that would be). Why they go is not fully explained either. My belief that it is nature's way of providing an imperative which cuts off the years of risk and provides a more relaxed future, safe from pregnancy, fits well with the dramatic disappearance of those egg-cells. It is otherwise an astonishing mystery.

But why are women plagued by the demands of a regular monthly cycle throughout their fertile years? It is easy to find an èxplanation for the continual fecundity of our species; in the wild we are weak and without muscle and claw with which to fight off a predator and it is clear that a high rate of reproduction was necessary for us to survive long enough to become civilized.

But the monthly cycle is difficult to explain. Every four weeks a new moist layer lining the uterus grows, matures, and is then expelled over a period lasting several days. If fertilization occurs the embryo embeds itself in this protective and nourishing layer in mid-cycle, and the menstrual loss does not come about. But in normal circumstances the cycle is repeated month after month for more than three decades of a woman's life. Menstruation is inconvenient and messy; it wastes valuable iron resources through the loss of blood (to such an extent that it has been suggested that half of any population of women is probably anaemic); and it causes hot flushes, back pains or cramps, and a degree of morbidity that is higher than in many widespread diseases.

Worst of all, in terms of personal misery, the continuous fluctuation of hormone levels that is involved during the monthly cycle causes psychological disturbances as well as physical manifestations.

Most women are well aware of this fact, and probably the majority of women suffer from it (some of them seriously). Yet little is said on the subject, it is rarely aired or even admitted to, and nothing substantial has been done to alleviate the feelings that distress so many normal women each and every month of their younger years as adults, until the menopause comes to the rescue. It is, to my mind, an astonishing perversion of societal attitudes.

THE CURSE

Menstruation itself has always been regarded with some kind of suspicion, and it is no credit to our era that we seem to perpetuate the same kind of superstitious approach to the matter. Pliny, writing a few years after the death of Christ, reported that a menstruating woman could turn wine sour and kill fertile seeds, and could even wither the fruit on a tree underneath which she sat. In some early cultures, women were segregated from the rest of the community during their periods, or were made to call out that they were unclean as long as the period lasted. In Mexico women during menstruation were banned from the silver mines, because they were believed to cause the ore to lose quality; in the Far East they were believed to turn opium crops bitter if they worked on harvesting during menstruation; and in European factories they were long held to spoil beer fermentations or to turn refined sugar dark in colour.

To this day it is possible to find superstitions of a similar kind; thus in remoter parts of Britain and the United States a woman during her period is believed to turn meat 'off'. Many girls are still given advice about their periods that range from 'do not wash your hair' to 'never eat an ice lollipop', and in many cultures they are warned against coming into contact with salt.

It is worth emphasizing that these quaint and distressing rumours are groundless (with the exception of the idea about salt, that is; the hormone imbalances of menstruation make women liable to retain water as tissue fluid, and this can cause headache and oedema – swelling – which extra salt in the diet can potentiate. So eating salt at that time is better avoided, though 'touching' it obviously doesn't matter in the least.)

No, the truth of the matter is very different. *It is also far more disturbing.*

Few people ever talk about menstruation or the problems posed to many women by their regular cycle. It was a small but significant step when the BBC broadcast a discussion which I chaired in 1974 devoted to the side-effects of the menstrual cycle, but even then one of their officials excised some of the words at the beginning of the tape. I mentioned that the topic was often called, 'something different; some call it the curse, others the plague. Most do not call it anything, for they choose not to refer to the subject at all.' Even though the Corporation were willing to transmit the discussion (much of which was subsequently reprinted in *The Listener*, 7 March 1974), they – or rather, the individual involved – felt that 'the plague', or 'the curse' were too strong for the listener to take. Shortly before transmission, therefore, the words went; a small though revealing example of the way in which the topic has been manhandled even when it has raised its head in the public arena. Presumably, at least half the audience not only were familiar with this type of colloquialism, but would have personal experience of the phenomenon.

And the experiences can be terrifying, not merely unsettling or irritating, but truly terrifying. Katharina Dalton, who has studied the mood changes associated with the cycle over many years, tells of a loving and devoted mother who – once a month, in association with her period – would dramatically change and beat her much-loved baby boy, even throwing him downstairs. Cases in which severe mood swings occur are very common; perhaps a third of all women, possibly a half of them suffer to some extent, and the figure could be higher if we knew more about the measurement of mood. The statistics available (and there are not too many of them around) show a disproportionate increase of disability of one kind or another associated with the paramenstruum – that is, the eight days around the first day of a menstrual period.

For example, there is a marked increase in the number of motoring accidents involving women around the paramenstrual phase, and according to available evidence, half of the admissions to hospitals of young children are associated with their mothers' paramenstrual phase. There is evidence that a schoolgirl's average mark in school will fall by some 5% during the paramenstruum and rise by perhaps 10% in the post-menstrual week; and that there is a detectable lowering in complex reaction time in women around the onset of menstruation according to work carried out by Jackie Bates in Belfast. Dr Dalton has shown a significant lowering in marks in girls who sat examinations during the paramenstruum, and, at the other side of the coin, has pointed out a change in the marking habits of women teachers at the same phase. Pupils sometimes learn how to select the best time to give in work for marking by a woman teacher. To quote directly: 'We found that in schoolgirls of 18, the prefects who were allowed to give punishments gave the majority of punishments during their own pre-menstruum. In other words, when they themselves were at their worst, they punished people most. And it's very likely that this sort of thing happens with magistrates and teachers and people in authority.'

Before you conclude that this astonishingly widespread finding concerns only females, and therefore that is why males do not bother to investigate it, there is every reason why males most certainly suffer from the female's menstrual cycle. Husbands are sometimes physically attacked by their wives, without any predisposition – like a row, for example – and children by their mothers. There are cases where the size of a salesman's pay cheque can be related exactly to his wife's menstrual cycle, and one where a regular row over the monthly bank balance was cured immediately when the bank was requested to alter the date at which the regular, four-weekly statement was delivered. Most men faced with this recurring situation accept it as part of the normal cut and thrust of marriage – and why not? Men are not gifted with an astonishingly even-tempered manner; I have said how there are good reasons to accuse men of being far more aggressive than women, and in that kind of balance it is easy to see how an extra row here and there is hardly noticed.

Of course this is not to apportion 'blame' on women, in some strange fashion. But it is a fact that hormone fluctuations *are* associated with mood change, and that there is abundant evidence that the menstrual cycle affects women's sensibilities and their attitudes. My own informal discussions with hundreds of people all around the world suggest more than that – that women are very often troubled and plagued by irritability and irrational changes of mood and awareness.

To me, the whole purpose of being alive is to enjoy the experience. If I see people trapped by convention or by the strictures of their way of life, it saddens me to think of the freedoms they might otherwise know. And when I think that women may lose even a single day of happiness and contentment in this rich and intriguing world of ours, it distresses me very much – particularly when we may be talking about a week or even more out of every month taken up with strange moods, mastitis, oedema or whatever throughout the fertile years of hundreds of millions of fellow-humans – a total of perhaps 15 years of ill-health in a lifetime.

We cannot, despite widely held views to the contrary, cure everything with pills. Our knowledge of the hormones involved is still scanty, and we have only a limited ability to predictably alter a woman's response so that she attains relaxed normality throughout her life. An alternative view, often extolled, is that women must simply learn how to cope and to adjust to their state – but how reprehensible that is! It is everyone's birthright to live within their mind and body in peace, and unless we are doing everything in our power to alleviate such a widespread form of morbidity then we are less than human ourselves.

Men have a burden of their own, and that is their masked aggression. Sitting at an office desk, liberating fatty energy reserves into the bloodstream as a raw material supplying energy for an outburst against some uncompromising superior (and building up deposits in consequence when the refinements of civilization demand that little is actually *said* to the man) is clearly the best way to guarantee a heart attack or stroke. Yet men do this, almost as a form of status acquisition, every day of their executive lives.

But that does not put men and women into the same category. Firstly, this is because the man's accumulation of energy-rich materials in his bloodstream is a natural part of his evolutionary background: he was, in short, prepared for a physical battle which never arrived. It is man's own fault if he sits around, stewing, when his instincts tell him to live more in accordance with his history.

There is no such justification for the suffering that so many women endure. Theirs is a peculiar consequence of some evolutionary trick, a piece of double-dealing that is somehow the price that must be paid for the monthly renewal of the womb lining. It is a tragic error, in some ways. The only reason you could possibly put forward for its occurrence is that a moody mate will repel a casual acquaintance, and attract no-one but a mate who loves her enough to understand it all. On that basis it could even be a kind of selection mechanism . . . but that is only a passing and unsatisfactory idea.

My greatest concern is that with the modern vogue for refusing to countenance more than the minimum areas of difference between the sexes, and in trying to inflict the unreal and unwarranted belief on the public that the sexes are pretty much equal and interchangeable, we will refuse to countenance that women are subject to this burdensome pathology, just in case it smacks of implied criticism which someone dubs 'discriminatory' or 'chauvinistic'.

A great many women are suffering, and so are their families. And the way in which we have encouraged men to cultivate stress almost as a badge of virility, and to adopt a life-style which exposes them to the rigours of competition, success, prestige and a whole range of other artificially distorted values and aspirations, is only adding to society's burden. The sooner all these aspects are re-examined, the better for all of us. Playing at propagandist politics and riding on the latest little temporary wave of fashion is doing no-one anything but profound and long-lasting harm.

We do not yet understand the full complexity of the sex hormone system in men or women. The idea that the male hormone is testosterone, just that, is too simplistic. There are many other steroidal molecules that seem to play a part and there are a series of so-called Releasing Factors secreted by the hypothalamus, buried in the brain, which regulate the liberation of other, more recognizable hormones. As well as oestrogen and progesterone, both of which are well known as the female hormones, there is also testosterone in the normal woman's body. And there are two other important hormones that have been extensively studied: the follicle stimulating hormone, known as FSH, which directly stimulates the follicles within the ovary and which in turn causes the liberation of oestrogen, and the luteinizing hormone, LH, which causes an empty follicle (after its egg-cell has been discharged) to develop into a yellow-coloured body which produces hormones of its own, some of which are essential for the induction and maintenance of pregnancy.

The point of interest here is that both LH and FSH have – since their discovery in women – been found to occur in the male bloodstream too, and they are most certainly involved in the correct regulation of male sexual development just as much as they are in women. FSH in men stimulates the production of sperm, for example, and if part of the tubules that produce sperm are destroyed, the levels of FSH increase so that extra sperm production is induced, in an attempt to restore the *status quo.*

The effect of LH in the man is to stimulate the production of testosterone. This means that if you increase the intake of testosterone in a man (by giving him a couple of injections, for example) there is next to no effect on the amount of the hormone that circulates in his body. What happens is that the extra amount of testosterone triggers a shut-down in the production of LH, and that in turn causes a lowered amount of testosterone to be released from the testis. The over-all effect, therefore, is that the man continues to have virtually exactly as much testosterone circulating in his body as before.

It is this feedback mechanism which typifies the way hormones balance each other in the body, and there are countless other examples of the principle. The concept is that of homeostasis, the keeping of a dynamic system in a steady state, and it is analagous to the way that you keep a car travelling at the same speed by alternately putting your foot a little to hard, and then not quite hard enough, on the throttle pedal. Without feedback or homeostasis, a car would either gradually increase in speed, or it would go progressively slower. But a conscientious driver can keep the speed pretty constant, no matter what comes along by way of hills and valleys, through careful use of the controls. And the balanced system of hormones in the human body is regulated, checked and controlled in just this way.

In men the rate of production of sperm is continuously high from the onset of fertility; quite why such huge numbers of male sex cells should be produced is not known, but it is probably safest to regard the system as being one of the ultimate in competition – the best sperm wins in the end. It is not a strong argument, but there are no clear candidates as yet for a generally-agreed alternative and so it must suffice. The fact that scientists are already studying half a dozen 'male' sex hormones is an important development which should remove idealized notions that it is all due to testosterone. But it is in the woman that we begin to encounter real complexity.

Here we are not faced with a single, continuous hormone system, but with a violently fluctuating see-saw that has many unanswered questions associated with it – perhaps the greatest being, why should it be necessary at all?

At the beginning of a new monthly cycle, when the menstrual period itself is just ending, a follicle is growing in one of the ovaries, its egg-cell destined to be the ovum chosen for release (and possible fertilization) this month.

As the follicle grows, it gives off a steadily increasing secretion of oestrogen. This in turn stimulates the release of LH, so that LH levels steadily rise. One of the principal results of LH secretion is the stimulation of further oestrogen liberation, and the two chase each other round a positive feedback loop until the dramatic release of the contained ovum in the middle of the month. Its follicle wall ruptures (with a tearing sensation that can be felt as a slight, sharp pain by many women) and at that instant the runaway increase is halted. As the LH and oestrogen levels suddenly fall, the now-empty follicle becomes a yellow body (the corpus luteum) and begins to secrete progesterone, the so-called pregnancy hormone.

Progesterone finalizes the preparation of the uterus lining to receive a fertilized egg-cell, if this eventuates, and it in turn depresses the production of LH. Eventually the womb lining is shed, there is an upsurge in the production of FSH by the pituitary, and that starts off the development of the new follicles so that the cycle repeats itself.

How follicles are selected, why the system is so remorseless, how menstrual loss actually works, and why it ever evolved to be so wasteful of time, energy, iron and inspiration . . . are just a few of the areas of ignorance which surround the topic.

In many mammals there is a simpler mechanism (thus in rabbits ovulation takes place on the stimulus of copulation, a far more satisfactory arrangement) and it could be that we were on the way to evolving one for ourselves when we became civilized. (See page 80.)

None of this means that a single answer is ever going to be found that will overcome all the symptoms, if it is symptoms we are going to treat; not only do women describe different kinds of response to their fluctuating hormone levels (headache, cramps, irritability, etc. – and sometimes nothing at all, of course) but the sequence seems to change from time to time, from month to month, in a single individual. It can occur that breast tenderness followed by, say, the retention of excess water signals the onset of periods for months on end and then for no detectable reason those symptoms may be replaced by something else. For women whose mood changes, the nature of the change may alter from time to time in a manner that seems entirely unrelated to anything happening in her outside life. So even though our knowledge is scanty, I hesitate to encourage anyone to imagine that rigid underlying mechanisms are going to be found. Above all, I have no doubt that a great many women who are being treated as mildly disordered are actually suffering from an internal chemical imbalance, and nothing 'mental' at all. It is an easy delusion that a woman who has an outburst against a child is releasing pent-up frustrations against that individual. In support of our handy diagnosis we can find plenty of predisposing characteristics in the child (insolence or untidiness) and any number of triggering factors (a hasty word or an ill-thought gesture) which 'explain' why Mother had her outburst.

But she may tell a different tale: that the child was no worse than usual, and that these 'triggering' factors did not – as a matter of fact – annoy her in the least. She may say that she is overwhelmed by feelings of what she recognizes as uncontrollable and unnecessary hostility and hatred. She may even describe the feelings of a hormone change as a noticeable alteration in her internal state; it is 'like being suddenly drugged', as more than one has said to me.

The convenient answer is to imagine the woman is mildly psychiatrically unsound, or depressed, and to put her on tranquillizing sedatives which dampen down all responses, good and bad. It is the mentality described in the Rolling Stones' number of a decade ago, 'Mother's

Little Helper' (the helper being a sedative pill) but in fact it is a more profound and widespread phenomenon than any of us imagine, and it deserves urgent and devoted investigation.

Meanwhile, how is this related to the fact that the cycle time in women is 28 days – exactly the same as the length of the lunar month? Many fanciful relationships have been discussed, including the widespread belief of the last century that the menstrual cycle was actually geared to the phases of the moon. But it is a fact (and always was) that periods occur at all phases of the lunar month and, simply, do *not* occur at one particular time. The length of time taken to complete the menstrual cycle in other species of animals which show similar behaviour varies according to a host of factors, the size of the species being one consideration. The length of the cycle in mankind is probably a coincidence, nothing more.

There is some intriguing speculation that one could entertain over the phenomenon of synchronicity in communities of women. It is known that a group of women living closely together (in a small dormitory at a nursing home, for example) will begin to move towards each other in terms of cycle timing until they may end up menstruating on the same days. How this is brought about is imponderable, but it does point to the limited understanding we have of the means by which we signal to each other, and the way in which the criteria we embody allow us to pick up these messages and interpret them as a chemical alteration of our bodies.

It is also important to bear in mind that the relationship between the chemical hormones and the mind is not one-way. The fact that the pituitary, which mediates so many of these phenomena, is located deep in the brain makes it easy to see how the brain might regulate the output of hormones directly, which is obviously a clue to what happens when periods become synchronized as just described.

But it also means that there can be a strong influence of mind over matter – which is why some girls faced with examinations find their timing is suddenly different, and periods come on when least expected. Other people will tell of the way that anxiety over a possible pregnancy can prevent a hoped-for period from appearing on cue, which in turn can cause embarrassing consequences of its own. And there are many cases (not all of them apocryphal) in which a child has been adopted by an infertile couple, who have then unexpectedly conceived a child of their own.

The obvious assumption here is that it was a level of tension which prevented conception in some way, and the arrival of the first, adopted, child laid those anxieties to rest. The result was a revival of the sexual phenomena in husband or wife to return to normal and a consequent pregnancy.

I have suggested that biological imperatives operate on communities that do not fit with the strictures imposed by nature's evolutionary overview. Could this mean that the kind of psychological mediation we have just considered could be triggered on a community-wide basis and act as a kind of pre-programmed contraceptive? It seems sensible enough – if worry about a period can prevent its onset, one can certainly speculate that a wider pressure on our sexual behaviour might be exerted by our innate abilities to translate community stress into personal sexual response. But (though the speculation may be sound enough) can we find evidence that the effect is real, rather than postulated? There is very little – but as this book was being completed, one timely example did indeed appear in the literature.

It concerned a study by sociologists from the University of North Carolina, Ronald Rindfuss, John Reed and Craig St John, who correlated birth-rate with the effects of anxiety provoked by an American Supreme Court's ruling. Their paper, published in *Science* in the summer of 1978, examined a hitherto inexplicable drop in the birth-rate of the southern States that occurred in 1955, at a time when there was a marked *increase* in other areas of the United States.

What Rindfuss, Reed and St John point out is that on 17 May 1954, the Supreme Court handed down its decision on the case of *Brown* v *Board of Education* – a decision which had marked effects throughout the southern States. It ruled that the segregation of black and white children into separate schools was unconstitutional, a judgement which the whites considered revolutionary, and which was seen as heralding a dramatic change in circumstances for the everyday life of the South.

'It is clear,' wrote the sociologists, 'that the court's unanimous decision struck at what many white southerners saw as the basis of their region's way of life.' The number of births nine months later was radically reduced throughout the South, most noticeably in the 11 confederate states where it fell by 8% over the figures for the same part of the previous year. Black rates fell a little, too, which the researchers conclude was due to their own uncertainty about the future.

The report concludes that, 'fear for the future led some Southerners to put off having children who would otherwise have been conceived during this period.' Now, that may be; but we should also examine the possibility that a more deep-seated mechanism was at work – that reproduction-regulating mechanisms which respond at a subconscious level throughout a society curtailed the increase instead. It is a facet of our sexuality which may help to explain how biological imperatives could be directing our species to adapt to circumstances on a subtler and more insidious level than we have previously suspected.

We have certainly interfered with our sexuality more than is widely recognized, and some of the beliefs we entertain are startlingly at variance with what even a superficial reconsideration can demonstrate. The most far-reaching has been our endless reiteration of the belief that the purpose of sexual relationships is the begetting of children. It is not. The sex drive is towards union with a desired sexual partner, and the purpose is gratification of sometimes overwhelming urges and desires. The arrival of a child nine months later is not related to the love-making for several reasons. For example, in most acts of sex, conception does not result. The desire for a child may make a frustrated young mother-manqué want to steal a child for her own, and take it away to protect it; it does not make her randy. No man who feels the urge upon him thinks: 'I could do with conceiving an heir tonight,' but something far more immediate.

It is the height of tragedy that we have put so much emphasis on procreation as being the only purpose of sexuality. In primitive societies we can imagine that sexual expression was free-wheeling and relaxing – until the weight of religious conscience was added to the balance. For centuries it has been taught that sex without the desire and intent to conceive a child is immoral (and the Roman Catholics persist in backing this absurd dogma with the weight of church law), whereas the sex desire is actually the best means we have of expressing love, caring, tenderness and affection.

This erroneous belief has been the sole factor behind the tragic fact that women have not, until recent decades, enjoyed themselves fully in love-making. We have been given an endless tirade about the selfish man who seeks only his own gratification and ignores his wife, but it is not as easy as that. Looked at as selfishly as you wish, a man would enjoy himself in bed with a wife who wanted to reciprocate, far more than he would if she was holding back from response all the time.

The truth is that for countless years child-bearing has been risky and often painful (expensive, too) and women who were in the act of copulation knew perfectly well what the result might be. They did not have an 'instinct' about it; they had been *taught* the fact. The pressures on even the most loving wife were great: she knew that what she was doing might cause a pregnancy, which could kill her, and if it didn't end her life might cause her physical or financial burdens; and she had been taught a code of criteria that held the sex act to be somehow 'dirty' and 'wrong' anyhow. Little wonder that women did not enjoy sex.

The introduction of safe methods of birth control, notably the pill, have freed women from those worries and has allowed them to re-establish their sexuality in a degree of expression that they must have known in primitive times. We have removed strictures, not imposed new freedoms, and it is important we realize that.

CEREBRAL ORGASM

A second trend has been towards the worship of the orgasm (approached from every imaginable physical angle) to the exclusion of foreplay, love and romantic attachment. This is most regrettable; marriages fail every hour of the day because of some minor incompatibility over the orgasm question, and the desire to copulate in increasingly athletic positions comes to take precedence over the voluptuous pleasures of extended love-making. We teach which areas of the body are erogenous, yet we all know that an unaroused person can have every item explored in detail and caressed for hours on end, but will fail to respond if the desire for sex is absent. Much time and paper has been devoted to the debate as to whether a woman's orgasm is clitoric or vaginal; but the orgasm of the woman (or man) in a satisfying union is nothing short of *cerebral*.

It is perfectly possible for a highly-aroused individual to experience orgasm without much in the way of physical contact at all, purely because of the immense satisfaction of sharing a bed with a loved one. We are all aware of the irrationalities of love, of the overriding importance of the pair-bond in human societies, and of the strength of these emotions, yet little attention is ever paid to them. Instead we imagine that bodies become mutual masturbating machines, and ignore the immense capacity we have for sensuousness and sexuality on a far higher and broader plane that defines vast areas of human interaction, and is immensely more important and significant in the ways of our kind than a quick poke behind the bike-sheds.

Even more absurd is that many of the acts of congress that have been known about and accepted for centuries (and practised for millenia) are actually illegal in many areas. The use of kissing, licking or sucking on the genitalia or nipples is widespread, and is for many people a highly arousing part of foreplay – yet cunnilingus (oral stimulation of the female genitalia) and fellatio (sucking and licking the phallus) are punishable by law in some Western states in the US. This, of course, is a hang-over from our fixation on the academic 'purpose' of copulation, and the denial of physical gratification which is not directed specifically towards conception.

Let us take one single aspect of the distortion of sexuality by civilized codes of behaviour – the response to breast-feeding. Most particularly in the United States, breast-feeding has increasingly been seen as 'animal' and 'degrading' and for decades has been discouraged. I will not be so uncharitable as to conclude that this was due to the lobbying might of the manufacturers of artificial substitutes, since a great many equally misguided fashions have been thrown up without such intervention, and, in any event, the trend is showing signs of reversing now. But the effects of discouraging breast-feeding have been many.

In the third-world countries it is particularly noticeable that bottle-fed children are more likely to die (the figure is a three-fold increase in a study of rural Chile, for example). The making up of synthetic cow's-milk-based drinks has an inevitable risk of introducing germs of one kind or another, whereas the mother's milk is clean; the bottle-feed may not be at the right temperature, whereas the mother's milk is; and the natural product is nutritionally better. It is not perfect, for it is low in Vitamin D (which in nature would be corrected by the amounts of Vitamin D manufactured in the baby's skin by the action of sunlight), but it is better than the substitutes. A mother's milk contains some immunity to disease, too, which is important to the baby.

The breast-fed child benefits in many ways, and is demonstrably likely to thrive better. It is likely to obtain more tactile stimuli too, and the bodily contact is doubtless an important part of the baby's cognitive and sensual development.

But we should not lose sight of the fact that the mother benefits as well. The obvious level at which she gains is in time and convenience. She does not have to wake up in the early morning to make up a feed. There are no measurements and volumes to be assessed, and of course she is in bodily contact with her baby when she may well need that stimulus as much as the infant. More to the point, the act of sucking from the child causes her to regain her figure quicker. Her uterus is directly stimulated to contract by the continued sucking, and it is this which is vitally important if the uterus is to regain its contracted and unobtrusive dimensions as quickly as possible after birth. The idea that a woman loses her breasts through breast-feeding is not true, either; the stimulus can have a positively rejuvenating effect.

The hormone oxytocin is responsible for the contraction of the uterus, and the infant's sucking stimulates the release of this hormone. Oxytocin also acts on the muscles within the breasts, and causes the ducts in which the milk lies to contract and 'pump' milk to the central area behind the nipple. I do not doubt that these effects are responsible for increasing the muscular tone of the breast, which is necessary for its recovery afterwards, and it might even increase the response of the vaginal muscles, aiding the recovery of that area too after dilation during childbirth.

THE OLDEST CONTRACEPTIVE

The most important aspect of breast-feeding in primitive mankind was its action as a contraceptive. As long as a baby is being breast-fed, the effect of the suckling is to prevent the mother from becoming pregnant. The mechanisms remain in dispute, but the hormone changes brought about in response to suckling clearly play a decisive role (though other factors, such as the state of health of the mother and her nutritional status, are also involved). In some primitive tribes of hunter/gatherers, who may provide a model by which we could assess our own social background, breast-feeding is prolonged, and a new baby appears on the scene a year or so after it stops. Studies of the !Kung tribes, a nomadic people, have shown that the !Kung mothers may breast-feed for 3½-4 years; if an infant dies, the mother becomes pregnant soon afterwards but if the baby is successfully reared (which is usually the case) then it is suckled for up to 4 years and the mother becomes pregnant again shortly after that.

A review by Robert May published in *Nature* (Vol: 272, 491-495, 6 April 1978) shows how important this period of suckling-induced contraception may be in the life of a !Kung mother. In her reproductive life-span a primitive hunter/gatherer female might experience four years of pregnancy, *and the same length of time of normal menstrual cycles*. This is an important fact – she spends 15 years without periods (or ovulation) caused by suckling her young. At 13 periods per year and 5 days per period, she therefore spends a life that is broken up very differently from our own civilized existence:

	!Kung Woman	*Modern Western Woman*
Total time menstruating	34 weeks	325 weeks
Total time suckling (state of natural contraception)	780 weeks	? nil
Time spent pregnant	180 weeks	72 weeks

This comparison is between a !Kung mother of five children and a Western mother of two who bottle-feeds her babies. The figures show that the !Kung mother spends, obviously, more than twice as much time actually being pregnant. But her Western counterpart spends almost 10 times as long menstruating! It can most certainly be argued that the experiences of primitive mothers like this have many lessons for us – the most important being that it is not necessarily 'natural' for women to menstruate like they do.

Much of our current practice over the use of contraceptive pills is based on a feeling that we have to allow women to reiterate their monthly menstrual loss by taking the pills in a regular timetable. That may be wrong. Some form of continuous medication might cut down the periods, or even banish them (regular, daily taking of many oral contraceptives abolishes periods in exactly this way), and it can be argued that this is in fact a *more* natural answer to the problem.

More conceptions are prevented throughout the world by breast-feeding, than by all the other forms of man-made contraception. That fact, and the likelihood that most normal women would probably prefer a life without regular menstrual periods, suggests to me that the most suitable form of contraception for the future would be a mild and continuous form of medication which did away with the inconvenience of periods, and helped smooth out the violent swings of hormone balance. In attaining this end we might be more closely approaching the condition of our forebears.

In my view, it is a safe principle for us to fit our modern, technological life-style as far as possible to the demands under which we evolved. A corollary to this is that we should not interfere with nature unless we have to, and in this framework of ideas the tendency to automate childbirth itself through the use of induction seems to be the ultimate sophistication - an unpleasant and unwarranted departure from biological normalcy. In recent years it has looked as though this form of technological invasion, so vital for the mother who is in difficulties, was going to take over every hospital delivery. Yet induced labour can be more painful (or alternatively, it can require more analgesics) and it makes the outside management of the event far more intrusive than it would otherwise be. And this presents us with the nub of the issue: we *can* modify the timing of birth, and we *do* have the facilities, but does that mean we *should* do it?

There is an automatic assumption that our ability to do something should be translated into actuality. It is affecting our lives at every turn; for example, we have suddenly begun to emphasize that many aspects of childhood are learned, and are based on behaviour which we teach. We recognize that male and female modes of behaviour can be influenced by this teaching. And again I apply my principle: we *can* modify things in this way, but simply because of that ability it does not follow that it is beneficial, automatically, to do it.

The essential nature of maleness and femaleness is predicated upon the genetic history of our species and is controlled (or at least initiated) by the hormones in our bodies. Men are more aggressive, more competitive, and perhaps that is why we teach them to be more protecting and guarding; women are more caring, and more changeable, and are rightly taught to behave and respond in ways that are non-masculine. I see no reason in the world why we should persist in spreading both sexes equally thinly through the whole spectrum of human endeavour - there never will be as many male nurses as female ones, or as many women miners as men. The woman's league of American Football never will boast as many football stars as the men, and men will never make such welcoming hosts.

We *could* make all that happen since our learning as children (and throughout adult life) is such an integral part of our development. But I do not believe that we would be so muddle-headed as to reject millions of years of evolutionary history and start to teach new, arbitrary values at the expense of the happiness of future generations. And even if we did, I do not think our inborn genetic programmes would allow us, even for a mere fleeting century or two, to get away with it.

CHAPTER FOUR

WHAT DETERMINES SEX?

The awareness of an existence of two, separate sexes is a fundamental part of mankind's insight. The term 'sex' itself derives from the Latin *sexus*, which in turn has its roots in the word *seco* – the verb 'to cut' – showing how it was regarded as an essential division across the human (and animal) population.

In fact it is not as simple. We can find many examples of intersexuality, and even in human society some people exist as males or females when they are biologically predestined to be the other sex. The boundaries are also blurred by some homosexuals who exhibit the traits of one gender, whilst living the lives of the other. And in the world of agriculture there are many examples of animal species in which the sexes may seem to merge. The capon, which is a male fowl treated to develop more like a hen, is one example; the freemartin (a genetically female cow with some secondary sexual characteristics of a bull) is another. Though the clear-cut categories of sexuality are well enough delineated in normal cases, then, there are examples where our comfortable categorization does not encompass the realities of nature.

The question 'where does sex come from?' is not easy to answer. Most people are aware of the X and Y chromosomes and their involvement in sexual determination, and it is tempting (for scientists as well as for the public) to assume that this explains everything. It does not. There are happily married women alive today whose only real complaint in life would be their inability to bear children, but who are genetically male. This may seem astonishing, and it is certainly in some respects unnerving. How such cases arise is a matter I return to in more detail when we consider the topic of intersexuality. But first we must examine what the mechanisms are which lay down the sex, the identifiable gender, of an individual.

If the sex chromosomes are not the only answer, what other influences are there? The main categories are as follows:

a) The sex-chromosome constitution

The existence of the correct combination of sex-chromosomes is the leading influence in determining the gender of an individual, and the discovery of this fact is one of the most important avenues of genetical history. However, the sex chromosomes are not the final arbiter, nor the only diagnostic criterion. Our understanding of the nature of the sexual imperative depends in part on this fact: we have to put the simplistic genetic basis of sex to one side when we begin to grapple with the reality, rather than just teach the theory.

b) The sexual anatomy

The structure of the gonads is of vital importance. Many a girl child with an over-developed clitoris has been raised as a boy and, conversely, boys in whom the penis is small and the scrotum divided (often in a case like this the testicles are undescended, which complicates the picture further) have often been reared as girls. The physiology of the glands is important too, particularly in examples where the gonads may be part-male, part-female. In such cases it has been known for the expression of sex by the gonads to vary at different times during the patient's life-span, and well-documented cases of sex-change are known to have been due to the failure of a mixed set of gonads to, as it were, make up its mind. There are several specific sub-categories of factor which have to be taken into account under this general heading. They are:

i: the anatomy of the gonads (what are the internal sex organs like, and how are they constructed?),

ii: the physiology of the gonads (how the sex organs function, and what products they excrete – hormones being the chief example to consider),

iii: the anatomy of the external organs of sex (including the size of the clitoris, the vagina, the scrotum, etc., and the existence of unusual or unexpected structures such as fistulae or other openings which may simulate a non-existent vaginal orifice, or a divided scrotum which can imitate the labia of a female),

iv: the structure of the sexual ducts (including all the tube-like structures in which the sexual products travel or are conducted, and encompassing many accessory organs associated with the sex organs.

c) The sexual characteristics of the body

Here we have to consider the disposition of hair, the quality of the skin and the cutaneous structures, the proportions of the skeleton (notably, but not exclusively, the pelvic girdle which in females is adapted to take the head of the child in birth), and the development of the accessories to child-rearing in the female, such as the breast tissues and nipples. There are also some characteristics that are harder to define, including the more rounded and gently tapering configuration of the body in mature women, compared with an angular and less graceful outline in men. This may in turn symbolize cultural roles or it may act as a signal of aggression or submission, but little is yet known of the way in which such intangible shades of differences can be interpreted by the eye and, more importantly, by the brain.

How much of what we perceive is predicated upon in-born codes of criteria, and how much is culturally induced, is equally mysterious. To add to our burden of ignorance is the fact that many of the criteria that we learn, that is to say they are culturally-dependent, we can also *unlearn* if we choose. It is part of the liberationist ethic that we seek out these factors and identify them as essentially arbitrary and out-dated. This may be a fundamental error, if learned codes of criteria do turn out to be vital ingredients of normal sexual development, and not mere arbitrary figments of a fickle imagination.

In either event, the power of the subtle differences that the distribution of fat in the subcutaneous tissues can generate in the eye of the beholder cannot be overestimated. It is a fact that, for all the understanding we now have of chromosomal constitution, hormone balance, chromatin testing, etc., the most telling example of sexual identification lies in the human eye. It may be the walk, it may be just the outline of the body; but in most cases you can tell the gender of an individual even if that person were to stand at a distance, back turned towards you. The fact that the human senses can make such distinctions on the basis of what would appear to be unquantifiable data in a time far less than it would take to draw up a scientific diagnosis, remains a perplexing mystery.

Although the division, the cutting, of mankind into two categories of male and female has an ancient lineage in our understanding of the nature of mankind, it is important to realize that understanding a relationship between intercourse and the conception of children is more recent.

The main reason for this was the relatively long time between intercourse and birth; and, of course, the fact that intercourse very frequently did not result in a conception at all. Of all the events preceding the birth of a child in a primitive society, intercourse must have seemed no more likely than any of the others as a 'cause'.

In some societies the dawn of awareness was perhaps disproportionately delayed: the Trobriand Islanders (their homeland is also known as the Kiriwina Islands in parts of Papua New Guinea) of the South-west Pacific have always believed that pregnancy is due to the occupancy of the womb by an ancestral spirit, and this view has persisted into our own era. It is a quaint, old-fashioned theory, you might think; but there is something in it. The idea that the womb is occupied by the spirit of a previous generation has something in common with today's genetic theories, even if the lack of awareness that intercourse figures in the pattern is perhaps surprising.

Earlier civilizations than ours had many different views on the determination of sex. In Aristotle's time it was popular to believe, as he wrote, that conception resulted from the interaction of semen and menstrual blood. There was no extension of this thesis to account for the origin of disparate sexes, though the philosopher Anaxagoras who lived during 500–428 BC claimed that the products of the right testicle produced male children and those of the left gave rise to girls. He stated that the reasoning behind this demarcation was based on the fact that the right testicle tends to dominate and to be larger (the 'stronger', as Anaxagoras put it) whilst the left testicle was smaller and 'weaker'. We may criticize the superficiality of his reasoning, but at that time there was little knowledge on which to base any firm conclusion – and of course in the sense that Anaxagoras deduced that the male sexual contribution was the sex-determinant he was anticipating modern genetic teaching, albeit accidentally.

The 18th-century biologist Procope Couteau gave some impetus to this view in his paper of 1748; he similarly concluded that the 'reason' why the testes in man were of different sizes was because one of them produced male-determinants, the other female-determinants. The English biologist J. T. Needham (who in another theatre of philosophy distinguished himself by being the last of the famous proponents of 'vegetative force' as an argument in favour of spontaneous generation) concluded in the following year that male and female semen existed. He proposed that particles representing every aspect of the offspring were inherited from both parents – a conclusion with which few would argue today – and that in some way a battle for dominance of maleness over femaleness took place between these 'atoms of inheritance'. Implicit in his view was the notion that the strongest would win out; but even in his day it should have been pretty obvious that dominant, feminine mothers did not always produce exclusively female children, any more than excessively aggressive and overbearing fathers were only siring boys.

A parallel view that persisted throughout this period was the so-called homunculus theory. This postulated that within the head of each spermatozoon was hidden a perfectly formed, miniaturized human being (some versions of the view held that the homunculus was concealed in a similar fashion within the ovum itself). The most conspicuous pioneer adherent to the homunculus theory was the Dutch microscopist Nicolaas

Hartsoeker, designer of what became known as the screw-barrel micro-scope (in its time the most widely used routine microscope in Europe). Hartsoeker claimed to observe homunculi within the head of human sperm cells, and his answer to the problem of sex determination was to argue that inside each homunculus was a successively smaller one, representing the countless generations yet to be born, constituted variously as male and female so that the distribution of male and female children in an entire family was predestined. This theory of *embôitement* – encasement – really suggested that humans were preformed within their sex cells in layers, like those of an onion. Hartsoeker was active in the late 17th century and one hundred years later his theory was being actively touted by Astruc, whose personal refinement on the question of sex determination had a marvellously simple, mechanical explanation. Astruc claimed that he had observed a tiny grooved aperture in the wall of the egg-cell itself, and in some ova it was larger than in others. He deduced from this that the determining factor must lie in the size of the sperm cells which approached the egg in the moments of conception. If a small one arrived first, it could enter through the small aperture. But if the ovum had a larger gap, a bigger sperm cell could gain entry. There was the difficulty that smaller sperm could have a choice of either size of groove, whereas the larger sperm clearly had to enter through a large aperture, which would have presented certain theoretical constraints . . . but in the 1760's this seemed a tiny objection and the theory attracted many adherents.

In the period following the mid-seventeenth century, when the existence of sperm became known, the number of theories on the origin of sex steadily increased. By the year 1700 there were at least 250; by the year 1900 the total had topped 500. Of the many alternatives, the view which gradually emerged as by far the most popular was that the two ovaries produced male and female ova respectively. This theory held that the sperm was merely the 'triggering' mechanism which set the ovum into development, whilst the ova themselves from, say, the left ovary were all predestined to become males whilst their counterparts could only become females. The practical result of the theory was that it became popular to believe that different positions during copulation would direct the seminal ejaculate to one side or the other; depending on which gender of child the parents wanted (and depending just as much on whose belief the parents accepted, as to which side corresponded to which sex), a couple could make love lying one way or the other so that the semen trickled downwards into the desired quarter, and a child of the desired gender would inevitably result. The fact that so many disappointments ensued was believed to be due to the uncertainty as to which ovary was which; and the theory died a natural death before any general consensus was reached. Meanwhile thousands of farmers mated their cows and sheep whilst herded onto a sloping field, in the hope of producing male or female offspring at will; and when Rumley Dawson postulated that the ovaries functioned alternately, it became popular to imagine that if conception of a girl child took place after a specified menstrual period, then every alternate period after that would correspond to a female conception. Count the periods, it was argued, and all your uncertainties were ended: even-numbered menstrual periods would produce female ova, odd-numbered ones males.

It had been the belief of Aristotle that very young and very old parents tended to have girls, whilst parents whose ages were more or less in the middle of the married spectrum were likely to have boys. This theory lingered on into comparatively recent times, too; around 1829 two research workers, Sadler and Hofacker, independently put forward the view that the sex of a child depended more-or-less on the gender of the older parent, with the majority of marriages where the parents are of roughly the same age having something near a fifty-fifty chance. It is true that women usually marry slightly older men, of course; but both these authorities overcame that difficulty by adding a bias of their own:

Age of parents	Sex of child
Husband much older	Male
Wife much older	Female
Husband and wife same age	Female
Normal marriage (i.e. where husband is slightly older than wife)	Male or female

The influence of parental age on the sex of their children according to the (independent) views of Sadler and Hofacker, circa 1829.

The belief that the sex of a child was related in some way to the relative vigour of the parents persisted until comparatively recently too. What became known as Girou's Hypothesis held that the child would have the same sex as the more vigorous parent. Now you may argue that this is absurd, since most families exhibit a reasonably random distribution of sexes in their children, and the everyday evidence against the dominance of one parent is so clear and unassailable that no-one could have held such a view for long.

The problem lay, however, in arguments about which effect produced which kind of child: thus the last of the proponents of a theory along these lines, Starkweather in 1883, held that the sex of the child was the *opposite* to the gender of the dominant parent. Either way, the uncertainty about matching results with expectations was always explained away by arguments about whose interpretation was the right one – and meanwhile the truth of the matter continued to evade discovery.

In our own era it is tempting to look back at such views and to decry their proponents for their naïvety or their gullible innocence. Certainly it makes one smile to imagine two rival views, one of them insisting that the most vigorous parent passed on his or her gender to the offspring, the other holding just as firmly to the exact opposite. But how different is it in our own era? We accept without demur that some doctors insist that exercise is the obvious treatment for a patient recovering from a coronary heart attack, whilst an equally convinced group teach that nothing but complete rest is essential. In a host of fields, from dieting to the treatment of mental illness, conflicting views are commonplace and diametrically opposed ideologies widespread. Yet we live with it all, we accept it with good grace as an indicator of present-day uncertainties. In much the same spirit I think we should look back at earlier conflicts in the theory of medicine; many of them fitted what was then understood as well as any of us could reasonably expect, and better than some of our modern controversies (of which vitamin C and the common cold must surely be the definitive example). Our modern era has fostered scientific arrogance as never before; and it comes at a time when our track-record shows how little we have to be arrogant about.

The death of these earlier theories followed speedily upon the widespread discussion of the experiments of the Czech monk, Gregor Mendel, in the early 1900's. The work itself had been more or less lost to view since it had been originally completed several decades before. Indeed on the 27th September 1870, Mendel wrote a letter to Professor Nägeli in Munich in which he suggested that sex might be determined by genetic factors (in terms very similar to those that we would accept today) but nothing further was then heard of the proposal. Mendel based his conclusions on a series of experiments which he carried out in his spare time at the Augustinian Monastery in Brno. His observations centred on the cross-breeding of garden crops, principally peas and beans, and he realized that specific factors were transmitted in clearly defined mathematical ratios, corresponding to what became known as dominant and recessive genetic characteristics.

Mendel's work neatly anticipated the modern study of genetics, but when he published it in 1866 no notice was taken of his portentous theory. He died in 1884 at the age of 62, his work secure in the annals of published science but entirely forgotten by contemporary scientific opinion. The true significance of Mendelism, the theoretical approach to inheritance founded on Mendel's observations, finds its expression in the field of genetics and in the claims of those who would like to introduce eugenics as a form of selective breeding aimed at producing a race of super-humans for the future. The greatest value of Mendel lies in the manner in which the behaviour of the characteristics he studied so exactly fitted the later postulations of geneticists. Mendel was observing the effect of individual genes decades before their existence was known about; in a perfect example of pure science he provided the confirmatory evidence for the existence of genes well in advance of their discovery. In science we are often tricked into mounting experiments which seek to provide technological confirmation of a preconception, or a personal hunch. The story of Mendelism is how science ought always to progress: in practice it does not usually happen along such high-minded and altruistic lines.

It was not until the year 1900 that Mendel's work suddenly hit the scientific headlines. His experiments were re-read by several biologists, all independently realizing their significance. The rediscovery of Mendelism was primarily the work of Correns, Tschermak and de Vries in 1900; then Bateson and Saunders in 1902, Castle in 1903, Doncaster (1904), Raynor (1905) . . . and so many others, all carried out experiments which confirmed the observations Mendel had so painstakingly made in the mountains of Czechoslovakia, working for nothing more than personal interest and inward satisfaction.

By 1908 it had become clear that sexual determination was another of these Mendelian characteristics, and was an inheritable factor passed on at the moment of conception. It further emerged that only one of the sexes (the male in mammals; the female in birds) carried the genetic information coding for sex. It emerged that there was not, as was at first suspected, one gene conferring 'maleness' and another separate entity responsible for 'femaleness'. Instead it was found that in one of the sexes the genetic make-up was complete, whilst in the other it was incomplete. What was happening was that in each cell of the adult body (or at any rate, since some cells - like the red blood corpuscles in humans, for instance - contain no genes at all, in all *typical* cells), there were two complete sets of chromosomes, one of them derived from the paternal gamete, the sperm, and the other from the maternal gamete, the ovum. Among these two sets of genetic information received from each parent was a chromosome of a particular kind, which was designated the X–chromosome. Every gamete undergoes what is called a reduction-division in the last stages of its formation, which cuts the number of chromosomes in half. This is an important mechanism to understand, since it is in many ways the key to reproduction.

Let us take an example. Suppose you have a creature in which each adult cell contains, for point of argument, ten chromosomes. Each chromosome is a ribbon-like structure embedded in which is a chain of genetic information, coded in the structure of that familiar complex, DNA (deoxyribosenucleic acid). Along the chromosome you may picture a chain of independent genetic messages, similar to the beads in those popper-necklaces which children love to play with. This is a simplified view, of course, but if the mental picture helps us to understand what is an otherwise imponderable concept then let us stick to it.

There are, then, 10 chromosomes in the cells of this mythical organism. Now, what would occur if a cell from each parent were to fuse and give rise to a fertilized cell - a zygote - from which an embryo would form? Their offspring would of course contain 20 chromosomes in each cell; their grandchildren 40; their great-grandchildren 80; their great-great-grand-children 160 . . . and within a score of generations the organism would outweigh the world from the sheer mass of its vast genetic hoard. The reduction division which takes place in the sex organs of adults is the mechanism we have evolved to prevent this unhappy accident from occurring. The process is known as meiosis (pronounced *my-osis*) and its effect is to halve the number of chromosomes that go into each gamete. Thus the sperm of the 10-chromosome father contain only 5 chromosomes each; and the mother's ova also contain 5 of their own. When these 2 cells fuse the original, mature complement of 10 is restored. In this way the chromosome number is maintained down the generations within each species.

Sex determination occurs in an extraordinarily simple manner. The X-chromosome is associated with femaleness (this is the case in mankind, and so we will make it the same for our mythical creature in the course of this explanation), and each adult cell of the female of the species contains 2 X-chromosomes. The egg-cells that are formed within the maternal ovary, with only half the normal chromosome number, will contain only 1 X-chromosome each.

Now, the male organism has a different chromosome constitution. Each of his body cells contains only one X-chromosome, and its opposite number is a smaller Y-chromosome. The genetic make-up of the female cells can be written XX, in a manner which is refreshingly algebraic and complicated-looking for any self-respecting biologist; and the male's sex-chromosome complement can be abbreviated as XY. When his gonads set out to produce sperm through the meiotic reduction-division, it is obvious that half the sperm will end up with one X-chromosome, whilst the other half will contain one Y-chromosome instead.

Here then is the basis of sex determination. If an X-containing ovum matches with an X-containing sperm, the resulting embryo will be XX - female. Conversely, if an X-containing ovum pairs instead with a Y-containing sperm the result will be XY - male. This is how the basis of sex determination functions in mankind, except that we have 23 pairs of chromosomes in each typical body cell, i.e. a chromosome number (or count) of 46. It is a fairly representative number, for it is certainly not true that the number of chromosomes has any bearing on the size of the adult animal, or on its state of evolutionary advancement. The cat has 38 chromosomes, for example; the dog 78.

It is clear that there is no such thing as a truly 'female' or 'male' chromosome, then. Instead we have cells in which all the chromosomes have an identical partner, which are the female or homogametic sex; and there are cells in which one of the pairs do not match – these being the heterogametic, male cells. In all animals we find a similar pattern; one sex has matching chromosomes, the other mismatching. But in different types of animal at different levels of organization we find that the converse may be the determining factor – that is, the heterogametic gender (males, in our own species) may be the females instead.

In the mammals, the heterogametic sex is male and the same is true of the molluscs and the starfish family of echinoderms. On the other hand in the reptiles and birds, together with many of the amphibians, it is usual for the heterogametic or mismatched gender to be the female. Might one not expect that there was a general rule that applied throughout the animal kingdom? Indeed you might – and why we have such an unexpected patchwork of assorted mechanisms is inexplicable.

In the animals in which the male is the sex-determinant, clearly the gender of the child is decided at conception – at least, it is in theory. In the species in which the female holds the trump genetic card instead it is a little more complex. During the later stages of meiosis, it is usual for the cells within the ovary to divide into 4, each of the 4 daughter-cells containing half the original number of chromosomes. But we do not usually end up with 4 ova. What happens to the others is that they abort, as it were; they form small rounded cells known as polar bodies and are wasted, so that only 1 giant ovum-cell out of the 4 remains.

During this last stage of the meiotic division in a heterogametic female, there is clearly a fifty-fifty chance that the ovum which results will contain either an X-chromosome or a Y-chromosome – the opposite number will have been extruded into one of those little polar bodies and been lost in the process. So in these heterogametic females, the moment at which the sex of the offspring is theoretically decided is at the time of the last of the reduction-divisions, when the ovum itself emerges. If it contains an X-chromosome, then the fertilization of that cell will inevitably result in an XX male. If the X-chromosome was the one extruded into the polar body, then the offspring will be an XY – which, for this species, will be a female.

There is an interesting consequence of this, for the manner in which the chromosomes are extruded by the developing ova can in some animals be related to temperature. There is at once here the possibility of predetermining, if not the sex of all offspring, at least the sex of the majority. In 1921 it was shown that the moth *Talaeporia tubulosa* was an ideal subject for the demonstration of this property. In that year, Seiler demonstrated that under low temperature conditions, adult females tended to pass the X-chromosome into one of the polar bodies, leaving a preponderance of Y-containing ova and in consequence they produced an excess number of female offspring. Raising the temperature caused the Y-chromosome to pass out of the developing ova, so that the resultant high proportion of X-chromosome cells gave a brood that was predominately male.

So far the picture seems reasonably clear. One sex will be homogametic, that is it will contain matched X-chromosomes, whilst the other will be heterogametic or XY; the only complication being that which sex turns out to be which depends on what kind of animal you happen to be. The temptation is to assume that here we have the answer to sex determination, but as you might already be beginning to suspect, it is not so simple. The overriding problem is that chromosome sex does not always concur with the gender of the individual concerned. But even this is not the only complication, for many animal types have since been shown to have a sex-determining mechanism that does not depend on the orthodox XX/XY system at all, but on some other singular variant for which no reasonable explanation can be found.

In 1916, H. B. Goodrich showed that the threadworm *Ascaris incurvata* has a sex determining mechanism depending on as many as 8 chromosomes. In some other genera, including the *Mantis*, the X-chromosomes exist in pairs, so that females are X_1X_2-X_1X_2 whilst males are all X_1X_2-Y. In other mantids even stranger patterns are found, for there seems to be an absence of Y-chromosomes (a feature of several other groups of animals, incidentally) so that the females (like humans) were XX right enough, but the males were designated XO.

In 1962 one member of the mantid family, *Rhodomantis pulchella*, was found to have males that were X_1X_2 whilst some other types have a compound Y-chromosome that still further complicates the picture. The XO type has probably evolved through the simple loss of a Y-chromosome somewhere during the rigours of the meiotic reduction-division. Obviously if the Y-chromosome was truly the male chromosome its loss would be a matter of great significance. But remember, the point is not whether the chromosome is present or not, it is a question of whether the cells have pairs that match (the homogametic cells) or do not (the heterogametic ones). By the same token that an XX is homogametic, and XO is a heterogametic mismatch just as much as XY would be. The phenomenon is not confined to the insect world, either; several mammals (rodents, in fact) are also now known to have XO males, the Y having been no doubt lost somewhere along the twisty backroads of evolutionary history.

But the different patterns that exist pose problems for the evolutionary specialist who tries to understand them. In some ways, of course, such divergencies can provide an insight into the relationship between groups and their taxonomic affiliations, which matter a great deal when we try to work out how to classify living things. In the past it has often been taught that you should select a given group of organs and utilize them as the basis for classification. But living species do not fit such arbitrary dictates. They have evolved in different ways for a multiplicity of reasons, and if classification is intended to mirror development and evolution (as all systems of taxonomy *must*, if they are to make any true sense of reality) then we must take into account as many disparate sets of data as we can. The patterns of chromosomal sex determination are one intriguing source of indicators of exactly this kind – though this should not make us overlook the very real nature of the problems they pose. For example, the majority of the joint-limbed arthropods (from crabs and shrimps to flies and mosquitos) have heterogametic males just as we humans do. The butterflies and moths, the group *Lepidoptera*, have heterogametic females and XX males. Why the unexpected reversal? No-one knows.

We now know, with all the confidence and blasé matter-of-factness that retrospection always brings, that humans have a chromosome count of 46 (23 pairs). But although the structure of the human cell nucleus has been studied for centuries one way and another, the relatively simple matter of how many chromosomes our cells contain is only a couple of decades old. In the early 1950's no-one was really sure.

It seems likely that human chromosomes were first observed by a microscopist named Arnold in 1879. In the 1890's, several workers tried to count the number, but they came up with totals far below the correct figure (between 20 and 30). In 1912 it was claimed that the number was 48 in women, 47 in men (the idea being at that time that men were XO rather than XY). This view persisted until the beginning of the Second World War, though in 1921 a cytologist named T. S. Painter had carried out some painstaking work using fresh testicular material and he came quite close to the right answer. Painter observed the Y–chromosome and wrote it up as a new discovery, and he also attempted to count the chromosomes in total. Try as he might, and the chromosomes of the testis are really to small to count in comfort, he could not confidently settle on a firm figure. He stated that the count must lie in the 45–48 range, though he did add that in the clearest examples he thought he had found 46. Had he stuck at that it is possible that this number would have become more widely accepted decades before it eventually emerged. Unfortunately, within a couple of years Painter had upped his bid to 48, along with most other cytologists of the age, and this remained the most widely-accepted total into the 1950's.

In 1956 J. H. Tijo and A. Levan settled the matter once and for all. They looked at the work of T. C. Hsu, who in 1952 declared that mankind boasted 46 chromosomes, and not 48 at all. Tijo and Levan cultured cells from foetal lung samples and spent a long time in making careful preparations in which the chromosomes were well spread out, and their number accurately counted. Their findings were conclusive: Hsu had been right, and mankind did, after all, have 46 chromosomes. From that time on there has been no argument on the matter.

So far we have admitted that the formal, basic idea of XX for females and XY for males – for all its merits as an aid to the teaching of simple genetic theory – is far from being the whole story. And if you were tempted to think that the oddities without Y chromosomes, or with two pairs of X's, were almost incomprehensibly complicated compared with the traditional basic pattern, well, you are in for yet further surprises. The normal number of chromosomes found in adult cells (for example 46 in man) is the *diploid* state; the 50%-of-normal condition found in the reproductive cells is known as *haploid*. In some species, one of the sexes is haploid. This means that every one of its body cells contains the same number of chromosomes as a sperm or an egg – and that is, of course, only half what it should be. The most familiar example is the honey bee, *Apis mellifera*. The males, or drones, all contain half the normal chromosome complement: they contain as many chromosomes as the sperm that they produce.

When, after their dizzying nuptial flight, the virgin queen bee copulates on the wing with the one drone agile enough to keep up with her, she takes into her sperm storage ducts enough of the male cells to last her a life-time (up to 5 years in many instances). At the end of copulation, the drone and queen separate; and the male falls to his death.

Within the community of the busy hive, the queen becomes nothing more than an egg-laying automaton, turning out a daily weight of eggs that weigh more than she does. If the eggs are fertilized, then they automatically regain their diploid number of chromosomes and so are predestined to develop into females. But many of the eggs laid by the queen are not fertilized at all: by a process of parthenogenesis – virgin birth – they go on to develop apparently normally into individuals with only the haploid chromosome complement. As such they become males, from one of whom the next generation's royal mate will eventually arise.

What is so interesting about the bee, however, is the role of diet in determining the way in which the larvae develop. If the fertilized eggs are reared in normal wax cells on the workers' everyday diet then they develop into workers themselves. But a small number of the larvae are reared in extra-large cells specially set aside for the purpose. Their diet is different, for they feed on a specially-produced 'royal jelly' and on the basis of this diet alone, they become the future queens. All the ordinary worker bees remain sterile females throughout their lives. Exactly what it is that makes royal jelly so special has yet to be definitively resolved. Meanwhile the product is harvested and marketed to susceptible, affluent humans who feel their ardour or fitness is in decline, and who have a touching faith in its restorative properties. In the medical research world it is now accepted that no benefit to humans can possibly accrue . . . to bees, of course, it is quite a different matter.

The reduction in importance of the male which we can observe in the honey-bee is carried to extremes in the marine worm *Bonellia viridis*. The female of the species is a fat, bottle-green worm with an unusual, segmented organ in the body known uncompromisingly as the 'brown tube' and an extensible proboscis which is exceedingly mobile and capable of being extended to great lengths. It lives in a hollow cavity on the sea-bed (perhaps a hollow under some stones or a hole in some submerged wooden structure like a pile or a pier) from the security of which it extends its proboscis in the search for food. So much for the female: but what of the male?

The male *Bonellia* is minute. It exists as a small organism, covered with cilia, looking like a dwarf flatworm. It has almost no internal organs remaining, apart from the testes, and would never be taken for a male *Bonellia* by anyone. This degenerate male lives as a small parasite swimming about within the large fluid-filled coelomic cavity that occupies much of the female's body.

The larval forms of *Bonellia* are of indeterminate sex. They look much like father, and swim about in the sea in a free-living independent phase. Those that continue to swim freely eventually develop into females, and become fully functional, large green worms in the normal manner. But those that come into contact with a mature female, either by accident or sometimes it seems by being taken in deliberately *via* the proboscis, enter the body cavity and develop into unmistakable males. This genus shows us a larva of either sex, which develops into a large female or a tiny, degenerate male, entirely dependent on where it happens to swim. This is sex determination by accident of trajectory – by flight plan, if you like.

Some marine animals show the characters of both sexes in the one individual. The little transparent arrow-worm so commonly seen in plankton bears a set of ovaries just aft of its mid-line, and a small testis behind that. In this way the worm, *Sagitta*, fertilizes its own ova with its personal supply of sperm cells from its tail. The edible oyster *Ostrea* enjoys an interesting variant on this basic pattern, by changing sex at intervals. Here the phenomena depend on environmental temperatures. Culture your oysters in water at over 20°C and they will become female once each year; at 14°C the change-over occurs three or four times less frequently.

The factors that influence sex are many, and the role of the chromosomes

– though they remain the basic sex-determinant – is often influenced by external factors. The final extent of these is something that science has still to unravel. In mankind the position is complicated by the unusual combinations of chromosomes that occasionally occur, which cause recognizable abnormalities. Chromosomes sometimes go missing during the manoeuvres of meiosis, or they may be accidentally duplicated, so that an abnormal combination of sex chromosomes occurs. One useful aid to diagnosis has been the discovery that a small dark blob of material is often found near the nucleus of cells taken from human females, when they are examined under the microscope, and this provides a handy 'instant sexing' technique.

The importance of this observation, first reported in 1949, is considerable. Earlier I have said how we can count the chromosomes of an adult human cell and see how many X and Y chromosomes it contains. That is easy to say, but in practice it is difficult to do. In the first place, chromosomes are very small. They are only a little larger than bacteria, and the smallest chromosomes in man are so close to the limits of the optical microscope's capacity to make out detail that we can only perceive them as minute, blurred outlines.

Secondly, it is never easy to be sure which of the chromosomes actually are the X and Y. Often it is said that they were named because of their shape and it is quite true that the X chromosome does have an X-shape, whilst the Y chromosome looks like a tiny letter Y. But 40 of the chromosomes look like an X, and the other 6 all look like Y's, so it is none too easy to be sure exactly which is the one we are looking for. The condition most of us know as Mongolism (more formally known as Down's Syndrome, after its discoverer) is due to the presence of an extra chromosome-21, for example; but though it was known for some years that there was certainly an extra chromosome in the Mongoloid individual – counts showed 47 chromosomes instead of 46 – it was not until the 1960's that the culprit was eventually decided upon.

The picture is complicated further by a very common misconception about chromosomes, namely, that they are simply lying there in the cell nucleus, just waiting to be observed. In most cells there are no chromosomes to study. The reason is that as a rule (and the only exceptions are such odd cases as the salivary glands of midges, where giant chromosomes are found which are always present and which – particularly in the case of the fruit fly *Drosophila* – have been a wonderfully useful research tool) the chromosomes only appear when a cell is in the process of dividing. In the normal, day-to-day active cell nucleus you can see nothing of the chromosomes. But as the cell prepares to divide, a number of fine undulating fibrils become apparent inside the nucleus, and these gradually become thicker and shorter until they actually 'condense' into the chromosomes. Once the chromosomes have appeared, they line up across the centre of the cell. Then, from each pole of the nucleus, a radiating structure of tubes appears, known as the 'spindle'. The chromosomes become attached to the spindle which looks a little like the radiating spokes in an umbrella, and they split down the middle; then the spindle contracts, pulling a complete set of chromosomes towards each pole of the now-divided nucleus.

As soon as the process of division is over the chromosomes begin to break down again and disappear. Where they go to in the nucleus between divisions is anybody's guess. The whole process of cell division (mitosis, in distinction from the reduction division, meiosis) takes less than an hour, indeed in some cells it can take a matter of minutes to complete. So if you examine a normal interphase nucleus – one between divisions, that is – you will see no chromosomes at all. If you try to look early in the process you will see nothing but a jumbled mass of intertwined chromosomes in the process of formation, whilst if you look too late you will see a radiating, star-like conglomeration of chromosomes in which no detailed studies are possible. Only when the chromosomes are neatly laid out across the cell's equator at the mid-point of mitosis can you hope to see the chromosomes separated out and clear enough to count. This can be for a matter of minutes, and only that, in a process of mitosis that for most cells is a rare occurrence anyway.

Obviously you have a long job ahead of you if you decide to take a random selection of cells from a given adult and use them as the basis for a chromosome count: you will have a long search before you to find a cell that is dividing at all, and even then there is a small chance that it will be in the moment of metaphase, when the chromosomes are on the point of being pulled apart.

Fortunately, it has been found that some chemicals have the effect of interrupting the process at exactly the right moment. They actually prevent the spindle from forming, so that the dividing cells in a culture keep on through the process of mitosis until they reach metaphase – and they stop there. Since the spindle does not appear, there is nothing to pull the metaphase chromosomes apart. They simply lie there, inside a cell stuck in mid-division, unable to proceed any further, until the microscopist comes along to count them at his leisure. If these substances are added to a culture of cells growing in the incubator, you can leave them for a couple of days which gives most of the cells a chance to divide. They all remain in the half-way stage, and by the time you come to make your examination you have a large collection of chromosomes to work with, all of them at exactly the right stage of cell-division to make the task easy.

The type of chemical we use is typified by colchicine, found in the flowers of the Autumn Crocus, *Colchicum autumnale* to the gardener; and an example of 'herbal medicine' if ever there was one. Its ability to halt cells in mid-mitosis has given it some uses as a means of arresting the growth of cancer cells (though it is too toxic to use in man for routine management, it has shown us a great deal about the way such growth-arrestors can be used, and has helped give some insight into the treatment of leukaemia), and in smaller doses colchicine is used to treat gout with some success. The pollen of the *Colchicum* flower is saffron, used to colour pulaw rice in India, paella in Spain and yellow saffron buns in Cornwall . . . an impressive list of benefits from a diminutive wild-flower of the woodlands!

Although colchicine has made life much easier for the cytologist who wishes to carry out chromosome counts, the process is still time-consuming and costly to use on a routine basis. An easier alternative would be the direct examination under a microscope of some cells from an adult, without waiting for them to divide. Now, that seems like wishful thinking; an idle dream of the idealist. But there is – quite by chance, for there is no obvious reason in the world why fate should have been so kind to us – a difference between male and female cells that you can observe in normal, interphase cells. It is this which has made the routine sexing of cells into a far easier business, and has brought the realm of chromosome typing into the realm of sport. Cytological examination can give a rapid answer to the question of intersexuality and this has assumed increasing importance over the past few years. The discovery that gave rise to this new branch of investigation was made – as so often happens – by pure chance.

During the 1940's M. L. Barr and E. G. Bertram were trying to demonstrate changes that took place in nerve cells when they were fatigued from electrical stimulation. This research was fashionable at the time, indeed the attention paid to the electrical stimulation of nerves in the 1930's and 1940's would surprise students of today. What Barr and Bertram hoped to do was show a series of changes within the cell structure and to relate these to the amount of fatigue the cell had experienced. A programme of work like this depends on careful and diligent microscopical examination of the specimens, and they began to realize that there was a feature of the cells which no-one had previously recorded. What they observed was a small blob of matter near the edge of the nucleus.

In preparing material like this for examination it is usual to stain the cells with a material like the dye gentian violet (like colchicine, extracted originally from flowers), and what they noticed was that this blob of matter stained very deeply. What was particularly interesting was that these tiny bodies, which became known as Barr bodies, were confined to one sex. Barr and Bertram were working with neurones taken from the domestic cat, and they demonstrated that the little dark blobs were found in a percentage of the cells taken from female cats but were absent altogether in cells taken from males. Quite by chance, at a time when no-one could have anticipated such a development, they had found a method by which you could hope to 'sex' cells on their own, with no need to set up cultures and wait days for the results. These particles were subsequently found in human cells, and we now know that in women around half of the cell nuclei will show the particle whereas in men it hardly ever occurs.

There is one easily-obtained source of cells that can be taken from patients without delay and without complications, and which is already used for routine examinations: the blood smear. Since the white blood cells all contain nuclei in the normal way, and they were already being studied routinely in the laboratory for other purposes, it was inevitable that, sooner or later, someone would look to see whether these little particles could be identified in blood cells as well. It was in 1954 that the truth dawned. The number of cells showing the special feature was far less than in the other cells taken from the body (only 2% instead of 30–60%), and they did not have the same appearance as the particles seen in other cells. Instead, they looked like tiny drum-sticks projecting from the edge of the nucleus like a tiny mark deliberately stuck on as an aid to identification.

The fact that they occur in such small numbers is a little inconvenient, but perhaps this is because in blood cells the nucleus always stains deeply and in the particular cells in which the drum-stick occurs (the polymorphonuclear leucocyte, which in school is often introduced to us simply as the 'phagocyte' which devours invading germs) the nucleus would prevent you from seeing whether a drum-stick was present or not, unless it was clearly sticking out from the edge. I think it is quite likely that many more of the cells possess a drum-stick, but as the cell dried on the slide the drum-stick came to be lying above the nucleus or below it, according to the luck of the draw, and so cannot be made out amongst the mass of granular material in the nucleus itself. Even so, you can safely say that if you count 300 such blood cells from a female then half a dozen or so will exhibit drum-sticks, whereas if you count as many as 500 cells from a man you will observe none. And there is an important relationship between the number of these features in a cell and the number of sex chromosomes within the nucleus. In some individuals you find more than one of these 'markers' in some cells, and it has since been shown that the maximum number is always one less than the number of X–chromosomes in the genetic constitution. A specimen of cells with no Barr bodies at all has $0 + 1$ X–chromosomes – that is to say, one; so we have a male. A specimen with a maximum number of one has $1 + 1$ X–chromosomes, making it normally female, XX. A specimen with two will be XXX, by the same reasoning; so here we have a precise means of examining cells and getting an immediate indication of the number of X–chromosomes in any individual. All you need is a gentle scraping from the cheek and a count of the Barr-bodies its nuclei reveal, or a rapid finger-prick blood smear and a quick check for the drum-sticks.

In either event we obtain a clear reading of the number of X-chromosomes in the specimen cells, and this can be of immense diagnostic importance. There is no need for incubators, cultures, colchicine treatment and the rest; that can wait for a confirmatory test on the occasions when something requires further investigation.

We now have a growing knowledge of the various genetic tricks that an accident of cell-division can play: abnormalities caused by the retention of an extra X-chromosome can give rise to XXX individuals and some cases of an XXXX constitution have even been reported. Sometimes a careful cell count has to be done to demonstrate the occurrence of a mosaic – an individual in which some of the cells in the body have one constitution, whilst the others have an abnormal chromosome complement. There have been cases where cells that are female (XX) and male (XY) have occurred together in the same individual; indeed in 1962 a hermaphrodite case was reported in which the cell make-up consisted of some XX cells, some XXY, and some XXYYY – an astonishing variety.

Such chromosomal accidents are an important cause of intersexuality. Yet we must remember that chromosomes are *not* the final arbiter of sexual determination, and some of the external influences exert effects of surprising potency. It has been shown that if you incubate a toad's eggs at different temperatures, you initiate the development of different sexes. At 10°C all the individuals resulting were females, at 27°C they were an assortment of males and females, though all the females reverted to masculinity as their maturation proceeded. That experiment was reported in 1930 by the Swiss experimenter J. Piquet, and similar tendencies for lower temperatures to favour the production of predominantly male offspring have since been reported in other amphibians.

Even more remarkable were the experiments of over-feeding in amphibia. It is known that if you over-feed some amphibia at the end of the winter's hibernation, when the individuals are starved, then a male will develop into a female. The testes become mostly reabsorbed during the winter's privations and are used up as a bodily food reserve, and instead of the testis regenerating, the gonad tissues produce an ovary. A similar experiment has been carried out with castrated male toads. If they are over-fed a rich and fatty diet, they develop into feminine-looking toads, and a new ovary develops out of abdominal tissue adjacent to where the gonads should ordinarily be.

So the factors that influence sex and the broader concept of gender are many. The discovery of the sex chromosomes, for all its importance, is not the whole story. As the varied interactions of diet, temperature and chromosome constitution bring their weight to bear on the developing individual it can clearly be seen that we must distinguish between the theory and the practice of sex determination. Sex is a property of mature individuals, acting as complex communities of cells. It is a propensity of adults, a set of attributes that become diagnostic criteria or behavioural norms.

Sex is not an abstract property of cells, nuclei, chromosomes or whatever. Indeed as we shall see, it is possible for the reality of adult human life not only to differ from the prediction you might make from a chromosome count, but in some cases the gender of the adult may be the exact opposite of what the chromosomes foretell. The sex chromosomes may well contain the basic blueprints of masculinity or femininity. But a lot can happen to a blueprint between the design studio and the finished product that comes out of the factory gate.

CHAPTER FIVE

VIRGIN BIRTH

Virgin birth, as a term, has much to commend it when we are talking about fatherless conceptions in mammals. But reproduction without males is very common in microscopic forms of many-celled creatures as well as in a host of plant types. It is also widespread in bugs and beetles. So it is probably better if we resort to using the biological term that embraces all these phenomena: parthenogenesis. The word is derived from the Greek *parthenos*, a virgin; and those with a humorous bent might wish to observe that the term might sound more fitting as '*no* Pa-thenogenesis', but that is quite enough of that. This is a serious topic.

Parthenogenetic reproduction is very widespread amongst the rotifers, a group of small, microscopic animals that live by hunting around amongst strands of pondweed. In some types the males hardly ever appear, the females simply continue reproducing by themselves for prolonged phases before returning to the more normal pattern. In other rotifers the males are unknown. These species are identified as females and as far as we know the male gender has become lost altogether during evolutionary specialization.

In theory all rotifers have males and females, and it may well be that in the exclusively parthenogenetic species as we know them, males do sometimes occur but have not yet been caught, as it were, in the act; or perhaps we might yet discover means of inducing the females to enter a different phase of reproductive behaviour where males do appear again. Meanwhile we are left with the fact that this interesting group of animals really does feature species that are all-females. For them the ultimate mystery of fatherless reproduction is not merely a reality but a mainstay of normal life. In the beetles and the group of insects including bees and wasps, virgin birth is a widespread feature, as it is in some bugs (such as the familiar greenfly of vegetable gardens and the rose-bed) and mites.

In the world of vertebrate animals, hens and turkeys have shown themselves to be capable of parthenogenesis under certain conditions. Coming nearer home, to the mammals themselves, the phenomenon has been observed in guinea-pigs, rats, mice and cats and has even been claimed to occur (without divine intervention) in mankind. Let us consider the groups in turn.

ROTIFERS

These are tiny, transparent animals which live in ponds, lakes and moist corners, like a rain-water gutter. Some of them live for the greater part of the year in dried cysts and come to life again as soon as they are moistened by a fall of rain. The ovary or testis is one of the largest organs in the rotifer's body. These organisms exist by swimming around as a rule, propelled along by what appear to be paddle-wheels at the front end. These do not actually rotate; they are arrays of finely beating hair-like cilia which thrash about in unison and give a rotating wheel-like appearance to the front of the organism. Rotifers are delightful creatures to study.

Yet for all the attention devoted to them, no male rotifer was ever discovered until 1848. All the common types previously identified were parthenogenetic, the females producing eggs from the ovary, which went on to develop into adult rotifers without the intervention of a male at any stage. Since then, males have been found for many rotifer species (though there is one large and important family, the Philodinidae, in which not a single male of any of the species has ever been found).

The reproduction of sexually-active rotifers runs through a phase of parthenogenesis before sex rears its head. There is then a mating period. In some types there are two of these sexual phases, one in Spring and the other in the Autumn; whilst in other groups sexual activity occurs in the Autumnal period only. The occasional types that live in relatively dry places are quicker to get on with sexual reproduction: very soon after a fall of rain they hatch out from their cysts, begin an active life as though nothing had happened, and are soon engaged in sexual reproduction.

There are two types of female rotifers. One always reproduces asexually, by parthenogenesis, the other may (but often does not) reproduce through sex. In this second type there are eggs which appear smaller than normal female eggs, which develop directly into males. Some of these smaller male rotifers eventually copulate with the females, inject sperm through the cuticle of the mate, and fertilize her ova. When this has happened she produces a clutch of similar eggs which she liberates into the water in the normal way, but which are larger than normal and have a thicker shell. They settle to the bottom and remain in this resting condition until Winter has passed by. In the warmer weather of Spring, they hatch out – always into females. The females then resume parthenogenesis until it is time for a sexual phase again, and in this way the cycle continues. This complex life cycle provides a model for the kind of male-less reproduction found in more complex forms of life.

A small group of animals related to the rotifers and known as gastrotrichs also exhibit parthenogenesis. Not all of them do it, though; half of them are life-long hermaphrodites.

CRUSTACEA

The little water-flea *Daphnia* is familiar to many people, either as a rounded translucent creature dancing through pond water or as dried granules as food for fish in ornamental tanks. *Daphnia* is very much more complex than the rotifers as well as being larger, yet it shares a similar pattern of sexual reproduction alternating with parthenogenesis.

It is during Summer that the males are dispensed with, as in the typical rotifer pattern. During this season the *Daphnia* females produce clutches of eggs containing yolk-sacs, rather like a minute hen's egg. These develop without fertilization into the female larvae which remain within the brood-pouch inside the mother's back. Eventually when sufficiently mature they are liberated into the pondwater around and continue to grow into adults.

Around late Spring, a change occurs. Male offspring are produced in the brood as well as females, and in time they become sexually active and fertilization takes place. From then on parthenogenesis proceeds alongside sexual reproduction. *Daphnia* produces resistant Winter-eggs each Autumn which can be dried out completely or even frozen without losing viability. These eggs, when they are formed within the ovary, contain a far greater amount of yolk than the normal Summer eggs and they develop more slowly. Before they start development, fertilization is necessary: then the enclosed embryo starts to form before suddenly ceasing growth. The egg then enters its resting phase and does not continue development until Winter has passed.

But the life-cycle does not seem to benefit from the presence of the males; they clearly share the mother's genetic complement with their 'sisters' and usually mate with them. So for all practical purposes the males do not seem to perform any biologically useful function. They seem to take quite well to performing their duties, though, mating with no thought for the morrow; for the male *Daphnia* the attraction of sex itself is clearly enough.

FLIES, BUGS AND LICE

Some insect pests rely on rapid rates of proliferation if they are to hold their own against predators, or in difficult conditions. Clearly there is a marked advantage in producing large numbers of offspring from a single mating (which many insects do as a matter of course) or even from no mating at all. It is this latter option which the bugs (such as greenfly) and the lice (including many parasitic plant-lice) have mastered most successfully.

Everyone is familiar with aphids. One day your roses or your broad beans are growing peacefully in the sunshine and fattening up their buds ready for a bumper crop; the next time you inspect them the growing tips have virtually disappeared under a mass of insect growth. The aphids have arrived. More than once, gardeners have observed to me that: 'they came so damned quickly I can't see how they had time to breed'. It is a pertinent observation. Aphids do not have time to breed, so they simply reproduce by parthenogenesis instead – it is quicker.

The fertilized eggs of an aphid only ever develop into females, never males; and these females are always capable of parthenogenesis. Eventually some of the parthenogenetic offspring develop as males from unfertilized egg-cells, and they show the kind of differences in chromosome count that you would expect to see in insects of different sex. In *Aphis saliceti*, for example, there are six chromosomes in the female, of which two are sex-chromosomes. In the male there are five chromosomes: four similar to those in the female, but only one sex-chromosome in addition. Clearly at the reduction-division you would expect to end up with ova from the female containing three chromosomes in each nucleus, whilst in the males you would find half of the sperm cells containing three chromosomes, and half two (that is, half female-determinants and half male).

Oddly enough, you do not obtain a brood following fertilization which is composed of 50% males and 50% females. Instead the result is exclusively female, all of them parthenogenetic – and so the cycle starts again. The reason seems to be that as the sperm cells mature, only those with the full complement of three chromosomes survive and the sperm with two die out.

As a result, all the eggs that form contain $3+3=6$ chromosomes, i.e. female constitution. When these females are due to begin the production of males, they lose one of the sex-chromosomes during meiosis, producing some larvae with five chromosomes instead of six. These, of course, become the males and in this way the sexual phase begins. It is a complex picture, and quite why it should function like this is anybody's guess.

An even more unusual form of parthenogenisis exists in a little-known group of insects which live on decaying wood. They are dipteran flies (an example is *Miastor*) and, like other flies, they produce maggot larvae from the eggs they lay. What is so remarkable is that the maggots do not go on to produce pupae and then adult flies – at least, they do not do so directly. The maggots themselves develop ovaries which mature before the larva itself is anywhere near maturing into an adult fly, so that instead of being mere immature food-gathering grubs, these larvae are able to reproduce themselves. They do so by a form of parthenogenesis known as *paedogenesis*, and each maggot can 'give birth' to as many as thirty 'daughter-larvae'. In human terms it is like babies giving birth to identical twins of themselves before becoming anything like mature in physical form.

During the summer a different kind of larva begins to appear amongst the paedogenic offspring, and this does form pupae. From the chrysalis emerges the adult gnat which only lives for a brief time – long enough to lay four or five large eggs. From these, the paedogenic larvae emerge, which carry on reproducing without males and without maturity until the cycle is repeated. In this insect the adults have been reduced to a minority generation, a rudiment almost; it is the self-perpetuating young forms which carry on the bulk of the business of self-propagation.

Elsewhere in the insect world the 'virgin birth effect' plays an important role in the maintenance of more conventional life-cycles. The casual observer of the bee would see little to suggest that anything unusual was going on, but parthenogenesis is responsible for the production of every male bee in the hive. The fertilized ova become females, the exact type depending on diet, but the drone results from the laying of unfertilized eggs every time.

For bees, as for aphids, thrips and some fungus gnats, parthenogenesis is a normal part of the life-cycle with a specific biological function. The phenomenon of virgin birth becomes even more interesting when it occurs in insects that do not ordinarily exhibit the phenomenon. It is justifiably true, I am sure, that the whole concept of virgin birth seems to most people a kind of freakish or unnatural idea which occurs when you do not expect it, and which has an aura of doubt surrounding it – you cannot help wondering if virgin birth was actually responsible, or whether some more natural process crept in unnoticed by the outside world. And cases like this certainly occur in the world of insect life.

One of the fruit flies, *Drosophila parthenogenetica*, is named for its proclivity to dispense with the male but the virgin birth phenomenon is the exception, not the rule, and the offspring themselves are weak and rather feebly developed compared to normal fruit flies. Of all the unfertilized ova from normal virgin flies which do begin dividing, around 80% die before they hatch or shortly afterwards. Careful searching and observation has shown that most species of *Drosophila* will reveal the occasional example of parthenogenesis.

Interestingly enough, the same is true of higher animals – some of them warm-blooded.

VIRGIN BIRTH IN HIGHER ANIMALS

If you take an unfertilized egg-cell from an amphibian (this has been done in frogs, toads and newts, for example) it is possible to give it a stimulus that starts it dividing. One of the simplest forms of stimulus is the pricking of the ova wall with a fine glass needle, and it has been claimed that this acts in the same way as penetration by a sperm. The ova, now reacting to the stimulus of what seems to be fertilization, can start to divide and give rise to an adult. The first time this was carried out was in 1899 when the French biologist (later to become an American) Jacques Loeb treated unfertilized eggs of the sea-urchin with a solution of magnesium chloride and found that they began to divide and to form an embryo. Loeb was astounded at the time, and said later that he was certain that he was mistaken in what he had seen.

Within a few years his compatriot Eugène Bataillon had repeated the experiment using fresh frog's eggs from an unmated female. His own reaction was that there must have been some stray male frog sperm cells in the supply of water he was using, but in fact he had initiated development of an unfertilized ovum. He had, like Loeb, taken the first steps towards the initiation of virgin birth.

More recently we have begun to recognize that accidental examples of developing embryos without fertilization occur in some domestic birds. In 1955, for example, an analysis was published of parthenogenetic development in hens' eggs taken from virgin birds. Just once in a while some growth of the embryonic tissues was apparent. In 95% of the cases, all that happened was the membranes around an embryo began to form, but nothing else happened. But in the other 5% development was more advanced, and evidence of early embryo formation was found.

Three years later an examination of Cornish Game Fowl revealed that more than half of a sample of eggs laid by virgin females showed some signs of parthenogenetic development of the embryo, and meanwhile a similar analysis of 2,537 turkey eggs laid by 79 virgin birds revealed that there were signs of development in 568 of them, eight of those reaching the stage of development of a normal embryo at nine days, and in four growth proceeded until sexual differentiation had occurred. All of these were male. Eventually over the next few years 68 of the parthenogenetically derived turkey chicks were hatched, although most of them died shortly after leaving the egg and none lived more than a matter of days.

What was interesting was an apparent association between the rate of parthenogenesis in the eggs and the existence of viruses in the hen that laid them. There was a far higher incidence in eggs from hens that had been vaccinated or whose dams had been vaccinated, suggesting that perhaps the virus in the vaccine was interfering with the normal processes of formation in the ova. You might also consider it possible that some undetected virus was involved – after all, turkeys are only vaccinated if there is a chance of infection (perhaps through their being raised intensively) and it is quite possible that some other infection was contracted at the same time.

In either event it has proved possible to increase the rates of parthenogenetic development by selectively breeding the birds. Various strains of turkey have shown increases of sizeable proportions.

Number of turkey eggs showing parthenogenesis (as percentages)

STRAIN	Before Selective Breeding %	After Selective Breeding %
A	1.1	18.6
B	4.0	21.1
C	16.7	40.0

The effect of selective in-breeding on rates of embryo development in unfertilized turkey eggs.

We have now to ask why the phenomena occur. There are several alternative explanations, all of them so far conjectural. Perhaps the chromosomes in the final egg-cell become doubled in some way, though it is difficult to see how. Possibly the reduction division of meiosis does not actually reduce the number of chromosomes by half as it should. Or it might be that one of the polar bodies formed during meiosis re-enters the cell and fertilizes it like a sperm nucleus would do. So far we do not know what the answer is and – though it would be interesting to find out what does happen in turkeys – it would interest me even more to know why it doesn't happen to the rest of us.

The desire to bring about parthenogenesis in higher creatures has given rise to a range of experiments with mammals. A series of experiments with rabbits produced many claims that heat shock (sudden changes of temperature, that is to say) or treatment with sodium chloride solution could stimulate rabbit ova to develop without fertilization. After treatment with cooling and the salt solution the ova were implanted into rabbits whose uterus had been prepared by treatment with pituitary extract, and who were already in an early false pregnancy. A number of offspring were produced, some of which were successfully mated.

IMMACULATE CONCEPTIONS

Claims of a virgin birth in humans are often put forward and there is nothing new in that. The unmarried woman with an unexpected pregnancy is the usual claimant, though others have insisted that their child was conceived through no act of sex either. Sometimes the woman is acting in good faith, since conceptions in people who have an intact hymen are well known to occur and if this is taken as the mark of virginity, then 'virgin birth' is not as rare as all that. I am not concerned with such honest misunderstandings, however; what we have to consider are possibilities that a child can be born of a woman who has had no sexual contact with a man, and in whom the ovum has somehow begun development without intervention from a sperm. This, barring divine intervention, narrows the search considerably.

The first scientific clues emerged in a paper published in 1939 by Stanley Reimann and his colleague Bernard Miller of Philadelphia. Knowing that many workers had induced the development of non-fertilized egg cells they turned their attention to human ova. Even at that time it had been argued that certain growths (including teratomas and dermoid cysts) might arise from some form of spontaneous development of a cell – perhaps an ovum – into embryonic tissues, and they decided to search for some evidence that artificial means could stimulate the egg cell to begin development towards the embryonic state.

They obtained the cooperation of surgical colleagues who were carrying out routine hysterectomies in women with conditions such as cancer. Reimann and Miller asked for specimens of the organs removed at the time most likely to correspond with fertilization (i.e. around the fifteenth day after the first day of the previous menstrual period – a figure which was a novelty then).

In some cases they were presented with an entire set of uterus, both fallopian tubes and both ovaries; in others nothing more than a single tube. Either way, the fallopian tubes were attached to a fine needle and syringe, and the contents were washed out into a watch-glass. If an ovum was there it settled down into the centre of the watch-glass and could at once be studied. Five ova were obtained and they gave an excellent opportunity to make some detailed examinations of these cells in the fresh and living state. But of the five, one was treated to induce cell division and to start it into development. The result is controversial and debatable – but it was something of a minor landmark in our quest for virgin birth.

The episode began on 17 July 1938 when a coloured woman of 35 was being prepared for the operating theatre. She had always had regular periods, though they were profuse and heavy. Her average cycle was the normal 28 days; her average period lasted five days. She was healthy apart from a fibrous tumour of the womb; it was this which the surgeons had decided to remove. Next day the operation went ahead, and it was successful. From the woman were removed two fallopian tubes, one ovary, and the uterus with its growth (a fibroleioma). The ovary showed signs of previous intervention, as it had been partly resected in a more conservative operation earlier in the development of the disease. The other ovary, however, was not removed this time. It showed no signs of disease, and its presence would continue to provide the body with its normal supply of hormones.

The specimens were at once rushed to the laboratory and the tubes were separated from the uterus. An ovum was soon found – it was now 15 days after the onset of her last period. It was rapidly transferred to a droplet of diluted blood on a microscope slide and kept in a warm chamber at blood heat. Then observations began.

It was a large, uniform cell under the microscope, with a darker area visible near the centre – which was presumed to be the nucleus – and a number of small yolk particles spread through the cell substance as nutriment for the first stages of growth. At one point near the edge of the cell a small body could be seen which seemed to be a polar body from the last stages of reduction division. When the cell was gently rolled over that impression was increased.

The cell was then lifted out and transferred to a solution of human serum containing a trace of the ethyl ester of acetic acid (a chemical which Loeb had shown to stimulate the ova of lower animals). The chamber with the ovum floating in its fluid medium was cautiously transferred to a microscope stage and the fine needles of a microdissector were brought into view. With the right-hand needle, pressure was brought to bear on the ovum, a cell no bigger than this full-stop. The ovum is covered with an elastic membrane, the zona pellucida, and it did not rupture. The point of the needle pushed the zona in, and as soon as pressure was removed it promptly moved out again, just like a rubber ball.

A second attempt succeeded in penetrating the ovum. The needle, this time brought up faster and with harder pressure behind it, 'popped' the zona and the tip entered the ovum. It was then quickly withdrawn. For the first fifteen or twenty minutes, nothing happened. Then the cell underwent a definite alteration in appearance. The zona pellucida seemed to become thin at one end of the cell and in the space of five minutes a rounded particle of protoplasm was extruded from the cell. A crater was left at the site from where this rounded body had become detached, but within a further five minutes this had been repaired and the cell wall was again unbroken.

After a further twenty minutes a similar phenomenon took place. This time the protrusion took longer to form, but after twenty-five minutes a second tiny body was ejected and its crater (this time not so deep as before) began to fill. The ovum then began to show signs of dying. Its surface became irregular and after five hours it was plainly beginning to disintegrate. But it had produced two tiny bodies which Reimann and Miller described quite certainly as small (but complete) cells. The ovum, they asserted, had been dividing until it died. They also observed a deep groove to form along one side of the ovum, and since this had been seen in earlier experiments with mammalian eggs they were certain this confirmed their diagnosis.

There are other explanations, though. Some cells do seem to put out rounded portions of this sort when they are damaged; but that is admittedly not such a sequence of coordinated events as this ovum extruding 'polar bodies' and then repairing its cell wall. It could have been an effect unrelated to division brought on by small amounts of calcium present in the medium; but reactions due to calcium usually require far higher concentrations and they occur far faster, too. So it is just possible that here was the first dividing parthenogenetic human ovum ever witnessed: the medical likelihood of virgin birth was beginning to come a little closer.

It was not until 1956 that the possibility of natural parthenogenesis in humans received its first qualified scientific support, when a search for British parthenogenetic babies was dramatically launched. The first rumbles had been felt when a lecture at University College London in October 1955 had described the parthenogenetic reproduction of certain fish, and there was the hint at speculation that perhaps this might somehow occur in mankind. London's medical journal *The Lancet* devoted a leader article to the subject the following week, Guy Fawkes' Day of 1955. It could not have been a better date, for the fireworks went up immediately.

The greatest interest in the idea was shown by the *Sunday Pictorial*, now defunct, and the mushrooming campaign to find possible virgin births was boosted by a paper published in Brazil, which claimed to describe a case in a young Peruvian Indian girl. The *Pictorial* published a sensational account of the revelation and asked its readers for information on any contenders for a British virgin birth that they could nominate. Nineteen firm testimonies from readers arrived. They were passed for examination to a British specialist, Dr Stanley Balfour-Lynn, and his findings were eventually published in the following Spring. He had been thorough, no-one could dispute that, and he had been given excellent advice and support from several eminent colleagues, including Professor J. B. S. Haldane, who advised on the serological tests and their interpretation.

The nineteen mothers who claimed to have experienced virgin birth were all asked to come to London for an interview. Their sincerity was, for the most part, unmistakable. Eleven of them were eliminated from the start, since they had conceived through sexual contact even though they had remained technically intact, that is to say their hymens had not been ruptured in the process of love-making. An intact hymen is regarded the world over as the touch-stone of virginity, of course, so in that sense these were easily mistaken by the women for virgin conceptions. It does not take full intercourse for enough sperm to gain entrance to the vagina for one of them eventually to succeed in fertilizing the waiting ovum (a fact which has become apparent too late for many unmarried and involuntary mothers). But the parthenogenetic birth has to occur without the sperm, so these cases, though of some interest from the medical viewpoint, were of no value to the survey.

There remained eight mother-and-daughter pairs. They were given code-names, the letters from the beginning of the Greek alphabet, and were all blood-typed. Four of the pairs showed good coincidence of the factors analyzed, which allowed them to be selected as possible contenders for the next stage.

Mrs Alpha	A1	Rhesus phenotype c̄dec̄de
Miss Alpha	A1	Rhesus phenotype c̄dec̄de
Mrs Beta	A1	Rhesus phenotype CCDee
Miss Beta	O	Rhesus phenotype CCDee
Mrs Gamma	O	Rhesus phenotype CCDee
Miss Gamma	O	Rhesus phenotype CCDee
Mrs Delta	A	Rhesus phenotype Cc̄Dee
Miss Delta	A	Rhesus phenotype c̄dec̄de
Mrs Epsilon	A2	Rhesus positive to anti-D
Miss Epsilon	A2B	Rhesus positive to anti-D
Mrs Zeta	O	Rhesus phenotype c̄cDE
Miss Zeta	O	Rhesus phenotype Cc̄Dee
Mrs Eta	O	Rhesus phenotype CCDee
Miss Eta	O	Rhesus phenotype Cc̄DE
Mrs Theta	O	Rhesus positive to anti-D
Miss Theta	A1	Rhesus positive to anti-D

The virgin-birth claimants: first blood group screening.

For this examination, more detailed blood-group studies were undertaken. They revealed discrepancies that were quite enough to rule out two of the mother-daughter pairs, but in the remaining two the degree of coincidence was good (see next page).

Mrs Beta and her daughter, together with Mrs Alpha and her daughter, were shown to have close matching from this more detailed scrutiny. But the Beta pair were eliminated on the basis of eye colour: Mrs Beta had blue eyes, her daughter brown. On genetic advice this made the partheno-genesis explanation seem highly improbable. But the match between Mrs Alpha and her daughter was close. So far they seemed to be passing all the tests hand in hand. Next came a series of further investigations.

First of these was the tasting of phenyl thiocarbamide, a chemical which some people can taste, and others cannot. Here both Alphas were able to

	M	N	S	P	Lu	Le a	Le b	K	Fy a
Mrs Alpha	+	+	−	++	−	−	−	−	−
Miss Alpha	+	+	−	+++	−	−	−	−	−
Mrs Beta	+	−	+	+++	−	−	−	−	+
Miss Beta	+	−	+	+	−	−	+	−	+
Mrs Gamma	+	+	−	−	−	+	−	+	−
Miss Gamma	+	+	−	+	+	+	−	+	−
Mrs Delta	+	−	+	+++	−	−	−	−	+
Miss Delta	+	−	+	+++	−	−	−	+	−

Second blood group analysis of four good-match pairs of claimed virgin birth mothers and daughters.

taste the compound at the same threshold value of 2.54 mg per litre. This is a degree of coincidence you would not expect to find – but it would of course be perfectly compatible with the virgin-birth hypothesis.

After that their saliva was examined for secreted components. Neither mother nor daughter secreted group-A substances in the saliva; and after a complex series of manoeuvres involving titration against antibodies they both had identical titres against A2 cells – there is no need to go into the technical details about this search for antigens but the coincident result was considered to be significant.

Thirdly they were asked to provide serum samples which were analyzed by filter-paper electrophoresis – a kind of 'spreading' process that separates out the components of such a mixture. The results stated unequivocally that mother and daughter gave identical patterns. In medical terms they were as good as being identical twins . . . almost as good as being the same person, in fact.

The final test involved skin grafting. A transplant like this is unlikely to 'take' if the two people who exchange skin are significantly different from each other. Between twins such a graft would normally be entirely successful, and in the case of a parthenogenetic mother/daughter pair the same would apply. The graft from daughter to mother was shed after four weeks, though the opposite exchange from mother to daughter remained healthy for six weeks before showing some signs it was losing its supply of blood-vessels. It was then wiped cleanly off with cotton wool. Neither graft actually 'took', then, and grew in place.

In favour of the two tissues being antigenically identical – which is what you would expect of identical twins or parthenogenesis – was the fact that in neither case was there any evidence of inflammation. The tissues were not being actively rejected. Against that explanation is the undeniable fact that the graft from daughter to mother was shed sooner than its counterpart. It is impossible for a parthenogenetic child to show any antigens that are not part and parcel of the mother's constitution, so – if any graft is to work – you would predict that it would be the graft from child to mother. The mother might, on the other hand, possess some antigens that were not passed on to her child; in that case you would predict that the graft in this direction would not take as readily. Now in the case of the Alpha family, it was the graft from daughter to mother which showed greatest signs of rejection, *not* what you would expect from tissues of common origins.

But this was the only suggestion that the tissues of mother and daughter might not be, to all intents and purposes, identical. Balfour-Lynn felt that, as all the other tests had seemed so conclusive, there was no point in raising this as an objection; and neither was he convinced of the value of carrying out further tests. He knew full well that a matter of this sort is basically a question of probabilities, and with the testing procedures available at that time he knew he had gone as far as you could reasonably expect. The scientific tests revealed no real evidence of incompatibility and there was no likelihood of foreknowledge of the factors involved on the part of Mrs Alpha or her daughter (she could have had no notion of the kind of tests that would be carried out or of their likely results) which, it was felt, increased further the likelihood that the case was genuine.

The report concluded that: 'This mother's claim must not only be taken seriously, but it must also be admitted that we have been unable to disprove it.' It does not mean that this was a virgin birth, then; only that we could not demonstrate that it wasn't. And are there mechanisms which could be put forward to explain how virgin birth could occur in mankind? There are several.

As we have seen, the reabsorption of a polar body by an ovum would provide it with a full genetic complement; a mosaic of XX and XY cells might occur in some rare cases and cause an accidental self-fertilization through the exchange of a nucleus in some fashion; so many factors could be put forward to explain rare cases like this.

And which mechanism was the reason for Mrs Alpha's incredible story? The answer was kept a secret for more than two decades, for it was not until 1978 that Mrs Alpha – in real life Marie Ammon, born in Germany and later a citizen of London – revealed that it had been sexual conception, and not parthenogenesis, that had given her a daughter.

Marie Ammon was born Emmimarie Sturm in Hanover and was brought up by her widowed father, a policeman. He was a strict parent, and taught his daughter nothing about sexual matters. She joined the Hitler Youth Movement in its heyday and by the age of 17, in 1943, she was called up for military service.

Almost immediately she was sent to an establishment at Furstenwalde, near Berlin, with a group of about thirty other attractive young girls. The atmosphere was that of a finishing school; the teaching involved Nazi propaganda, classes on the prospects in the war, and lessons on deportment and behaviour in addition to broader education designed to bring out 'the social airs and graces'. It must have been an astonishing change of life-style for a girl brought up to a life of stricture.

At intervals, senior officers came to stay for a few days on rest and recuperation – and, though Marie Ammon says she did not suspect it at the time, for the opportunity to take part in eugenic breeding experiments. One night she was introduced to a good-looking young man named Peter with whom she danced and drank the night away. Mrs Ammon believes she was drugged, for the next thing she remembers was awakening next day in bed. There followed a series of medical examinations and some injections, she says, and she was later sent back to Hanover without any further explanation.

At that time she was being courted by a young soldier in the German forces named Hans Ammon. Hanover was repeatedly bombed by the Allies, night after night, and the two sometimes took refuge together. One night after a severe air-raid they lay together and made love (Marie now suggests her motive may have been 'gratitude' as much as anything, for she says she was very scared at the notion of sexual penetration) and after two weeks she went to see her doctor following an attack of vertigo. The examination showed she was already three months pregnant.

She married Hans Ammon to provide her child with a father even though she had had no sexual contact with him at the time of the conception and she knew he could not have been the father.

The baby was born in February 1945 in a barbed-wire-surrounded Sonderlager in northern Germany. It was not an easy confinement and Marie Ammon was given a considerable amount of nitrous oxide during labour. To her embarrassment she called out the name 'Peter' several times to the staff.

After the war she drifted apart from her husband and was eventually divorced. With her baby, Monica, she tried to eke out an existence amongst the ruins of her home town until she fell in love with a British soldier who gave her and her child some food. In due course they married (this time, she says, out of her gratitude) and she settled in England.

So it was that in 1955 she wrote to the *Sunday Pictorial* to claim a virgin birth. Throughout the investigations she said nothing of her experiences, but seemed more intent on proving that her conception had indeed been done without sex. The tests, as we have seen, did not disprove her claim and Marie Ammon became widely believed to be an example of a mother whose pregnancy was a confirmed example, albeit a somewhat surprising one, of parthenogenesis in a human.

Meanwhile what happened to the daughter, now in her mid-thirties? Marie Ammon says that they have little contact now; she is married and has children of her own and though she did not invite her mother to her wedding, Mrs Ammon turned up of her own accord anyway. And so it seems that – even if Monica Ammon was not conceived by parthenogenetic means – she was probably a result of Hitler's Aryan eugenic plans to breed a race of superior whites as a force for the future of the Third Reich. It is a remarkable climax to an unnerving tale.

Yet what does this tell us about the actual chances of parthenogenesis occurring in humans? It would be wrong to feel that the surprising conclusion to the saga of Mrs Alpha shows how silly we are even to speculate about virgin birth in mankind, for there is no reason we know of that prevents it from seeming possible, or even likely.

It remains a singular fact that biological mechanisms have evolved that prevent us from undergoing parthenogenesis, even if we try to use as much scientific might as we can to get the process started. Parthenogenesis ought to work, and science has no means of explaining why it doesn't.

And what of the ultimate question: are there examples of partheno-genesis awaiting discovery? With the knowledge we have, all I can say is that there ought to be examples. Yes, they would be rare; certainly, they are an unlikely prospect. But we have no knowledge of any mechanism which we can demonstrate which makes parthenogenesis any more improbable in mankind than it is in, for instance, turkeys. Putting the idea in its most tempting form – there might be some examples of parthenogenetic conception waiting for us to identify. One thing is certain – we could carry out far more detailed scrutiny of the antigenic status of tissue samples than was the case in 1955, when Marie and Monica Ammon were tested in London.

And if no examples of parthenogenesis have occurred in mankind we are still faced with the need to find out why, and this is a mystery almost as great as virgin birth itself.

THE PREGNANT MALE

The most easily-recognizable example of a pregnancy that did not involve sexual intercourse is of course when a man – or a boy – is pregnant. There have been examples of this aberrant phenomenon, which seems to betray the most fundamental concepts of biology, yet the prospect has attracted more incredulous attention than serious investigation. Though there has never been any shortage of rumour and speculation about sexual peculiarities of this kind, there was never any reliable documentation in earlier centuries. But in more recent times this incongruous phenomenon has at last been confirmed.

On 8 March 1964 a baby boy was delivered at the Queen Mary Hospital in Hong Kong. The mother already had ten children, all of them normal; none of them twins. At two months of age he was a happy and healthy child, feeding well and putting on weight – indeed he seemed to be putting on too much weight, for he began to develop a distended abdomen. In the family it was jokingly said that the little one looked as though he was 'expecting', and this was exactly so, even though no-one suspected the fact at the time.

He was brought in to the hospital when the swelling became an embarrassment, and was examined. To the doctors' surprise, the little boy's abdomen contained a large and rounded lumpy mass, which was not apparently causing him any great trouble and was certainly not involved in any obstruction. What is more the mass was easily movable. A series of x-rays was taken. It was then that the truth suddenly became plain, for inside his body were the skeletal outlines of a developing foetus. The baby was pregnant.

At the university's Surgical Unit, the boy was seen by Edmund Lee, the surgeon, who decided to operate as a matter of priority. Much to his surprise, he found three developing foetuses, each with an umbilical cord, bathed in fluid and lying in an embryonic sac of membranes. The first of the 'triplets' was six inches (150 cm) long and was developing rapidly, but it did have spina bifida, and its skull was not properly formed from firm cartilage but was described as 'gelatinous'. The second was imperfect: an oval mass of tissues on which limb buds could just be made out. The third, however, a tiny healthy human of two inches in length, was a well-formed foetus. A blood supply ran to the umbilical cords of the three foetuses from the boy's iliac vessels running inside his pelvis.

The operation took place on 1 June and within eight days the little Chinese boy was well enough to be discharged. He made an uneventful recovery.

On occasions an abnormal foetus has been known to develop with another inside it, a condition known as *foetus in foetu*. Usually it seems to be a form of 'inverted' twinning, although on occasions it may be that a subsequent pregnancy has begun and the already-forming occupant of the womb has taken the newcomer into his or her body through some inexplicable mechanism. Alternatively, I am tempted to speculate whether the little invader might not arise from a spontaneously dividing body cell of the unwitting parent through a form of parthenogenesis.

But Mr Lee's case does not quite come into this category. The patient was no foetus, but a well-formed and independent child. His triplets – though imperfectly developing – did have their own blood supply and were being nourished much as a normal embryo would be; and they were floating in a fluid-filled sac in a perfectly acceptable manner. We lack the technology to keep such immature foetuses alive but if we were able to offer some kind of placental substitute it is possible that such tiny individuals might even have been raised to term.

It is a remarkable instance of the unexpected behaviour of sexual reproduction in a bizarre guise – when pregnancy occurs in a human who is not only unable to have conceived, or to have had sexual intercourse, or even to be the right age and size to survive it; but who is also the wrong sex. What more bizarre evidence of nature's occasional fickleness could you find?

CHAPTER SIX

DEAR SIR OR MADAM...

It is eight-thirty in the morning in the mountains as a bright, trim-built shapely brunette collects her mail from the box and, pausing only to check that the day's fresh adornment of cosmetics has a precise and professional appearance, re-enters the kitchen and affectionately kisses her husband. Mrs Loretta Martin* enjoys an interesting life; she enjoys sex with her spouse, likes to sing and play tennis, has a penchant for gardening, and drives with confidence and skill. Her husband loves her to distraction. She needs protection, and he knows it. He fully understands that their persistent failure to conceive is a burden which she would give almost anything to shed.

They have recently been to an adoption agency, and it looks as though this may be the only way for them to start the little family they so deeply hope for. Medical checks came before that, of course. Her husband's sperm count was normal, and the sperm cells themselves seemed to be active enough and perfectly capable of reaching their target. The doctor had carried out an internal examination of her genital tract and had sent off some specimens for examination. Later she had even been seen at the hospital in San Francisco, where a warm and friendly specialist had explained that – though she would always enjoy a perfectly satisfactory sex life (she had coyly confirmed that on that score neither she nor her husband had a word of complaint) she could not conceive. He had told her that something had simply failed to develop properly, and there was no sign of the normal connection leading up from the roof of the vagina through the cervix – the channel through which sperm cells could enter the uterus and through which, in time, the new-born baby would emerge. It was of course a bitter disappointment, and it is the kind of blow one usually has to suffer alone, since the normal married woman who is perfectly well able to conceive can never appreciate the sense of loss and anguish that so many would-be mothers experience when that realization dawns for the first time. Men, of course, are even more unsympathetic. Their reaction is

* Loretta Martin is a fictitious name.

generally that, well, at least it saves bothering with contraceptive precautions. Her husband was not like that. He understood. He had spoken at length to their doctor, he knew the score, and understood her well enough to try and build some compensations into their lives.

Though the doctors had been helpful, sympathetic, and genuinely wanting to help as far as they possibly could, there was one fact they had not mentioned to either of the couple. It was quite simply that this sparkling-happy, vivacious, securely-married young woman was nothing of the sort. She was a man. In spite of her feminine appearance and her wholly satisfactory life as a married woman, her internal sex organs were masculine. Instead of ovaries she had two undescended testicles. There are hundreds of people like her in the United States; perhaps a few thousand world-wide.

The phenomenon is known as Testicular Feminization, and as far as one can deduce it seems to be caused by a gene present in an X-chromosome, which has the unusual effect of preventing the body's tissues from responding to the presence of the male sex hormone, testosterone. The person does not become a mere half-way individual though; often these individuals may be voluptuous and exceedingly attractive-looking women. One study has boldly asserted that cases occur as photographic models, airline hostesses and prostitutes . . .

One intriguing case is on record of a woman who was mother, grandmother and sister to victims of the anomaly. She exhibited a most unusual bilateral asymmetry of secondary sexual characteristics. The left half of her body bore a rounded and well-proportioned breast and, in the groin, a healthy growth of pubic hair. By contrast, on the right side there was no pubic hair at all (pubic hair is absent in victims of the condition itself) and the breast was markedly underdeveloped.

This is an interesting syndrome, because the bodily and psychological attributes of the patient are entirely, almost seductively, feminine. There is no uterus, a vagina that is typically under-size, and a pair of testes lodged in the abdomen in which – in some cases at least – fully-formed sperm have been observed. It has been reported that the testicular tissue has a greater than normal likelihood of becoming cancerous, and prophylactic removal of the organs has been suggested. Unfortunately if they are removed before puberty then the breasts will never develop.

The testes normally produce oestrogen as well as testosterone, and it is believed that in these people it is this female sex hormone that is responsible for the development of all the feminine characteristics that appear. Castration prevents maturation from proceeding normally and so, although it is arguably helpful in removing an increased cancer hazard, most doctors prefer to leave the testes where they are until adulthood.

This is a rare condition, but (although the patients themselves are sterile and never menstruate) a familial distribution between cousins and other close relatives is often found. Testicular Feminization forms an endlessly intriguing study: it presents us with a personally tragic situation, and one in which counselling must be carefully and responsibly carried out. But in addition, it shows that – for all their admitted potency in inducing sex differentiation – the role of the chromosomes can be overruled by a single gene. The woman who is man poses many issues to social philosophy, and presents interesting challenges to many of the most fundamental concepts we grew up with.

There are many genetic abnormalities which produce more devastating consequences. One of the commonest of these is named, after its discoverer, Klinefelter's Syndrome. The patient has an extra X-chromosome, making his complement up to 47, XXY. He is undeniably male, but often of a somewhat pear-shaped, listless, somehow feminine outline. The testicles are very small, usually less than an inch across, and within them sperm production is absent or, at the very most, slight. Many victims of the abnormality exhibit mental retardation, though it would be wrong to assume that this is, to a greater or lesser extent, an invariable consequence of the condition. One of the features of Klinefelter's Syndrome is the variability of the various diagnostic signs and symptoms, and this is a case in point for – although many of the victims are retarded – a considerable number are mentally normal. Similarly, it is said that breast enlargement is frequently found although there are many individuals in which this sign is not present at all. Associated with these factors is the occurrence of a small penis, the signs of eunuchoidism (which include the development of a 'pendulously' obese, tall physique) and a somewhat feminine distribution of facial and body hair. Some of the individuals who have been reported in the past have proved to be fertile, but it seems probable that this is an illusory association: what is probably happening is that these individuals are mosaics, i.e. many of their body cells are indeed XXY, and show this pattern on culture and chromosome count, but a proportion of their cells may be normal XY in constitution, and if the percentage was high enough, clearly normal sperm production could occur.

Within the Klinefelter's group there are many sub-types of the condition, in which extra X-chromosomes occur. Not only are mosaic mixtures found of XY and XXY, as we have already seen, but individuals whose cells are XXY and XXXY are known, and in some rare instances the complement has been reportedly as high as XXXXY or even XXXXXY. These rare examples, though, produce more severe effects and mental retardation becomes severe in many of them.

The incidence of Klinefelter's Syndrome in newborn babies is fairly low; roughly two per thousand is the generally agreed rate. Often sufferers turn up in clinics where they present symptoms such as marital difficulties, sterility, impotence or whatever. The figures imply that in a crowd at a sporting fixture, for example, there could be dozens of victims of Klinefelter's Syndrome. It is not a matter to be ignored by the medical profession, then; it is a cause of significant personal difficulty, and not merely a medical conundrum of academic interest.

Klinefelter's Syndrome came to light in the early 1940's. The parallel condition in women results in an XXX configuration, and was not discovered until the late 1950's. Because of the possession of an extra X-chromosome in female cells, the term 'super-female' was suggested for the condition. It is a term which does not really match with the reality of the situation, and perhaps it is fortunate that it has not stuck. Just as in Klinefelter's Syndrome, XXX individuals show a remarkably variable degree of incapacity. Some of them are married women who have given birth to babies with normal chromosomes, which has encouraged speculation that in some way the defective ova are weeded out. It may be that the fertile XXX mothers are really mosaics and contain a significant percentage of normal cells. If that proves to be the case there is one way in which the normal ova could be produced in an entirely regular way, and we would not have to invent as yet-undiscovered mechanisms to account for what is an otherwise inexplicable phenomenon.

Like their opposite numbers who suffer from Klinefelter's Syndrome, these women tend to show interference with the normal development of mental function and the sex organs. Retardation is often reported, and so is a varying degree of poor sexual function. The menstrual periods are frequently scanty, irregular or even absent altogether and under the microscope the structure of the ovaries is frequently abnormal. The breasts are often smaller than average, too, and in the more severely-affected patients the secondary sexual characteristics are poorly-developed.

The incidence of the condition in the population as a whole is difficult to ascertain, but the most widely accepted estimates suggest that the incidence is slightly over one per thousand births. As one would predict to be the case, in view of the association of the condition with mental retardation, the incidence in women from mental institutions is higher, around four per thousand.

So far, in considering the effects of three sex-chromosomes on the development and appearance of the individual in whom they occur, we have considered XXY and XXX. The third possibility is an XYY individual, but it was not until 1962 that the first of these was reported. The patient was normal, a well-built man who was fertile. Later examples that came to light suggested that he might have been a lucky exception to the general rule in such cases. Twenty-one cases of men with Barr bodies (suggesting that they contained abnormal X-chromosome allocations) were subsequently examined in two groups of high-risk mental patients, all of whom had been detained in the British State Hospitals of Moss Side and Rampton because of uncontrollably violent and aggressive behaviour.

More than half of the sample turned out to suffer from Klinefelter's Syndrome. But seven of the sample had two Y–chromosomes. Five of them were XXYY and two contained XYY cells in a mosaic mixture of XYY and XXYY. A subsequent examination of more than three hundred patients in the male wards of these top-security establishments turned up a dozen more individuals with the same kind of abnormality, the majority being the basic XYY type.

As a result of these findings we now have a pretty clear picture of the characteristics associated with the abnormality. Most interesting of all is that the extra Y-chromosome does not produce any consistent physical handicap; quite the converse, in fact, these men are abnormally well-built and the great majority are over six feet tall. However, there is evidence that a lowering of intellect is usual. Above all, it is quite clear that these men show extra aggression and antisocial behaviour and the fact that this makes them into what you might call 'genetic criminals' is borne out by the observation that the brothers and sisters of these double-Y criminals have a tendency towards crime no greater than any other section of the community, whilst the siblings of criminals with normal genetic make-up are far more likely to commit crimes themselves. There is a social or environmental pressure on youngsters who become criminals, in other words, and the pressures apply across the board to all members of a family unit.

The XYY male, by contrast, is an exception to his family's rule. The fact that he is larger, taller and more aggressive coupled with a lowering in mental capacity makes such a man almost predestined to carry out antisocial or even violent acts.

There is a valuable pointer in all this towards the essential, inborn nature of sexual behaviour in humans. We often hear that the sexes are acquiring their disparate behaviour patterns from societal pressures, and from family conventions that we should now discard. But the XYY male may show that this modern belief is erroneous. These men have, as it were, an overdose of masculinity. They possess twice as much of the male-inducing genes as a normal man with one Y-chromosome. The effect of this double doseage is to increase stature, to increase aggression, to increase 'dominant' behaviour. Does this make them super-men? Sadly for the victims, it does not. The effect of the chromosomal mismatch takes a toll of its own and induces mental retardation which as a rule prevents the patient from utilizing his physical and emotional attributes constructively: rather than becoming a gentle giant, he becomes a mindless brute.

But it is noteworthy to my mind that the characteristics associated with the condition are exactly those that parents will say are associated with boys, rather than with girls. The lesson of these tragic men is that the Y-chromosome truly does convey specific physical and psychological attributes. Our vogue for construing sex-dependent behaviour as nothing more than a series of learned responses will not do, since so much of the stereotyped idea of maleness is genetically programmed into the constitution of a man. We can argue about the extent of the effects and even their relevance. But few can deny that there are clear evolutionary and social benefits in having a man who is physically and emotionally adapted to protect and defend his otherwise defenceless family. And the examples of the XYY males – the men with a double share of maleness – provide yet more evidence that these characteristics have a fundamental, genetic basis. On that Y-chromosome is predicated, not only the look of a man, but much of his innate behaviour too. In my view, civilization has only become possible because that is so.

The question of the incidence of this condition is not easy to answer. As I have said, a characteristic of the victims of this chromosome error is that they are not physically deformed. It is accepted that the incidence may be something near two per thousand, but far less than that number are ever reported by the medical profession. If this is the case it is likely that the majority of XYY males exist in society without their problem ever coming to light. We do not have a quick and convenient means of screening cell specimens from newborn baby boys like the search for Barr bodies in girls. Detailed chromosome counts are tedious and costly to mount on a large scale, and so the exact incidence must remain, for the time being, an unknown quantity.

So far we have considered disorders in which there are extra sex chromosomes. Occasionally the opposite happens, and we are left with an incomplete set of chromosomes instead. The classical example in this category is Turner's Syndrome. In an interesting reversal of the XYY condition we have just considered (where an essentially normal physical development is accompanied by a greater or lesser degree of mental incapacity), the victims of Turner's Syndrome are women with marked physical deficiencies, but with little or no evidence of mental retardation.

These individuals can be identified at birth since they are clearly girl babies, but their cell nuclei show no sign of the tiny tell-tale Barr body which is characteristic of female cell types. The number of X-chromosomes in the nuclei of a cell specimen is always one more than the maximum number of Barr bodies. The evidence is clear, then: these little girls possess just one X-chromosome.

The adults they develop into show several clear-cut diagnostic signs, which were first recognized as a distinct clinical entity by Turner's original studies prior to the Second World War. They are short women, almost always five feet tall or less. The neck is short and the skin on either side, under the ears, may be extended into a web as it joins the shoulders. The skeleton does not develop well; there may be a high arched palate and a receding chin is often found. In these individuals it is common to find that the teeth do not meet properly because of the deformed jaw. It has been shown that after injury the skin of these patients tends to heal by forming large, lumpy keloid growths (keloids are a form of benign tumour) and pigmented naevi or moles are common too. To the pathologist, the most consistent sign is the so-called 'streak gonad', a line of pale tissue with only the slightest resemblance to a normal functional ovary, which is found where an ovary ought to be.

This is the prime cause of the effects of the condition: without ovaries, normal sex hormones are never produced and for this reason the secondary sexual characteristics do not appear. The Turner's Syndrome adult has no menstrual cycle, no periods, and she cannot produce ova. The saving grace of the condition, if you will allow that such a term applies, is the lack of mental retardation. The women are, as a rule, of normal intelligence.

As far as incidence is concerned, Turner's Syndrome is mercifully not very common. The figure is around one case in two thousand females. Once again we have to realize that the exact total is difficult to obtain and the number of mosaic mixtures is known to be higher than appears to be the case with the other chromosome abnormalities we have discussed so far. One combination is of Turner-type cells with normal XX cells, which results in an intermediate state between normal female sex and the abnormal condition. Interestingly enough the exact site of the chromosome abnormality – that is to say the particular cell in which the discrepancy occurred in the earliest divisions of the zygote immediately after conception – dictates the areas of the body liable to carry a predominance of affected cells. It can be, for instance, that a woman will present to her doctor as being predominately normal in bodily constitution but can still have malformed ovaries even to the extent of the 'streak gonad' type.

An alternative error is the omission of the Y-chromosome in a developing male embryo, so that he develops to show a mosaic mix of normal XY cells and Turner cells bearing just a single X. The range of development can therefore cover the entire span between virtually normal male to sterile Turner's Syndrome female, depending on the ratios of the two cell types. This is certainly the widest range of diversity found in any of the regularly-occurring chromosome disorders, and diagnosis of such cases can be difficult. Here, though, we are talking of unusual examples that feature only in perhaps one birth out of thousands. Even less predictable are the individuals whose chromosomes exist in normal numbers, but not in normal shape and size. They may have X-chromosomes with abnormally long or short arms, or an unusual dwarfed Y-chromosome. Needless to say there is no hard-and-fast correlation between these abnormalities and the effects they produce, as so much depends on where the extra length came from, or exactly which of the genes (in a short chromosome) have been lost.

Finally in this group, a puzzle. The classic case of Testicular Feminization – the woman who is man – is startling enough. But what of that very rare, but undeniably genuine condition, of the man who is really woman? Testicular Feminization may be unexpected, it may be astonishing; but it is certainly explicable. The cells do, after all, contain an X and a Y chromosome and (since the X confers femininity in the ordinary way) there is at least an X-chromosome in each cell which could express itself by inducing femininity. The capacity is there.

The man who is woman, on the other hand, is at first sight an impossibility. These individuals, normal men in every obvious respect (and with a perfectly average sex-drive), have an XX constitution. How can they develop masculinity? The male-inducing Y-chromosome does not appear in the picture at all, and it would therefore appear impossible for masculinity to find expression – the capacity is altogether lacking.

What are these men like? In external appearance as in behavioural terms they are entirely normal males. They may well have proper-sized testicles, though their internal structure will not allow them to produce sperm in the normal way and so the individuals remain sterile throughout life. Their libido is in the normal range, and may be high.

What explanation can we put forward for these unexpected results? One obvious possibility is mosaicism: that the men contain knots of XY-cells which were responsible for the production of the masculine features, these cells being for the most part lost amongst the welter of XX cells which seem to make up most of the body. It is a convenient answer but hardly the right one. Geneticists have looked at many of these cases with exactly this possibility in view, but so far mosaicism has not emerged as the explanation.

Alternatively you might suggest that the genes coding for masculinity in the Y-chromosome have become transferred through some mechanical accident within the cell to the X, or to some other chromosome in the set. It is hard to show that this is not the case, and I suppose this might turn out to be the answer. But there are no suitable parallel examples known, and so it is probably more realistic to categorize that explanation as a handy theory which is too far-fetched to be the answer.

There is also the possibility of sex-reversal. In the goat it is known that you can find an ostensibly normal male equipped with nothing but female X-chromosomes. The 'polled' gene is a recessive characteristic which induces sex reversal, and when present in the chromosomes inherited from both parents the recessive character emerges and becomes expressed. In short, the female goat contains sex-change genes, and switches during development to becoming a male instead.

There is a possibility that much the same can happen in mankind. In 1959 a survey of 2,000 boy babies turned up five whose chromosome pattern was exclusively XX – they were genetic females. An editorial in *The Lancet* discussed the merits of the sex-change hypothesis, and pointed out that the result would certainly fit neatly with the observation that there are 106 boys born in Britain for every 100 girls (perhaps three of the boys were actually genetically female, so that the actual ratio was 103:103). The article added that if the results were of general applicability it meant that in every battalion of the British Army there were two women 'masquerading' as men.

That's putting it too strongly, I believe; so far as the individuals are concerned, men is just what they are and there is certainly no masquerade involved. It is true that their chromosomes would imply femininity, but clearly some triggering effect – like the 'polled' gene in the goat – has set the embryo developing towards masculinity instead. The adult life-style adopted by such a person is nothing more than an honest acceptance of their anatomical and psychological gender. Cells are not really of one sex or the other, even if they do have the capacity to carry messages that seek to preordain sexuality in the adult human they eventually form.

Can such sex-reversal genes account for that most tantalizing abnormality of the sex-chromosomes – the hermaphrodite? Perhaps so. Hermaphrodites are people whose gonads contain both ovarian and testicular tissues. The term does not cover individuals with intermediate external genitalia more correctly termed pseudohermaphrodites, for they do not conform to this essential bisexuality at the gonadal level. There are three distinct types of hermaphrodites, depending on the combinations of testis and ovary that are theoretically possible.

a) The lateral hermaphrodite
has an ovary on one side of the body, matched by a testis on the other. Both organs are normal under the microscope, though because the testis is retained within the body it does not produce sperm.

b) The unilateral hermaphrodite
possesses, on one side of the body, a composite organ composed of ovary and testis (know as an ovotestis), and on the other *either* a normal ovary *or* a normal (but sterile) testis.

c) The bilateral hermaphrodite
exhibits a composite organ in the form of an ovotestis on both sides of the body. The sections of the gland that are testicular show an essentially normal pattern, though sperm do not mature; whilst the ovarian tissues are likewise typically non-functional.

Hermaphrodites are typically sterile, and they show a range of physical forms that extends from the feminine to the masculine. There may be a blend of both. Cases are known in which there is a phallus and male-type body hair, accompanied by a rugged bodily contour and a masculine physique; but the face is mostly free of any traces of a beard and there are well-developed sensuous breasts. Self-fertilization in hermaphrodites is impossible because of the lack of any anatomical connection that might conduct sperm and egg into a meeting-place. But it would be theoretically possible to transplant the site of attachment of the testis into a scrotum or something like it in order that sperm might form, and to bring sperm and ovum into contact. This would give an offspring that for the first time came close to the traditional idea of cloning – where the child had the exact chromosome complement of the parent.

Whether the hermaphrodite development would follow is of course speculative. But any repeat of the experiment would produce exact identical copies of the first-born child, twins of different ages. It is fortunate that our generation exerts social constraints on adventurous biologists who might be tempted to try the idea in practice without any deterrence from the personal consequences for the child so unnaturally conceived. But surgical treatment of such a hermaphrodite could one day enable such a procedure to be undertaken and if an opportunity arose it is possible, even if only that, for a reckless experimenter to take the step.

The chromosome complement of hermaphrodites was assumed to be a mosaic blend of XY and XX cells, and it does seem likely that in some cases at least the phenomenon is brought about by two sperm cells (one X, one Y) entering the ovum at exactly the same moment and producing a 'double fertilization'. But in the majority of cases XX cells are all that can be found. It may be that there are a minority of XY cells hidden away, indeed in the case of a bilateral hermaphrodite child reported in 1965 XX cells were isolated from the skin, bone marrow and blood and even from the testis, but a second examination of the cells from the testis did eventually reveal some XY cells too. A form of sex mosaic may be the answer.

But the lesson of the man who is woman, mentioned earlier, does suggest that perhaps there are people in whom a sex-reversal gene can occur in a wholly XX constitution. If that is so then it may be hermaphrodites result from the partial expression of a sex-change gene inducing masculinity in what would otherwise be a normal woman. The relative rarity of these abnormalities makes scientific study difficult, though it is of course most fortunate that the sufferers of these agonising, tragic conditions are limited in number. For those who live in ignorance there is some hope of a normally fulfilling life but in some of the cases the deep-seated longing for some form of normal sexual identity can cause distress. The final extent of the distribution of every kind of possible abnormality remains unknown, of course; already we know of many mosaic combinations of cells with widely varying effects.

X/XX
X/XX/XXX
XX/XXYY
XY/XXXY
X/XXXY
XYY/XXYY
X/XX/XY
X/XXY/XXYY
X/XY
X/XYY
XY/XYY
X/XXY
XX/XXY
XX/XXY/XXYYY
XY/XXY
XXY/XXYY
XXY/XXXY
X/XXX
XX/XXX
XXX/XXX
XX/XY/XYY

Known sex-chromosome mosaics in mankind.

It is possible to calculate what other combinations are theoretically possible. This may give us nothing more than a range of isolated possibilities which are hypothetical models, and which do not exist in life. But, knowing the fickleness of the way chromosomes seem sometimes to behave, it is quite likely that such predictions may one day be recognized in some previously unsuspected new condition.

Sometimes it is not only the sex chromosomes which double up in this way; instead of the diploid number of chromosomes in the mature nucleus it is possible that a triploid constitution will be found instead – that is, there will be three sets of the 23 chromosomes in the normal gamete instead of only two, making 69 in all. We would expect to find such examples at least on the basis of comparison with other forms of life. In many plants, triploids are the rule. They occur in the fruit-fly *Drosophila*, so often used for genetic experiments, and triploid amphibians are also known. In higher animals, though, the result of the triploid state is incompatible with life. It has been said that 1% of all human conceptions results in a triploid zygote, which is a surprisingly high total, but the condition is rarely seen at birth as most cases abort spontaneously. Of those that do mature for the full nine months of life in the uterus, almost all die at or shortly after the birth process and the few who survive do not live longer than a matter of weeks. They show small and poorly developed bodies, possibly because the triploid cells take longer to divide, with the extra set of chromosomes to manipulate. They have ambiguous genitals and show many of the signs of intersexuality. Abnormal baby boys in this condition may present with a small, but normal-looking, penis *and* a uterus. Perhaps it is a form of evolutionary benevolence that, sometimes, these devastating abnormalities are incompatible with survival.

But what happens to the thousands of victims of the sex-chromosome abnormalities who do survive until adult life? Many of them are recognized by their doctors and adjust to a contented and fulfilled existence. Some, like sufferers from Klinefelter's Syndrome, often live their lives without their specific problem ever coming to the notice of the medical fraternity.

As for the intersex child, here we do encounter real problems which a change in current practice could ameliorate. The child's sex is diagnosed instantly after birth, at a glance. 'It's a boy' or 'It's a girl' are the words every new mother in the labour ward wants, and expects, to hear. In normal circumstances a glance at the genitalia is indeed sufficient to diagnose the sex of an infant, but it is in the case of the intersex child that difficulties arise. In many cases a child with an enlarged and rather masculinized clitoris has been raised as a boy, taught masculine values and encouraged to aim for manly targets of attainment; yet all the time the child was genetically female and ought, by rights, to have had the upbringing of a girl. There are similar mirror-image cases of boys born with undescended testicles who are at a glance confined to femininity, and in cases like these it is usual that the first doubts as to the sexual identity of the individual are never raised until adolescence.

By that time, of course, social relationships have become established for that person and it is simply not possible to approach old friends or close relatives and say: 'I was a boy, and you always thought so, but I am really a girl and I will be a girl from now on' and expect that to be the end of the matter. Sexual curiosity being what it is, and societal norms being as strong as they certainly are, the stigma of a supposed 'sex-change' in such circumstances would linger for a life-time. How tragic it is that such consequences can. follow from a simple error made at the moment of childbirth more than a decade before.

Perhaps it would be sensible to argue that screening facilities should be more widely available, and more widely publicized, so that doubtful cases could be speedily referred for a smear count or a detailed chromosome analysis. Surgery can do much to modify and improve the function of malformed sexual apparatus in half-way children, and well-planned hormone treatment might do much to assure the patient of a recognizable and – for him or her – satisfying sexual identity. On the other hand you may argue that the intersexual state is capable of its own form of fulfilment and the individual given such an unusual assortment of chromosomes should enjoy the special privileges of the half-way state.

But it is easier to argue that case if you do not suffer from the anguished uncertainties that some of these patients experience from time to time. In the last analysis, these conditions are a deviation from normal, a break with the pattern established by evolution and – most important – a clumsy ill-assortment of mismatched chromosomal elements. Our insight can restore a measure of normality to the victims of sex chromosomal abnormalities and free them from the strictures imposed by a trivial accident in the body, when a tiny ribbon of protein found itself accidentally ensnared or caught up in the wrong place just at a critical instant, and this should be our prime and overriding aim. At the same time, the search for sex-chromosome mismatch could help us anticipate difficulties in later life. Counselling and special assistance at the right time could enable us to help that person lead a constructive life, rather than being trapped on a downward escalator imposed by a genetic accident that we do not yet understand, and are powerless to prevent.

The ultimate sanction against nature's vagaries must be the termination of pregnancy in cases like these. If you believe that all suspect foetuses should be identified and turfed out of the womb before they come to anything then I would disagree with you. A suspicion is not enough; and the possibility of a mild form of abnormality is not sufficient to terminate a pregnancy when a fair percentage of 'normal' folk are more than usually destructive and malignant. But we ought now to be able to tap off some of the cells a foetus liberates into the fluid around it (through the process known as amniocentesis) and look at their nuclei. If a massive, life-threatening abnormality is present then certainly it would be reasonable to offer the chance of termination to the mother-to-be.

In either event, the options available to the doctor are many, whether we are talking about surgical intervention, hormone treatment, or the radical abortion of a pregnancy. But the first step in tackling the practical problems raised when mankind's chromosomes fail to keep themselves sorted out is to recognize the existence of the abnormalities, to discuss them, to become attuned to what they mean.

Finding answers, if there are effective answers to find, comes later.

CHAPTER SEVEN

SEX CHANGE

In the year 1474 in the Swiss town of Basle, fourteen years after Pope Pius II had founded the town's University, a witch was strapped to a stake of hardwood and set on top of a pyre of brushwood to burn. The death was a noisy one, but it relieved the town and its new-born academic population of a burden of unease. The witch was a cockerel: its much-publicized crime had been the unnatural act of laying an egg.

The domestic fowl is peculiarly liable to undergo sex change in adult life. Many different techniques can be used to divert a selected bird from its natural destiny, and for centuries they have been used in agriculture. The poularde is a masculinized hen produced by the removal of the ovaries; a capon is a feminized cockerel produced in analogous fashion. Both have exactly the same bodily appearance so far as plumage is concerned: they are, if you like, a 'neutral' fowl capable of acquiring either destiny.

The influence of hormones on sexual development is well understood to be profound, but I know of few animals in which the effects are as dramatic as they are in the domestic fowl, *Gallus domesticus*. A normal and intact cockerel treated with thyroid hormones will soon develop plumage exactly like that of the female of the breed. It is a remarkable phenomenon, for the thyroid has a function that is primarily concerned with metabolic regulation, rather than the specific control of sexual characteristics.

It is known that in the normal hen, only the left ovary functions whilst the right gonad becomes atrophied and exists in the adult only in rudimentary form. Now, what happens when the functioning left ovary is removed? You may be inclined to assume that the hen will from that point on become sterile, which is a sensible enough conclusion.

But the remarkable thing about the hen is that the dormant gonad becomes resuscitated, but it develops into a testis! The result of removing the functioning left ovary of a chicken is to convert the bird, eventually, into a cockerel. Please don't ask why. If you implant a testis into a normal hen, she develops the upright comb of the male, but retains her feminine plumage. Much the same happens if a testis is transplanted into a poularde: the comb increases in size and becomes typically cockerel-like, whilst the features hardly change at all. On the other hand, if you transplant ovarian tissue into a capon, his next set of plumage (after a moult) becomes exactly that of a hen.

It often happens that the plumage forms whilst the gonads are still in a developing state, and adult feathers are produced before the sex hormones start to be liberated. If this happens, you may end up with a capon looking like a kind of hen, but which (when the testes suddenly begin operation) starts acting like a cock; or conversely, you may have a poularde with every appearance of being a cockerel in the making, which suddenly begins to lay eggs. This was doubtless what lay behind the Basle 'cockerel' of 1474, which suffered the indignity of being spit-roasted without the expedient of being painlessly dispatched beforehand.

Chickens can also show actual sex-change during life without any experimental intervention from outside. They occasionally suffer from tumours of the ovary and when this occurs the functioning left ovary may be destroyed. Should this take place, the right ovary develops into a testis (just as occurs under laboratory conditions) and a fully-fledged and functional hen can truly change into an ostensibly normal and sexually active cockerel.

In the previous chapter we saw how extensive is the range of intersexual conditions that abnormal chromosomes produce. Many of those are due to some form of sex-change in the developing embryo, and many apparent examples of sexual reversal in adults or adolescents are probably due to the delayed expression of true sex in an individual who was accidentally brought up in the wrong sexual identity. But now we must look into the non-chromosomal effects on sex differentiation. There is nothing 'wrong' with a hen that loses its only functioning ovary – it exchanges a female identity for a male one as though this was the most natural thing in the world. To many other kinds of animal, such behaviour is indeed all part of the normal pattern of life.

The most ancient references to hormone-induced intersexuality concern the freemartin, a sterile cow which is chromosomally female right enough, but which looks like a castrated bull. Varro wrote about them one hundred years before Christ, as did Columella in 100 AD, and both of them recognized that the freemartin was usually the twin of a normal bull calf. It has since been found that the phenomenon occurs when a pair of twins, one of each sex, is conceived and as their placentas develop within the uterus a bloodvessel forms that unites their circulations. In this way, it was argued, testosterone from the bull foetus could get across into the blood system of the unborn cow, and would effectively masculinize it. As a result, you would find that a normal bull was born and the freemartin twin which emerged at the same time had female-type genitals, but a greatly enlarged, phallus-like clitoris and a much shorter vagina than normal. The ovaries are reduced in size and do not function; what is more, they contain pockets of testis-like tissue. As far as I am aware, no attempts have been made to induce such an intersex cow to produce sperm and ova (perhaps surgery could allow a testis to develop and produce sperm, which could be stored at low temperatures; and then the ovaries could be induced to mature and give viable ova). That might provide an interesting demonstration of genetically identical calves.

Unfortunately the explanation given above is unlikely to be the real answer to the origin of freemartins. You can treat a pregnant cow with male sex-hormones in such a way as to induce the freemartin state experimentally in the female foetus, but you do not get the expected result. The calf that results certainly shows signs of masculinization, but the ovaries develop too. You obtain a masculinized cow – but it is *not* a freemartin.

It seems as though the ovaries in freemartins develop normally for a while and actually change towards the ovotestis state after the bull twin's testes have formed. Some female XX cells have been found in the testes of bull calves from freemartin twinnings, which suggests that there might have been an exchange of cell types, and it has been put forward that perhaps the freemartin acquires a proportion of XY cells in her developing ovaries, which are responsible for the formation of the testicular tissue. But there is no real evidence for this happening, and anyway it is odd that freemartins are found so consistently in cattle, goats, pigs and sheep, but do not occur in the majority of other mammals.

It is interesting to add that the production of freemartins has had a profound effect on the development of the hormone theories of sex differentiation, but for the wrong reasons. It became so widely accepted that the freemartin was masculinized by the bull twin's male sex hormones, that this was used as a teaching model to account for the importance of hormones. Every medical student was taught about the effect, and many still are. The artificial attempts to induce freemartin births, however, have persistently failed. So that cannot be the real explanation of the effect – there is still an unexplained force at work which needs to be unravelled.

It is very much in line with the widespread ignorance that we still share over the topic of sex and sexual differentiation, that this text-book example should have had such a profound effect on scientific thought in this field, and yet be wrong all the time.

Intersexuality is commonest, perhaps, in the goat where in some breeds as many as 15% of newborn goats can be classified as having a mixture of male and female characteristics. It is relatively widespread in pigs, where roughly one pig in five hundred is intersexed. Lower down the evolutionary scale, sex change becomes more common. Frogs can be induced to change from one sex to the other by several means, and in one experiment a sex-reversed female became not only masculinized but actually copulated successfully and fertilized a brood of spawn. As you would expect, from such a female/female mating, the whole brood developed likewise into female adults. Similar reports have testified that the reversal of sex in chickens – occuring naturally after the destruction of the functioning ovary through disease – has had a similar result. A chicken which had produced fertile eggs after normal mating, and reared them successfully, eventually developed into an entirely normal cockerel which mated and became the father of a second brood. To become a mother and a father in one lifetime is an experience denied to most species. And it is most surprising to find examples of complete sex-reversal like this in an animal as advanced as a warm-blooded vertebrate.

In our own kind sex change is very far from being ordinary or predictable. But it can, and does, occur. How often this is due to psychological factors which cause an individual to feel an irrepressible identification with the other sex, and how much of it is caused by medical abnormality, is difficult to know. The physical causes are undeniably easier to explain and to identify.

One of the most disturbing of these is gynaecomastia, in which a man, quite quickly, sprouts breasts. I am not thinking of the overweight and flabby man in late middle-age whose breasts expand in a desperate attempt to cope with the burden of obesity, but the patient who develops the breasts of a woman. One of the commonest times in life for this to occur is adolescence. A boy in mid or late teens, in the process of what seems to be a normal adolescence, begins to notice that the breasts become enlarged and tender. They may increase in sensitivity and become pleasurable for him to caress. As a rule he becomes embarrassed by them, and consults his doctor. But treatment (even if it is offered) is rarely necessary. This is a temporary phase of puberty, and the breasts later diminish in size and regain a normally masculine contour.

It is sometimes a more serious matter when the phenomenon occurs in later life. Here it may be associated with a disease of the hormone-producing glands, and it may follow the development of a tumour of the testicles which is affecting the cells responsible for the production of female sex-hormones (a small amount of which are necessary in all normal males). A more severe cause may be chronic liver disease, and gynaecomastia can also follow the thyroid disorder known as thyrotoxicosis. Sometimes there is evidence of a more deep-seated cause: the testicles may be small and non-functioning, or the body show the signs of Klinefelter's Syndrome (of which gynaecomastia is a fairly common side-effect). When it presents as a symptom of a deep-seated hormone disorder, gynaecomastia calls for prompt and efficient treatment.

On occasions the condition actually *results* from medical intervention, and when this happens it is more predictable. The usual origin is treatment of cancer of the prostate with female sex-hormones such as oestrogen. The effect of the hormone is to dampen down the enlargement of the prostate gland but its presence invariably incurs the risk of feminization of the patient. Discontinuation of the treatment will lead to a cessation of the effect but (like the effective treatment of thyroid disease) though the breasts stop enlarging there is no guarantee that they will ever reduce in size as do the temporarily enlarged breasts of the male adolescent. The answer then becomes surgery, and the offending breast tissue is removed.

This is an example of partial sex-change, then; a move towards femininity in an otherwise normal male, or in a male born with some genetic defect, which stops well short of actual reversal. No-one in a case like this expects to end up as a female, living a woman's life instead of a man's. But in occasional instances this ultimate experience does occur.

The first time that sex-change caused an international scandal was in 1934, during the first-ever World Women's Games, which were held in London at the White City Stadium. The 800-metre contestant entered by Czechoslovakia was a strapping woman named Zdena Koubkova who easily won her event. The result produced protests from representatives of other teams and after a brief reconsideration Miss Koubkova was disqualified. She returned to Czechoslovakia and entered hospital for medical treatment. After an operation she emerged again as a man, and lived the rest of his life (see how immediately that juxtaposition tends to jar on the senses?) as a normal male. Zdena Koubkova, as she was born, became Zdenek Koubkeck until the day he died.

A similar episode occured four years later when Adolf Hitler was trying hard to ensure that his own breed of superior athletes obtained all the best results, and the high jump record was broken by Dora Ratjen, representing the women of the Reich. Her leap of 5ft 7in (170cm) astonished many of the spectators and three days later the German Athletics Federation issued a statement to the effect that the organizers of the European Championships in Vienna should know 'Fraulein Ratjen has no entitlement to compete in women's competitions'. She was disqualified and the title passed instead to the Hungarian woman who had come second. The women's high jump world record was meanwhile restored to Miss Dorothy Odam, and Dora Ratjen quietly slipped back to Germany. After she retired from athletics she underwent surgery and the last I heard Hermann Ratjen, as he became known, was working as a waiter in a Hamburg cafeteria.

In the European Championships for 1946, the French entered a woman athlete from Lorraine named Lea Caula who has since married an attractive young wife and successfully fathered several children.

The controversy over the sexual nature of athletes is important, since here more than in any other area of life the gender of a participant has a vital role on one's right to participate. This is because men are better at athletics, on the whole, than women; a direct consequence of their leaner and more muscular build, their inbuilt competitive spirit which societal conventions seek to exploit to the fullest extent, and their biological function as protectors of a family. Isolated cases (like those I have referred to) have occurred from time to time, which raised the question of 'what does "sex" mean?' in a casual, almost flippant manner. But in 1966 the sporting world was rocked by the results of introducing strict sex screening for the eighth European Athletic Championships held in Budapest.

Until 1964, women were admitted to events on the basis of common consent or (for specially controlled major events) on the strength of a doctor's certificate. But in 1964 the International Amateur Athletics Federation, at their conference in Tokyo, passed a resolution that at all major international events women must undergo an examination by a board of three independent (female) gynaecologists. Masculinized females crossing the border in the opposite direction were not a problem, of course, since they were only going to compete against tighter standards in the men's events. But the introduction of rigid sex controls and nuclear sex-tests brought to light the existence of many competitors in women's events who might be stealing an unfair, intersexual advantage or who – in some cases – were certainly men.

In the field of athletics, English, Russian, Dutch, French and German girls who were not entirely female have since been identified. During the 1966 Budapest games, four of the most successful Russian woman competitors did not turn up, including the famous Press sisters: Irina, who was the Olympic pentathlon champion at the time, and Tamara, whose well-built body had given her the world record for both putting the shot and throwing the discus. The lead coach of the Russian team, who led the delegation, explained that they had decided at the last minute to leave some athletes behind since they were 'borderline cases' and he did not want them to be put through any embarrassment. It had been rumoured for some time that the Russian sporting authorities had been capitalizing on Tamara's admittedly somewhat masculine build by treating her with male sex-hormones, and a friend of hers was reported as describing her personality as 'desperately unhappy', living in a limbo of in-between, half-way people.

Other competitors turned up with their teams but did not submit to the required medical examination. The world champion high-jumper, Ilanda Balas, refused to turn up for the tests and issued a statement saying that, because of leg trouble, she would not be able to compete, and was therefore withdrawing from all the preliminaries. She had held the world record for eight years at the time, and no other women athlete had shown any sign of bettering her result. Some competitors took the tests as a slight, or a personal insult. At least one girl, the Italian long-jump competitor Maria Trio, declined to be tested on religious grounds and did not compete either, although no-one at the games (including her intimate friends from the teams of rival nations) doubted for an instant that she was a girl in every sense.

Though the sporting arena is the prime target for sex testing, and therefore throws up more borderline cases than you might expect from other walks of life, it is also arguable that intersexed individuals are selected for sporting careers as a direct result of the pressures and the nature of the challenge. A part-male woman athlete, with a narrower pelvic girdle and less subcutaneous fat to burden her, has a constitutional ability to better other women competitors. The discipline and the sense of personal acclaim that attend success may also play their part at a subconscious level. But of course we must not overlook the examples of sex change that occur in other walks of life.

The eighteenth Baron Sempill had two children, William, who became the famous air pioneer and eventually the nineteenth Baron, and Elizabeth, who was born in 1912. Elizabeth grew into an intelligent and studious teenager who went to medical school and qualified as a physician. She settled in the Scottish village of Alford, Aberdeenshire, as general practitioner (now known as a family practitioner in Britain).

The surprise came in September 1952 when – at the age of forty – Dr Elizabeth Forbes-Sempill of Alford announced her intention to change her name to Ewan, and her gender to male. The change did not seem to come as a surprise to the patients or the villagers in general. And a month later, Dr Ewan Forbes-Sempill married his housekeeper (also aged forty), Miss Isobel Mitchell.

The Sempill family had expected the news for years, since Elizabeth had for some time tended to dress more and more noticeably like a man. Less phlegmatic was the reaction of the pillars of society who have to work out the implications of such a dramatic reversal, including the College of Arms, who require the submission of evidence to the Standing Council on the Baronetage before anyone can inherit a baronetcy, and the legal authorities who were faced with the question of deciding who the heirs to the nineteenth Lord Sempill's estate might be. Mrs Ann Moira Chant, his daughter, became Lady Sempill in her own right. But male heirs traditionally take precedence, even though in this instance the estate – according to *Burke's Peerage*, the great authority on the British titled classes – passes to 'heirs and assigns whatsoever', without stipulating sex. The involvement of a male heir presumptive who began life as a female had no precedent and the College of Arms in London were faced with a decision that seemed to raise more questions than it could ever solve. Of course, though Dr Forbes-Sempill had changed gender, in the practical sense, it is difficult to know whether cases like these represent a change of sex. It may be in many instances that the person was wrongly attributed at birth through a too hasty examination and the real gender emerged only later in life.

This is not truly a sex-change, then; it comes closer to the emergence of sex later in life. But where an individual does bear both ovarian and testicular tissue, the sex does actually alter in every meaningful sense. In that case, a person born as a girl does die as a man. Which explanations apply to which cases it is difficult to know, and few doctors would want to inflict on an uncertain and shy patient a prolonged period of probing and examination in the interests of medical curiosity.

But at least Dr Forbes-Sempill developed towards manhood in the fulness of time and did not require surgical intervention. Most examples of sex-change occur in the opposite direction, from male to female, and some anatomical help from the surgeon is usually essential for the transition to be complete. The trans-sexual patient in this category is often aware of a feeling of unease at his upbringing as a boy and usually longs to become a woman, the feeling increasing strongly during puberty, until he begins to dress in women's clothing (often his sister's or mother's). But trans-sexualist adolescents will go out with girls, and they may engage in close petting and in romantic, relatively stable pair-bonding. It is when sexual intercourse looms up that the problems may occur. To the trans-sexual, the outward manifestations of maleness are wrong, they are abhorrent. It is a frequent sign that they experience erection and penetration quite normally when stimulated by a girl's closeness and her erotic presence in a sexual situation, but will lose it if the penis itself becomes a centre for manual arousal. There is an association of penetration and of the actions of a copulating male with unwholesomeness, and it appears that trans-sexuals will frequently turn to a prostitute for their sexual initiation. When this happens it is often a disaster. The professional bed-mate knows that direct and positive stimulation is what a man may need to engage him in successful intercourse, and it may be just what he lacks at home. Manual arousal of the client's phallus is a usual preliminary to coupling. The trans-sexual may have such a profound disassociation from his masculinity that the last thing he wants is for any attention to be paid to his sexual organ. He fails to respond, and the attempt at initiation is over.

This is not an invariable consequence, however. Some men acquire an association between sexual activity and illicitness. To them, sexual intercourse becomes spicy and enticing if it is surrounded by an aura of the forbidden fruit, or, as one of them put it, 'of dirt'. Should this overlayer of stimulation prove strong enough, the penis can respond, driven by the excitement for copulation that results from the illicit connotations of love with a woman who has known countless other men.

Trans-sexuals can marry, and some of them sire children. In many cases the urge to change sex becomes overwhelming and the individual will then seek medical assistance in converting himself into a fully-fledged female.

There are two aspects of the change itself. One is chemical, and involves the establishment in the bloodstream of optimum levels of hormones for the anatomy to begin to change towards the female form, and for the personality to take on a more feminine nature. Sex-hormone therapy has the two important effects of causing the penis to wither and the breasts to enlarge, and these are both signs to the patient that he is casting off his unwanted masculine identity and entering a world of feminine purity and sensuousness. This is usually nothing more than an illusory distinction, however. The Dutch Health Council investigated medically induced trans-sexual changes during the early years of the 1960's, and concluded that no difference or improvement in the patient's attitude resulted from the treatment. But, of course, to a patient who feels his true identity is being denied him, the mere fact of being treated, and experiencing some of the signs and symptoms of femininity, is itself at least gratifying. His attitude may not improve at the end of it all, but his frustrations at least find some short-term satisfaction.

This drug treatment can go on for years, a decade being commonplace. But then the surgeon comes on the scene. Initially the only intervention is electrolytic control of excessive beard growth, which the female hormones tends to reduce but which will not cease altogether. In some patients who have developed the normal signs and secondary characteristics of masculinity, beard growth may remain stronger than average even after years of hormone treatment, and for these men intensive electrolysis is often necessary. But this is only the beginning. Eventually comes the time for the sex-change surgery itself.

First, if castration has not been carried out before, the testicles are taken out from the scrotum. By the time of the operation they are probably much reduced in size; and if the patient is a true intersexed individual they may always have been more or less rudimentary. The erectile contents of the phallus are excised and the penile skin is used to fashion a lining for a new 'vagina' which is produced by turning the tissues, as it were, inside-out. Around the entry to this vaginal opening, the scrotum is adapted to form two labial structures, imitating the labia of the normal human female, and the urinary duct is brought to the surface through a new site chosen by the surgeon (which may be within the 'vagina' itself, at the site of the original opening of the penis, now turned inside the body).

After the operation the patient will take time to adjust, for obvious reasons; and more important in the immediate post-operative phase is the management of pain. Some of the body's most sensitive tissues have been assaulted surgically, and the discomfort consequent upon that can be intense. In compensation for that, of course, the patient is left feeling that he has exorcised his previous, wrong identity. He is now a she.

The perceptive reader will ask: 'but is that true?' and it is certainly too simplistic a view to assert that the change in physical appearance, coupled with hormone therapy, has done anything more than force a certain femininity onto an essentially masculine individual. It is undeniably true that the sex hormones exert a strong effect in deciding gender, but this is what happens when they exert their effects on sexual organs that have been developing since long before birth. The treatment of a man with oestrogen will certainly act against his penis, and will stimulate the growth of his breasts; but it is too late by then to produce any real degree of total feminization.

In the world of sport such effects may be a real problem. In 1978 the world heard much about the way in which the sex-change tennis player Renee Richards – who spent the first forty years of life as Dick Raskin – was fighting for acceptance as a woman competitor. Here was an example of long-term treatment with hormones, followed by radical sex-change surgery. 'And now,' Renee Richards stated, 'I want to be the Wimbledon Ladies' Champion.'

Many of the tennis stars objected; their argument was that this player is really a man, and has male advantages over women. They thought that any player born an unmistakable man should not be admitted to women's tennis – why just one man allowed to have this privilege, and not all of them? On the side of the new woman player was the argument that therapy and hormone treatment had converted him into a woman. There was no advantage of maleness, because the maleness had been excised.

It is difficult to know where to turn for an answer. All one can do is assert the facts. It is true that many men, who are constitutionally male in every sense and who are composed of pure XY cells, fail to acquire masculine identity because of parental or family pressures. A common feature in the background of these people is the presence of a dominant or over-bearing mother. The Dutch report referred to earlier concluded that in every case they examined there was no evidence of any constitutional abnormality, but all the men had been the victims of a psychological trauma in early childhood. It seems to have been so in Renee Richards' case, where father was reportedly absent for much of the time and mother was dominant in her influence and, to use Richards' own term, 'overloving'.

Is it therefore justifiable to use surgery to alter someone's physique to fit their erroneous preconceptions of their own identity? The Dutch report considered that the answer was a firm and unambiguous 'no'. Since no improvement in the patients' mental abilities or attitudes appeared the operation was considered unethical. Renee Richards has stated that the effects of the operation were negligible in psychological terms, without there being any noticeable change in what you could call 'inner personality' at all, apart from a tendency to express more emotional reactions to stress – crying, for example. You might argue, however, that this was merely the release of a mode of expression which the strictures and social pressures of manhood suppress, rather than a profound alteration. But here, too, we are on unfamiliar ground; one's instinct is to shy away from making hasty decisions and reaching superficial conclusions, for this whole area is one where our knowledge seems to be so slight and so tenuous that hard-and-fast rules simply cannot be applied.

In some cases the courts seem to concur. Thus stated Justice Joseph A. Sarafite of New York City in 1966: 'The syndrome of trans-sexualism involves a truly untrodden, controversial and largely unexplored field of medicine.' Justice Sarafite dismissed an application by an unnamed man who wished to compel the authorities to change the sex listing on his birth certificate, and made his findings clear in a judgement running to seven pages. His ruling was that the birth certificate attests to the facts of a birth, and not a later condition. The applicant was said to lead the semblance of a woman's life, nothing more. On a more observational note, the judge added that one specialist in the field of trans-sexual medicine had described the people who undergo sex-change surgery as 'among the most miserable people I have ever met'.

This of course brings us to the core of the problem, so far as the patient himself is concerned. He is a normal male on physical and chromosomal grounds, perhaps diverted from his biological destiny by an over-indulgent or an over-prominent mother. The result is an overpowering dislike of his maleness, a desire to become a woman and to shed the unclean, embarrassing accoutrements of masculinity – the penis being top of the list. In areas where gender dictates personal habits (such as where to buy clothes, where to go to the toilet) the sex-changed person that results is obviously a woman, with a woman's role in life.

But on the sporting field it is not so simple. If you argue that it is mechanical factors of bodily proportion and basic anatomy that dictate a degree of excellence on the athletic field, then someone who has grown up as a man could be argued to have unfair advantages associated with other, normal males. Thus the woman's extra-wide pelvis, specially adapted for childbirth, might be construed as a sex-determined disadvantage. Perhaps the degree of muscularity of the male body as it develops over childhood and adolescence confers another sporting ability that is peculiar to males. If that is the case, then a man who has undergone sex-change treatment might still retain enough of these ineradicable factors to possess advantages

145

over the opposition.

It is certainly the case that an individual so burdened with feelings of maladjustment and unhappiness is not likely to excel in sport to the same extent as a dedicated, settled and well-adjusted woman opponent. The sex-change woman athlete (or tennis player) is not an automatic challenge to the stars at the top of the tree. It may be that the biological advantages of a youth spent in manhood could raise a mediocre competitor into a top-rank one. But then, no-one would suggest that you remove from the ranks of tennis players all women who, for instance, do not seem to be fertile, who do not menstruate, or who have a pelvis that is uncharacteristically small; let alone exclude those with musculature that is well-developed, angular, or 'mannish'.

Yet beneath all the external facade, and unclouded even by the uncertainties posed by this most vexatious problem, it cannot be denied that no amount of hormone therapy started late in life (after adolescence, that is) can take away the clear-cut physical proportions that typically belong to men. No degree of surgery could eliminate those Y–chromosomes from every cell and replace them with an X instead. The sex-change patient who is given his femininity by the surgeon's knife and the pharmacologist's prescription may be a woman in appearance, but to a cytologist, an anatomist, a scientist and sometimes it would seem, even to a judge, such a person remains a man. An unhappy and uncertain individual teetering on the boundaries of trans-sexuality, fighting a battle with an unwanted inner sense of identity perhaps; still a man.

If we knew enough about the programming of the human mind in the early years of childhood then perhaps we could, at a stroke, rectify the wrongly acquired criteria and allow more appropriate ones to develop. As the evidence of the patients shows, they do not seem to develop a more settled personality after the operation, which suggests strongly that the basic psychological wound remains unhealed and unaffected. Only when we can tackle this problem at its source will there be the hope of real treatment for these people. At present, all too often we are left with a bizarre and unhappy addition to the list of the *man who is woman*, and the *woman who is man*: the *woman who is man, and who knows it all the time*.

There is a footnote to the discussion which puts it more accurately into perspective. It is that there has to be an extra factor which operates, perhaps at a level we do not even suspect, since of course not all men from dominant, assertive or 'overloving' mothers become trans-sexuals. It may be that there are factors which predispose a man towards trans-sexuality whilst he is still a foetus in the womb (an abnormal, undetected level of circulating testosterone from the mother, for instance or, alternatively, an excessive exposure to oestrogen during a critical stage of sexual development in the uterus). Some of them may be mosaics with a

146

percentage of cells bearing an extra X-chromosome – indeed in one or two cases this has been shown to be the genetic constitution of cells from trans-sexuals, though it does not apply to all.

In many forms of sexual abnormality an individual is turned away from behaviour that would allow him to procreate, and I believe this is a form of evolutionary safeguard which ensures that a species continues to transmit essential codes of behavioural criteria to successive generations, and eliminates the sexual deviant. But for typical trans-sexuals there is an extreme urgency, a profound distaste for their biological destiny, a desire to seek surgical mutilation almost as though it was some form of expiation or penance.

The man who models himself into a woman against the dictates of sex-determining factors in a deliberate and artificial manner is one of the most disturbing and problematical of phenomena. How it starts is a mystery; putting an end to the problem an enigma. If a chicken changing sex is to us such a remarkable thing (for all its biological 'normality'), how much more poignant is the spectacle of a sex-change patient enduring curiosity and titillating gossip? Is it an attempt to masochistically endure self-inflicted embarrassment and privation as a means of retribution for sins unperceived? Remember, this is a human we are talking of, not a bird; a person driven by desperate longings to submit to surgical mutilation – the ultimate in self-abuse.

CHAPTER EIGHT

SEXUAL VARIANTS

There is nothing inherently right or wrong, good or bad, about sexual activity, over and above what we have been brought up to instinctively accept and approve of, and biologically the end result of sexual awareness must be the carrying out of successful copulation and procreation. We have a whole range of instinctive desires which direct us towards survival, like hunger and thirst, for instance, and a feeling of revulsion from certain acts that in societal terms would harm our species' chances of survival. So anyone who experiences an instinctive and unreasoned antipathy for sexual aberrations is manifesting what is, in my view, a natural response to something which is biologically undesirable.

Homosexuality is not as unfamiliar as parthenogenesis or hermaphroditism. Everyone is aware of the phenomenon. Here too, one can experience instinctive revulsion for the idea and it may be that there is a sound biological principle at work by diverting our attention away from the abnormal, and towards sexual normalcy.

One has to be wary in applying terms like 'normal' and 'abnormal' in an area like this. As any gay person will quickly tell you, heterosexuality can seem profoundly abnormal to them. Gays tell the joke of the guy who went away for the weekend with a woman and spent much of the time in bed. Later he was asked what it had been like; and he replied, 'It was good, but not like the real thing.' By 'normal' in this sense, then, one has to confine one's meaning to sexual activities that mankind – in the broad spectrum of evolution over millions of years – has developed to be compatible with procreation. Let no-one be so naïve as to object, citing for instance intercourse involving the use of contraceptives as being 'abnormal' in this sense, because conception cannot then occur. It is a basic tenet of what I am saying that sexual norms are developed for the prime purpose of ensuring that the race survives. Something which is derived from such behaviour (like heterosexual intercourse), is clearly in this normal category, whilst homosexual buggery or fellatio, if used as a substitute for normal sexual climaxes, is not.

On the other hand, it would be a brave fool who tried to suggest that missionary-position copulation was the right and proper destiny for all sexually normal adults, irrespective of their desires for fore-play or experimentation with different positions, or their occasional indulgence in masturbation (which can be seen as a sexual exercise entirely compatible with maintaining a desire for intercourse). To a gay who insists that homosexual love is as normal to him as breathing is to you or me, I say that on a personal level that is undeniably so, but in a biological perspective similar to the situation in which our species evolved, it is anything but normal. If 'abnormal' is too strong a word, and I am inclined to think it is, then *variant* is perhaps better.

This relationship between sex acts as we now practise them and our evolutionary background is important. Man has not merely happened, he has not idly turned up in a civilized state by some quirk of chance or a galactic time-slip; he evolved, subject to the constraints of the environment, and has adapted himself to a set of physical and behavioural conventions that ensure his continued survival. When I am asked what diets are 'normal' for mankind, I look to the diets which impelled us to evolve as we have, and to search for areas of compatibility between our ancestral habits and those we now form. We have developed social conventions, for instance, which take us far from the strictures imposed on our primitive forebears. There seems to be no doubt, as I have explained, that this is why we are bedevilled by the coronary heart attack: we liberate those fatty energy reserves into the bloodstream when angered, but then – instead of giving vent to our anger – social conventions take over in their arbitrary way, and we sit at the office desk quietly fuming. The fats, unused by the energetic response nature intends, lie around in the blood vessels and tend to clog them.

In planning our future I have always held that we ought to make our life-style nearer to what we have become adapted for and this principle of compatibility surely applies more profoundly to sex than to any other field. Actions that are part of the evolutionary momentum of our kind are as basic and as necessary as hunger, thirst, and the urge to breathe; those that are not (no matter how enjoyable, how socially acceptable, how harmless or how fashionable they may be) are clearly variants.

HOMOSEXUALITY

The classical teachings of psychology suggest that we are all homosexual at some stage of life, and later evolve towards heterosexuality. According to this view, the homosexual adult is a person whose sexual development has been arrested at an essentially early or immature state; and many psychologists have written of gays as suffering from psychosexual infantilism, a hangover from what Freud regarded as the polymorphous perverse stage of sexual development. More recently, others have argued that homosexuality develops from our current 'group life' (to use the term which Marshall C. Greco used as the title for his book on the subject) rather than being a mirror of early experiences.

It is for psychologists to argue that out, not me: but I have in the past pointed out how easily we assume that we have solved a problem, when all we have really done is to describe it, sometimes in classical terms. 'If you cannot solve the problem, then translate it into Latin,' is the motto, and in some of these areas I am inclined to the view that this is all we are doing. Whether we are witnessing the persistence of an infantile sexual picture or not is, in pragmatic terms, neither here nor there. What we have to ask is, firstly: why do some people develop the trait, whilst others do not, and secondly: what biological or evolutionary purpose does homosexuality embody?

The idea that there may be an evolutionary function of homosexuality derives directly from what I have already said about the need for us to view mankind in the light of his past development. It is often said that a homosexual is determined by genes; but there is evidence from the study of twins that this is not the root cause. Others have suggested that it is hormonal, but in many cases this is not true either. Some homosexuals may have an irregular chromosomal complement, or be mosaics or even latent hermaphrodites, but it is clear that in the preponderance of cases the individuals have been unwittingly brought up to their condition. They learn from their parents and the family situation. Some people call it conditioning, others imprinting; I have outlined my view that we can clear many of these ideas in our minds if we regard the process as the learning of codes of criteria with which we learn to select our options. This is a convenient solution to the problem; it enables us to put sexual responses on the same plane as any other sense, such as hearing, or sight. Here too we have to learn codes of criteria that enable us to identify apparently random configurations of signals at an impossibly complex level of intricacy into stimuli corresponding to the sound of a voice, or the look of a person's face. To give an example of the miraculous nature of this selection process, let us visualize the oscilloscope tracing of an orchestral concert – on the screen, in the form in which the brain receives the stimulus, it is a scrambled mass of wavy lines, an incredibly complicated tangle of frequencies and amplitude. If you looked at it for an hour you would not learn to decipher more than the beat, if that.

But the ear can pass this encoded information along the electrical pathways of the brain until it is sifted through those codes of learned criteria and becomes, not just the sound of a recognizable tune, but – to the trained ear – a specific singer, a recognizable orchestra, even a specific concert hall. Similarly the eye trains itself to make sense and colour out of a web of electromagnetic stimuli. In just this way we can account for all of mankind's sensory and interpretive mechanisms.

And so it is with sex. What we need to learn are codes of behavioural criteria that will give rise to successful offspring. There is a clear evolutionary benefit to any organism that learns to apply sanctions to behavioural defaulters. Now, what does this say about homosexuality? Does this mean that the children of homosexuals inherit, through their training, their parent's variant?

This is certainly not the conclusion. It is more remarkable than that by far. The parents of homosexuals are often entirely heterosexual themselves, but there is evidence that they are not (in the biological sense of the term as defined above) always normal. That is not to say they may be inferior, nasty or perverted; but it does mean that they may not be in the ordinary way biologically acceptable in their relationships. Perhaps (and this is a common finding) there has been a recessive father and a dominant or over-protective mother. What does this mean to the child? It certainly does not imply unhappiness, nor does it necessarily imply insecurity; but it is a pattern of parental influence that does not fit with the evolutionary traditions of mankind.

It does not mean that the parents are unhappy, either. They are likely to be as happy with their lot as anyone else; and it is no right of someone who doesn't live that way themselves to decry such a mode of behaviour. However – and this is the crux of the matter – this is not the way we evolved. And the way nature responds is not what you might at first expect. The children of such a relationship do not, as it were, grow up the same way themselves; it is not that the mother 'forces' her view on a child, making him or her see the role of motherhood differently from the norm. No, nature reacts in a manner that is at first sight absurd. She turns the children of such a pair into homosexuals. They are pre-programmed to adopt this aberrant means of reaching sexual fulfilment. It is, to put it simply, the evolutionary machine's way of ensuring that behaviour patterns that cannot be correctly taught from one generation to the next die out.

Obviously it would be convenient if there were a genetic explanation of homosexuality; if it could be found to occur on a particular abnormal chromosome structure that you could identify in homosexuals and their progenitors the problem would be solved. Alternatively, if it was a behavioural explanation that you wanted to put forward as the answer instead, then you should be able to demonstrate a link between effeminacy in father (or masculinization in the mother) and homosexuality in the child.

What I believe may be the answer is distinct from any of these views: it is that we carry in our genetic make-up the (usually dormant) proclivity for homosexuality. In a normal childhood it remains masked, as the child learns a series of complex behavioural norms that will fit him or her to normal parenthood. In an unhappy, insecure, unfulfilled or impoverished family there is no interference with the sequence I have described. But in a couple where the relationship is such that abnormal, i.e. evolutionarily unacceptable, patterns of behaviour would be taught and handed down to the offspring, nature applies the ultimate sanction – homosexuality implies, at its worst, that the child will never breed, and so will not pass on its behavioural burden to a new generation.

The ban on breeding thus imposed is not invariable, of course; the obligate homosexual is effectively sterilized by his condition, but lesser degrees may be facultatively heterosexual to an extent. A significant proportion of gays marry in order to acquire a veneer of social respectability (a convention that was forced upon them more in the past than is the case in a more open society) and only a generation ago in Britain, homosexuality in men – though not in women – was an offence punishable by law. There are today many men and women with marked gay tendencies who have reared children, but who 'take time out' to revert to their variant alternative. Mild degrees of homosexuality like this are subject only to a lesser version of nature's sanction, therefore; but they are not happy individuals as a rule, and their spouses suffer too, either through the tensions of acceptance, or suspicion; or perhaps more often through the subliminal failure to relax as much as they should.

Homosexuality is in evolutionary terms a profound state of sexual abnormality. But within the life-span of an individual it is no bad thing to be gay. A great many of our leading visionaries, writers and actors have leanings of this sort, and more than once has a connection between creativity and homosexuality been put forward as though it had a cause-and-effect relationship.

There is one way in which there could be an element of truth in this attitude, of course, and that is that a person denied the creative opportunity of making new people is diverted instead into other forms of creation, of an artistic or intellectual kind. It may be that feelings of inadequacy impels such a person to seek success or acclaim on the stage; or that there is an element of exhibitionism, perhaps even a hiding of one's (unwanted) personality through acting a part in the theatre . . . there are many alternative possibilities which might explain how homosexuals are more intent on personal fulfilment and public success than heterosexuals might be.

In some ways this is almost compensation for the sanction against procreation. If homosexuality does lead to a potentiation of creative abilities (for whatever reason is immaterial) then you may certainly argue that gays might be, on average, more gifted, or more able to exploit their latent talents, than society's straight majority. Whatever the root cause, it is difficult to 'disapprove' too heartily of any influence which potentiates the human ego, and invigorates an individual's abilities. We know well enough of Plato's writings that suggest Socrates might have been homosexually involved with his students; Aristotle was certainly gay, in all probability so were Virgil and Horace; and the list goes on from Oscar Wilde and Michelangelo to Walt Whitman and Tchaikovsky . . . indeed it has even been suggested that Shakespeare was homosexually inclined. If the potentiation of one's abilities is a concomitant of homosexuality, then many people would argue that it is a fair deal.

My view on this *purpose* of homosexuality provides one important item of insight without which it is impossible to account for the most common finding in the homosexual's nature: that a gay is essentially inclined to fear the opposite sex. The lavish and over-protective loving kindness of a devoted mother, which many psychiatrists associate with the potentiation of homosexual impulses in man, is not very likely to inspire feelings of instinctive repulsion – gratitude, perhaps, or you might even argue that a desire to escape from all the smothering would be the result in an extreme case. But the development of repulsion bordering on actual trepidation and instinctive dislike of the entire feminine gender is an illogical 'learned' response to kindness!

No: I postulate that we are witnessing the unmasking of an innate biological protective mechanism against the passing on of unwanted, undesirable patterns of behaviour and in this way homosexuality is a mainstay of cultural normalcy. Historians may go further, and might investigate the frequency with which the breakdown of civilization is associated with an increasing level of sexual abnormalities of this sort; if it is true that variant sex is the result of biologically unacceptable patterns of behaviour, then both might be said to lead to the breakdown of organized civilizations. The dictum that 'moral degeneracy' precedes cultural regression is dangerous if we take that to mean that a departure from a given code of political criteria is self-evidently undesirable; but sexual norms are predestined and are predicated upon biological necessity, rather than the whims of political extremism. They might be said, then, to supply an objective means of assessing what it was once popular to describe as 'the moral health of the nation'.

The liberalization of our attitudes to homosexuality has come at a time when, by any standards, such reform was overdue. Suggesting that variant sexual behaviour of this sort is part of nature's control over wayward or fruitless behaviour patterns is one thing: condemning it as obscene or criminal – as many societies have done in the past, and as some still do – is quite another. Homosexual love is capable of being as binding and as passionate as heterosexual relationships, it is just that the expression of pair bonding instincts, when directed in this way, will be not passed on to a future generation. Typically, homosexual bonding occurs between effeminate and masculinized members of the same sex: a butch woman, say, wearing 'manly' clothing and adopting what are construed as 'manly' social conventions with a soft and feminine (sometimes unkindly known as a 'bitch') partner. Comparable pairing situations occur in males. And this at once brings us to the realization that, contrary to popular belief, not all gay women are butch, any more than all gay men are effeminate 'pansies'. As many as half of each group are outwardly straight in their manner and behaviour. Conversely, there are many effeminate men and masculine women in society who betray such characteristics as part of an entirely heterosexual make-up.

The terms used to describe gay folk are almost invariably derogatory (at least, until the term 'gay' itself came into prominence). The gay is 'queer', 'bent', or 'kinky'. Though the mutual stimulation of two partners to orgasm in the context of romantic love is perfectly acceptable to straight people in the context of heterosexual lovemaking, it seems to inspire revulsion and repugnance when visualized as occurring between homosexual couples.

Why is this? Some commentators have, in the words of Albert Ellis, suggested that 'an individual who exclusively desires sex relations with the members of the other sex . . . who is utterly afraid of trying all non-heterosexual outlets and is compulsively tied to heterosexual ones; - then that person is indubitably neurotic'. Ellis explains that this definition includes someone 'marooned on a desert island with only members of his own sex for a long period of time' and I am prepared to concede that, in such a circumstance, a highly-sexed individual who was not prepared to experiment with surrogate sexual partners until restored to heterosexual society might be said to exhibit an obsession that was arguably neurotic or, at least, excessive.

But the basic principle that it is just as extreme to be exclusively heterosexual as to be the converse - and this is a view that has gained some considerable currency in recent years - is in my view a fundamental error. The distaste that straights have for homosexuality, as revealed through their instinctive desires and through their choice of derogatory terms to describe gay practices - is a result of a biological imperative. This is part of our developmental programming: just as the cuckoo flies to warmer climates thousands of miles distant in order to survive, so we embody mechanisms that make us fly from sexual patterns that are incompatible with the survival of our kind.

My viewpoint is one that bears directly against the view of gays and bisexual people that homosexuality is entirely normal, an equivalent substitute for heterosexualism and - as some argue - the real McCoy. But for all the biological fruitlessness of the condition (an unarguable truism that makes the colloquial term for homosexuals, 'fruit', ironic) the view I am advancing is sounder by far than such condescending comments as those in Vendervelt and Odenwald's book *Psychiatry and Catholicism*: 'There is no justification for regarding homosexuals as . . . depraved and degenerate. They, like all sick people, deserve to be . . . given sympathetic assistance.' Homosexuality is no superficial sickness, no temporary illness of the psyche that a quick re-educate will cure. It is no bent substitute for the more rewarding 'real thing'. On the contrary, it is a natural and essentially wholesome instinct revealed in those of us who are taught to acquire codes of criteria that do not help the future of our species; a substitute for heterosexuality, certainly; but a diseased form of it? Never. In terms of biological imperatives, then, the gay is abnormal: but he is not *unnatural* by any means.

There is an additional corollary to my interpretation, and that is the relative paucity of success in psychotherapy for homosexuals. If a gay has merely learned an aberrant behaviour pattern or has simply not progressed along life's sexual highway as much as he might, then re-learning should be a simple matter. All the therapist need do is inculcate the right desires by suggestion, and help the homosexual complete his metamorphosis.

In fact, exactly as my view would lead one to predict, it is not so easy. As psychiatrist John Randell admits, psychotherapy cannot 'claim much in the way of successful treatment for homosexuals, despite the claims of some respected analytically oriented colleagues'. What more fitting evidence could one find that homosexuality is a latent trait with a firm biological purpose. We are faced, not with a series of wrongly learned attributes that are amenable to correction, but the potentiation of a defence mechanism for our species brought on by the triggering effect of behavioural aberrations in parents. Imitation, then, is no part of the homosexual's training; and imitation is equally unlikely to be part of his hoped-for 'restoration' to the heterosexual state. You may certainly create a conditioned aversion for homosexuality. Therapists tell me of electric shock treatment administered when homosexual pictures are shown on a screen, the administration of emetics to make the homosexual vomit, or the insistent retelling of nauseous stories that are associated with images of the loved gay partner: 'As you go over to Ralph you see him lying on his bed, his penis fully erect. The feeling of nausea is now overwhelming; you stand over him as he masturbates and feel the spew welling up in your throat, then you sick up all over his body, his degraded, filthy, body . . .' which is calculated to put anyone off anything.

Such operant procedures are unlikely to create a positive *liking* for anything else. To distort the gay's appreciation of what is for him an entirely natural and fulfilling means of sexual gratification is an assault no-one should tolerate for an instant.

Occasionally, though, homosexual practices are clearly founded on a learned code of criteria from childhood. Thus we can easily understand the case of the gay student who entered his parents' bedroom in the middle of the night when he was six or seven, and saw his mother engaged in fellatio (the sucking of the phallus) on his father. On a later occasion, this time feeling sick through some minor illness, he went for help and found them engaged in conventional, i.e. 'missionary' intercourse. The first visit had not resulted in his parents noticing him watching their love-play, whilst on the second he was seen and was sent away in anger.

It is clear why he grew up with an association of positive criteria with fellatio and strongly distasteful, negative ones for conventional intercourse. He spoke of a strong desire to suck his own phallus, and succeeded eventually in perfecting the somewhat athletic contortion necessary to carry it out. His love-making as a teenager centred on fellatio with a male companion.

In this instance it was his introduction to an experienced prostitute well versed in the technique herself which 'cured' him. And the transition of the stimulating orifice from mouth to vagina was an easy one to make. This, though, was the result of the learning of aberrant behaviour by mimicry; the potentiation of homosexualism by the experience of parents who are not in balance with the dictates of successful child-rearing is an imperative from which 'escape' is not so easy – and is neither necessary nor even useful.

The commonest homosexual activity between gay partners is mutual masturbation, which may be manual or oral. Fondling of the breasts and genitalia in women gays is as frequent as it is when men make love to women; and stimulation of the thighs, the scrotum and the anal area is the counterpart in men. The act of anal intercourse (which, as buggery, remains a legal offence in Britain and elsewhere no matter how private may be the circumstances or how consenting the participants) provides an effective substitute for vaginal penetration in male homosexual love-making, but there is no somatic (i.e. bodily) substitute for women. The fingers may be inserted into the vagina, and artificial aids may be employed instead – ranging from electrically powered vibrators to the neck of a bottle, a 'Coke' bottle being for some reason the most frequent candidate in sex night-clubs – and in some women pairs the clitoris may be large enough (perhaps several centimetres in length) to act as a substitute penis. The dildo is an artificial penis which was once made of wood or rubber, but nowadays can be bought as a plastic model phallus, complete with the grooves and surface blood-vessels of the genuine article, which straps around the waist of the 'dominant' partner in the love act, sometimes with a self-stimulating backward-projecting dildo at its base.

Aberrant behaviour may be associated with homosexuality, of course, as it is with heterosexual practices. Coprophilia, an addiction to stimulation through the sight or feel of excrement, is not infrequent and in this syndrome the idea of contact with the partner's faeces *per rectum* acts as a stimulant. Other coprophiliac gays use smooth mud as a substitute, and more than one example involved bathing in a secluded spot on a river-bank followed by the insertion of the erect penis into a cavity in the mud.

Adornment of one's body is stimulating to many gay males, as is 'unadornment' or the adoption of harsh and unflattering clothes by many gay women. The elaborate liking for dressing up in many religious orders has a strongly sexual connotation for a proportion of their number, and in some people there is a desire to adorn the organs of sex themselves (one example is of a youth who liked to stick glittering Christmas decorations to his phallus with adhesive tape, and Dylan Thomas writes of the decoration of the breasts with lipstick in his *Under Milk Wood*). There is an echo of all this in the use of cosmetics.

The shame that is attached to homosexuality, even though I have explained that this has a clear biological function, is itself unfortunate for several reasons. Firstly it gives the homosexual a head start in neurosis. For orthodox psychology, homosexuality is a symptom of a deep-seated neurosis, whereas I would contend that there is evidence to suggest that it may be quite the converse: that neurosis develops because of the reaction of outsiders to the gay's condition. He becomes neurotic because of his condition, and not the other way round, according to this view.

Secondly, the gay is less inclined to approach a doctor for treatment if he suspects that he may have contracted VD and for this reason alone, rates of syphilis in homosexuals are higher than they are for straights. Roughly 5% of the population are exclusive homosexuals, whereas as many as 14% of new cases of VD seen at clinics are homosexual.

Gays are also subject to a series of unrealistic stereotyped ideas that persist, for all the attitude of quasi-enlightenment in which we live. People feel them to be untrustworthy, for instance; or they may be seen as distasteful to such an extent that they become cut off from social contact and ostracized by people who were their friends before the truth emerged. For many people, this is understandably a considerable burden. The relationship with their parents is uneasy, too; in some ways this is at a conscious level, because the parents feel they may miss an opportunity to see grandchildren; but on the instinctive level of which I have written it is an inevitable consequence of the distaste we feel for homosexuality if we are heterosexual ourselves.

Insight into the origin of the condition is no real answer to the problem, either. If the parents can now feel that their son, say, is as happy and as secure with a gay partner as he would have been with a wife, he may blame them (or they themselves) for a series of accidental, subconscious impulses transmitted to him unwittingly and without any malice, or conscious neglect of parental duties.

Finally there is the likelihood that on average a gay pair are not going to find the depth or permanency of bonding that may be found in heterosexual couples. The sexes are what they are for strict and immutable evolutionary reasons, their physical and emotional configuration matched for each other in a way that is programmed and carefully matched for the reality of procreation and child-rearing. An abhorrence of one's opposite gender, driving a gay towards his own sex, is not as likely to give fulfilment for the pair. This is not to say that gay pair-bonding does not work, for manifestly it can. But the chances for permanent, stable bonding are I think considerably less in homosexual relationships than they are in heterosexual pairing – though of course the best and most successful gay couples experience far more genuine warmth, love and physical passion than the majority of run-of-the-mill straight marriages.

There is also the vexed question of the legal status of gay pairs. Some have entered into formal marriage, having lived together as man and wife for a time beforehand, without anyone realizing that they were actually of the same sex. Such an act is clearly unlawful, since it involves the making of a false declaration of 'fitness to marry'. In many cases, sympathetic ministers of religion are now willing to offer a parallel service to that of the consecration of marriage, a form of gay dedication, as it were, which is held to be as binding and as permanent as marriage itself.

More difficult by far is the question of lesbian couples adopting or fostering children. This issue became a matter of public concern in Britain in 1977, when some authorities were supporting such an application on the grounds that it could only be to the benefit of a child to have two 'loving and devoted parents' even if they were both genetic females. There may even be something in the argument, insofar as the outward behaviour of such a couple may conform perfectly to what you would expect of an orthodox man/woman pair. It might be argued that such patterns would even inculcate in the child a perfectly balanced and viable set of behavioural codes – but this is not, I fear, enough. There remains the fact that the parents are of the same sex, and that this may well cause the child acute embarrassment or difficulties at school or in later life. And though it can be argued with unquestioned authority that, according to our orthodox view on the nature of homosexuality and the new trend towards liberal acceptance of what was once thought to be unspeakable behaviour, public attitudes are changing, it is incompatible with a deep-seated biological imperative that makes us avoid abnormal sexuality, whether you are a normal gay who avoids straights, or vice versa. To teach a child codes of criteria based on maleness and femaleness experienced at the hands of two women is a weighty responsibility. When there are *prima facie* reasons against it, then it would be too much to risk.

At least homosexuality is now more widely accepted and more frequently discussed. To some extent, this trend has gone too far; at least one commentator has gone so far as to suggest that the American novelists represent a daisy-chain of 'failed queers', and in the words quoted by Dennis Altman, an Australian homosexual writer, we have almost reached the stage where 'the love that dared not speak its name' became the neurosis that did not know when to shut up.

And let me use that telling phrase to reiterate one further example in support of my contention that it is the reaction of outsiders to the gay predicament, rather than homosexuality itself, which actually causes this neurotic condition. Juveniles who engage in homosexuality - at school or in a youth movement like the Boy Scouts, for example - do not enter into it after some prolonged period of neurotic disturbance. As a rule they are as well-adjusted to that as most children are to whatever sexual activity they may have discovered - masturbation, for example. It is only when the names start: 'faggot!, queer!', and when the outside world begins to make its disapproval felt, that neurotic tendencies creep in. For children who are maintained in single-sex schools, transient homosexuality is common and can be easily accounted for as being the use of whoever is available and willing for the purpose of instinctive gratification.

But for those whose homosexuality is predestined, who have been given this alternative outlet as a sanction against unwanted behavioural patterns, the pressures have at this stage begun. It is the relief of that weight, and the understanding of the biological purpose of homosexualism, that can do much to integrate homosexuals into society, and an understanding of homosexuality into our minds.

CHAPTER NINE

DEVIATION AND
THE SEXUAL PERVERSIONS

It is difficult to encompass mankind's varied sexual experiences without being simplistic. So many are aspects of each other (thus masturbation, which when carried out excessively, is certainly recognized as a perverted form of sex by workers in that field; but in lesser forms it is entirely 'normal' and forms a part of regular love-making for couples of all nationalities, to some degree; thus – what is 'excessive'?); so many variables are implied in normal sexual patterns; and a few are represented in societal conventions of a non-sexual nature – from the dressing up of men as women as fun, in pantomime, or in fancy-dress, to the embracing of schoolgirls as a conventional cue for friendship of a platonic nature – so that it is hard to call them transvestite or homosexual (lesbian) manifestations. It is a matter of degree. The pathological killer who murders his victim in the course of sexual assault is undeniably perverted to an extreme degree, of course; but if lovers nibble and sometimes bite each other painfully in the expression of sexual ecstasy, who is to draw a specific criterion of distinction between one part of that spectrum and the other?

But, though the colours of a spectrum form a continuum in which it is impossible to draw strict boundaries, the principal colours are identifiable, right enough. You may argue about turquoise belonging to the greens or the blues, but no-one will argue about buttercup yellow being yellow, or the crimson of blood being red. So we can certainly examine the key colours on the spectrum of human sexual activity. And, as there are colours that do not appear on the rainbow spectrum at all (such as lilac, grey or brown) we can outline the categories of sexual deviation which by any standards must be perverse, if that word has any meaning at all: activities which are destructive, or which would seem to have no echo in sexual activity that has an evolutionary role.

TRANSVESTISM
The semantics of this term are unmistakable; it means across, or from one

side to the other (Latin prefix *trans-*) and clothing (Latin *vestire*, to clothe, from which 'vestment' and of course 'vest' derive). Very well then, but it is not quite as simple. Men and women dressed as each other have long formed a part of entertainment (the pantomime dame and the principal boy in traditional British Christmas-time theatricals have long been played by members of the opposite sex), and though there are transvestite overtones there is no great capacity here for sexual stimulation on the grand scale.

Student rags and a host of similar festivities have for a long time given people a chance to dress up in clothes from the other sex, and the same idea regularly figures in pram races and other events at carnivals, fetes and so on. In espionage a change of sex has often been arranged for an agent or a criminal, who wishes to cross boundaries undetected, by the use of conventional disguises. You may argue that Uncle Wilberforce dressing up in garish clothing at a Christmas party has some sexual connotations, and – depending on Uncle Wilberforce's preferences – it's just possible that you are right. But there is nothing kinky about a suspect who protestingly dons a feminine wig and a false brassière in order to slip past the police.

It is also treading on touchy ground if you wish to point to the wearing of trousers and slacks as transvestism in women. Most women wear slacks because they are comfortable and because they keep them warm. A few women wear them as part of a true transvestite desire to mimic men, to feel masculine, in some cases to be taken as the male (butch) partner of a lesbian, or to express male-type aggression. So the wearing of trousers as part of a transvestite syndrome can certainly have some clinical significance – but it is now so widespread a social convention that for the majority it would be absurd to try to advance such an explanation. It is possible to draw a distinction between the motives of women choosing trousers today and those who chose them in, say, the 1920's and 1930's. The act of wearing trousers then (like the carrying by men of anything that could be designated a 'handbag' in the 1960's) was a criterion diagnostic of a given behaviour pattern and although there were clear-cut exceptions to the rule – no-one, even in the bad years, would have condemned as gay a man holding his wife's handbag at the glove counter or a woman wearing protective trousers in a factory, though they might have been teased a little – such behaviour was considered more significant than it is now.

It is not the act itself, or any aspect of its true meaning that matters. Once a gesture or a sign has acquired a learned value, no matter how spurious, it becomes a criterion by which a generic class can be selected. Universality can, in the end, sterilize such a distinction. That is what has happened to the wearing of slacks by women, for even twenty years ago a trouser suit was considered remarkable in Western society – a fact it is difficult to recall today.

The trend towards women's liberation has given us what could be called political transvestism: the adoption of a recognizable male uniform or costume by women who wish to make a political gesture, or who have come subconsciously to accept the criteria of those activists who want to break down societal barriers. The wearing of tweed jackets, flat hats, waistcoats, heavy boots and other male apparel is an example.

And it tells us something of great interest about the movement itself. The origins have been claimed to derive from the need for women to assert themselves as equivalent to men, i.e. having the same value, and not being regarded as secondary, inferior citizens. Few political movements can have been more overdue. The systematic under-payment of women who were in the same jobs as men is one example of the abuse of women, whilst the astonishing convention of addressing all tax correspondence to married couples in Britain to the husband, by name (even to the extent of making out rebate cheques in his name when they were due to the wife) – which was still going on in 1978 – is another. The pressures against women for the first three-quarters of this century have been unwarranted and degrading, and a society that manages to perpetrate any such system is manifestly short-sighted and downright cruel. The move for equality however, has often failed to take women onward towards a state of feminine equivalence and liberation. There has been a strong move to make women virtually the same as men, and this was reflected in 1970's fashion.

Women saw a trend towards the masculinization of their clothes design. Instead of a great upsurge of confident, outgoing, assertive womanhood revealed through a newly liberated and free expression through clothes, there was a sudden flooding of the market with essentially male apparel, boots, trousers of a heavy and manly design, jackets, waistcoats and severe hats. The movement attained a cheap and unsubtle imitation of maleness.

There was much talk of unisex fashions. They were not unisex at all, when we get down to it; who suggested that men wore dresses or skirts (on the face of everything far easier to get on than the buttons and zips of men's clothing)? Quite the converse: it is women who were adopting the narrower confines of men's fashion.

Womenfolk of the West were conveniently convinced that their best hope of equivalence was equality – and the best way of obtaining that was to dress up to look *not* like an independent and free-thinking woman at all, but like a watered-down imitation of the male of our species.

Transvestism is often associated with a neurotic personality (whether by cause or effect remains unresolved) and it is of course a symptom of trans-sexuality. So it may be that the origin of a move to liberate women by ensnaring them in the same fashion conventions as men lay in the charismatic effusions of a few sexually deviant campaigners who were motivated, not merely by a desire to put men in their place or to show women that it was high time they asserted their own individual equivalence in society, but by an envy of masculinity and a desire to act and dress like a man.

Women, by taking up the campaign for equivalence (*not* equality) showed that they were the first group in society to set about rethinking our traditional criteria and remodelling our values. They have grasped the chance to eliminate much of the mindlessness of conformity which has dogged our heels for centuries. But the cult of political transvestism implies stricture and convention rather than showing men what real liberation was all about.

THE CROSS-DRESSED MAN

Political transvestism is essentially public. It is a symptom of an openly expressed movement. But the typical transvestite is a man who is motivated by internal desires and wishes of an essentially personal character. Quite simply, he wants to look like a woman to please himself, and to satisfy his sexual leanings.

The transvestite man when cross-dressed is not only playing the part of a woman. Many such people derive pleasure from their secret knowledge that they are male, and do possess a penis and testicles beneath the soft folds of silken knickers stolen or bought for the purpose. The behaviour usually becomes manifest in childhood or adolescence, when the boy will obtain a pair of pants from a female relative and put them on in the bathroom, displaying himself before the mirror with the security of a locked door to protect his secret. Transvestites like to look at themselves in the mirror, in acts of pure narcissism, and will put on a nightdress or a frilly gown in order to display at themselves in the looking-glass. Sometimes the parents know about the habit and may accept it, and even encourage it in rare cases where the parents longed for a girl instead of a boy. Once in a while, parents actually bring up a child dressed as a girl, knowing him to be a sexually normal boy, and send him to a girl's school. Whether this can be grouped under the heading of transvestism is arguable, since the condition has external, rather than internal and personal, origins.

It is quite frequent for a transvestite man to carry out his experiments in cross-dressing occasionally, when no-one suspects anything. Such people living alone (perhaps for a short while, when a wife is on holiday or away visiting) can cross-dress and then go for short expeditions acting out the role and attitudes of a normal woman. Less frequent is the family situation in which the condition is known about by the wife, and even encouraged by her. Some wives enjoy the cross-dressing for sexual reasons of their own, whilst a significant number become what Robert Stoller has called 'succouring wives' – they actually help their transvestite husbands to choose clothing and to make themselves up correctly, and may go out with them, addressing them by an adopted female's first name and pretending to be sisters or schoolfriends.

On occasions, transvestism may even be known and accepted by the social circle with whom the couple are intimate, and it may even be that the children of the marriage know of the trait of their father and come to terms with it. You may say that this is entirely natural and even obvious, but remember that this form of behaviour clashes profoundly with those innate codes of sexual criteria which I have described in earlier chapters. Therefore (though the acceptance of transvestism in this way is in many ways admirable) we must not assume that those who are instinctively repelled are being in some way antisocial or deliberately cruel. They are mirroring a biological imperative with an honourable and important evolutionary pedigree.

Where does transvestism of this sort come from? There is no easy answer to that question, and it is in my view clear that we are regarding, not a disorder, but a symptom when we see men cross-dressing in this manner. Perhaps for some it is a sign of a deep-seated neurotic complaint, or perhaps it is the result of traumatic early experiences which teach a code of aberrant criteria that manifest themselves as transvestite behaviour.

Some people who behave as transvestites are latent trans-sexuals. Others are certainly homosexual (about 50%, if survey data are reliable) and they use masturbation whilst cross-dressed as a sexual outlet. In some people, this has the effect of causing a feeling of revulsion and in these cases the phase often dies out before adulthood asserts itself. There are many avenues through which the patterns of sex unravel themselves in which revulsion for the act itself contrasts forcibly with the overwhelming desire that expresses itself as fantasy earlier on. It is true, for example, that in other sexual deviations such as paedophilia, it is the desire for sex in this way which is so strong and so tempting, but only as desire – only as a fantastical possibility. Once the act itself has been completed, and the longed-for dream has become reality, it is sometimes found that the individual experiences revulsion for it and for everything associated with it. In cases like this (which are, regrettably, only a minority) it is the chase that satisfies, not the conquest.

Homosexuals are not permitted to join the Beaumont Society, an organization of transvestites who are named after Chevalier Charles d'Eon Beaumont, a noted cross-dresser whose name was used by Havelock Ellis in the earlier twentieth century in his coinage 'eonism' for the syndrome. They have meetings where transvestites – often accompanied by their wives or girl friends – can be accepted without malice or embarrassment. Beaumont himself, a French nobleman of the eighteenth century, served his country well by acting as an agent whilst playing the part of a woman.

Philippe, Duke of Orleans, who was brother to the Sun King, Louis XIV, of France, was another noted transvestite and an early governor of New York, Lord Cornury, was also occasionally seen in public dressed in women's clothes. The incidence of the condition is hard to assess; but it is usually accepted that around 1% of Western males are transvestites.

Why is it that males dressing in women's clothing should be regarded as more outrageous and unacceptable than a woman wearing slacks or a trouser suit? This is an apparently anomalous distinction to draw – in the words of John Randell, a noted English psychiatrist, 'clothing is after all merely a covering for the body (and) logically there is no reason why a male wearing female clothing should be regarded as more abnormal than a woman wearing a trouser suit.' Logic, though, is the greatest obstacle to clear thought I know: there is no more powerful means of compounding conceptual errors that have their origins in a mistaken notion of reality. What concerns me far more, is how we recognize reality in the first place – what are the criteria we utilize to distinguish one 'true' interpretation from a range of options? Once you adopt this alternative means of analyzing the matter, the apparent conundrum solves itself.

The point is that the present state of society does not utilize the criterion of 'trouserwearingness' to delineate transvestite sexuality any more. Women who wear slacks are accepted as being in the normal or acceptable range of our experience, and that is purely a matter of fashion. Men, on the other hand (who could certainly *in logic* expect to get away with wearing loose dresses or pretty floral hats) would clash with the learned and accepted fact that such behaviour is recognized as a criterion that distinguishes a group of abnormal, effeminate, repulsive men. The logic in that is minimal. But once we see how learned criteria act, and how they interact with fundamental interpretations of sexuality at an inborn level, we can begin to accept that cues of this sort – no matter how insubstantial they may seem on critical examination – can trigger off whole-hearted feelings of the strongest kind.

What we are witnessing is the potentiation of latent impulses that our species needed (needs?) to survive and develop. It does not matter what the criteria themselves are. Mankind did not acquire an inborn dislike of flowery hats on men's heads way back in palaeolithic times, or anything like that. But we did, most certainly, evolve with the ability to assign criteria to conceptual events – such as the recognition of individuals as belonging to our sex or not – and once we have learned them the diagnostic weight we accord them is overwhelming. When the criteria reinforce inbuilt associations, and this could be said to apply to many of the sex-dependent conventions of dress, the effect is redoubled.

So there is indeed nothing in logic that makes a man wearing female apparel and going about his normal daily activities seem, on the face of it, repulsive or disgraceful. But once we see the value of our learned codes of criteria we can at least appreciate where the discrepancy lies. The strength of reaction that most people can detect (and which they may know to conflict with reason, objectivity or the humanitarian feelings they would ordinarily show) is a reminder of our inborn defence mechanisms against the evolutionarily counterproductive forces that surrounded us throughout our development as a species.

To reject them, to wish they were different, even to seek to modify them, are all understandable reactions. But to ignore them, or to pretend they are not there, is devastating and could confuse and undermine the foundations of human culture.

FETISHISM

I have said that a male transvestite may begin to acquire female undergarments and use them as the starting-point of a wardrobe of feminine clothing. Not all young people who start by borrowing a pair of girl's panties go on to become cross-dressers. Sometimes the garments are worn (a condition often referred to as 'adherent fetishism') but often they are merely possessed and used as a stimulant during masturbation. In this case we are concerned with association. The individual, known generically as a fetishist (Portuguese *feitico* – 'a charm') uses objects from a love target as a symbol of the absent partner. Soft and feminine clothing is one obvious choice for a male fetishist; feminine hair is another – indeed there have been reports in the press from time to time of girls on a bus or train finding bits of their pigtails mysteriously missing at the end of a journey, which was clearly an example of a hair fetishist at work.

The fetish need not, however, be physical. There are case histories of individuals whose fixation was on a behavioural characteristic. The most remarkable of these is perhaps the man who was brought speedily to masturbatory orgasm on hearing a patient in the hospital where both were confined coughing in a paroxysmal fashion. The stimulus was greatest for the sound-fetishist when the coughing reached its height. The association was with his mother, who was a consumptive, and with whom he had a strongly oedipal relationship. He used to hear her coughing at night, and his sexual associations with her memory were triggered by the coughing spasm he heard in hospital.

A more common form of this behaviour is when a sexual story or the sound of sexual swear-words becomes the stimulant. In one form or another this is often found in normal marriages, where allusions to sexual performance and whispered descriptions of the delights in store serve to heighten passion. A parallel may be drawn between the speaking of sexual words in a case like this, and the writing of the words on walls. The stimulus may be direct, as when the words are spoken during sexual activity, or it may be referred to another person. This is clearly the case when an individual indulges in sexual graffiti: he is being stimulated by the idea of shock or surprise in the mind of whoever reads the words, and the assault to the senses which he associates with them is itself stimulating. Sex-word graffiti is a form of associative fetishism, then, just as sounds or words being spoken (often known inelegantly as 'acoustic' fetishism) is audiofetishism. The growth of tapes and discs with recordings of simulated sex sounds and of sexual acts is a symptom of growing interest in the possibilities for audiofetishism.

Here, too, we have to be careful in the matter of definition. Many people find such recordings stimulating for quite different reasons. These may be *either* because they serve to stimulate an atmosphere of sexuality during foreplay and coition, and as such are an adjunct to heterosex; *or* because they provide a titillating insight into what other people are up to, and in this case we have a parallel to voyeurism. Audiofetishism is really concerned with the adoption of the sounds of sex, or sounds associated with sexual activity, *in place of* heterosexual stimulation rather than to supplement it.

Some forms of the syndrome may have evolutionary components, such as the state of 'adherent fetishism' in which contact with smooth surfaces (silk, rubber, plastic) is greatly desired. This tactile response is present in most people; smooth silky sheets in bed, for example, are frequently used to increase the pleasures of sex. I have little doubt that this is because such materials are capable of producing cues that are recognized by our innate codes of criteria as pleasing – because they mimic the touch of soft skin. As a sex cue this is a fundamental pleasure trigger, and at this profound level clearly we need to identify sensuous intimacy – represented by contact with these silky-smooth textures – as a desirable end.

It may be that the olfactory fetishes of those who treasure soiled garments, sweaty shirts, aromatic underwear and the rest, are potentiating a similar code of criteria. Pheromonal attraction is well known in the animal world (some male moths can detect little more than a few free molecules of an odour attractant from a mature female a kilometre or more distant) and the large sums expended on perfumery in Western society and elsewhere shows how well-recognized is the power of scent as a sexual stimulant.

Musk, which is obtained from preputial secretions of the Musk Ox, is a sexual stimulant and the faintly fish-like aroma of secretions in humans is associated with sexuality and has, for many people, a potentiating effect. Other scents may be learned to fit the pattern. The aroma of sweaty socks or armpits is favoured by some, and some underground and fringe publications carry advertisements for soiled undergarments, a fetish that has been dubbed osphresiolagnia.

Finally there are the fetishes associated, not with the forms and figures of lovers, but with parts of their bodies. This trait, known as partialism, is typified by the foot fetish, in which the shape of a foot (particularly the foot of a loved one) becomes an object of desire and a source of great stimulation. Others may have a fixation for hair. It is possible that the toes are seen as surrogate and non-threatening penises, or hair as a more portable version of the pubic adornment of a loved one.

An extreme form of fetishistic association with the products of excretion, rather than with the smells (*vide supra*) is found in undinism (urolagnia in the United States) and coprophilia. Here the individual wishes to come into contact with urine and faeces respectively.

Undine was the mythological spirit of water, and the syndrome of undinism centres on the watching of people in the act of urination, and can take more extreme forms. Thus, some prostitutes will offer to urinate on their clients for a special fee. Occasional undinists like to drink their partner's urine, a parallel to cunnilingual masochism. On a more subtle plane, the male undinist will occasionally prefer to wear a sanitary towel in his underwear, having moistened it with urine.

It is the excremental associations of these seemingly bizarre rituals that provide the typical feeling of disgust, even nausea, that you may experience whilst reading this account – but there are some underlying and inborn codes of criteria that might enable us to see where undinism (at first hearing an absurd and unappealing act) might have its roots. Urine is a saline solution, not unlike sea-water or the amniotic fluid in which as embryos we developed; and there is nothing in the least repellant about contact with the balmy waters of the tropical oceans or the Mediterranean. Chemically and physically, bathing in a warm sea is a close parallel to immersion in urine. Perhaps the undinist has triggered off a distant memory, and is indulging a fancy that has its origins in something more romantic by far than the bizarre prospect of being pissed on by a whore.

A desire to associate with faeces is known generically as coprophilia (Greek *kopros*, dung), and in children signs of interest in faeces, such as handling of a stool or wiping a little with one finger across the lavatory wall, are common. These symptoms are not in the least significant; they point to nothing more unusual than a developing interest of an individual in his body and its products. Some psychotics, though, show a marked desire to associate with excrement as adults. They can find it exciting as a masturbatory stimulant, and may reach orgasm during masturbation only when confronted with the products of their own bowels. It is possible that the liking for contact with mud, which I described earlier, is a related phenomenon.

An extreme form of coprophilia is coprophagia (Greek *phagedaina, phag-*, eat) in which the individual actually eats his excrement or, rarely, the excrement of associates. Cases are known where a coprophiliac, on bringing himself for the first time to taste his own faeces, quickly experiences a consequent orgasm. Though anal intercourse is usually seen as the use of the anus as a vagina substitute, it is likely that some homosexuals who are partial to this form of union do so out of a desire to associate with the partner's faeces. It may be that certain tactile stimuli are identified as pleasurable, or that there is a childhood association with 'dirt' or 'filth' with the sex act itself. In a case where excreta are used for what the individual himself describes as self-defilement, such an association seems very likely.

EXHIBITIONISM

It is natural that men and women should, in some way, take pleasure in revealing their bodies. A well-cut garment is designed to do this. Women wearing see-through blouses or a plunging neckline are displaying their attributes; so are men with clinging suits and trousers cut to reveal the outline of the genitalia ('on which side does the gentleman dress?' – i.e., against which leg does the penis and scrotum hang, is the tailor's traditionally discreet enquiry). It is not, then, only men who can be associated with a desire to exhibit their sexuality in public. There is at least one example on record of a young woman in London who was visibly wearing no underwear in the street – her body was clearly seen through her clinging outer clothing – and she was charged with indecent exposure, a charge usually associated with men exhibiting their genitals to girls in the park!

The sexual exhibitionist, however, is not restricted to such relatively inoffensive acts. Instead, he likes to hide in an inconspicuous corner until the moment is ripe, and then he will suddenly reveal a penis (often erect) to the gaze of a lonely and startled female. He may hide behind the corner of a wall and come out in semi-darkness; he may rely on spatial isolation for security, and accost young girls in open daylight when he is sure no-one else is near enough to cause trouble. Sometimes he may expose himself from an upstairs (bedroom) window to a woman passing beneath. And some exhibitionists construct special garments with the crotch cut away, or even with no covering around the waist at all but merely a pair of cut-off 'dummy' trouser legs that end above the knee, where they are tied with laces and concealed beneath an overcoat or mac.

This form of exhibitionist, who approaches his target and then opens his coat for a moment, is known as a flasher. He is not uncommon; indeed this is the commonest of all the sex offences for which prosecutions are brought. He is also a figure of fun, and no comedian fails to get a laugh for turning his back on the audience and mimicking the action of a quick flasher at work . . . but it is not so funny for the victim. Fear of rape, a very real fear in many areas, is in the minds of women who are confronted with a sexually active and exposed man in such circumstances and their situation is potentially frightening. Our ability to laugh whole-heartedly at the flasher is all very well, but it would be more appropriate to restore the balance with a show of concomitant sympathy for the target.

An exhibitionistic tendency is often manifest in normal marriages where large mirrors are installed along the bedroom walls or ceiling, but this fringe of the category takes us into the broad belt of normal behaviour and shows us how – in its context - exhibitionism may be said to derive from a harmless and wholesome desire to celebrate one's sexuality and to revel in the sight of a partner's body which becomes offensive only when it acquires the pathological overtones of an unwanted visual assault on an unsuspecting victim.

The habitual exhibitionist becomes disordered, to a greater or lesser extent, during his act. He may be breathing heavily or perspiring, and showing obvious signs of sexual excitement. Some seem to be clearly dazed or in a detached, trance-like state at the time and it would be interesting to know whether there is some hormonal control (like a flush of some gonadotrophic hormone, for instance), and – if so – whether private masturbation could be used to relieve the sexual sensations in a less disturbing fashion than exhibitionism itself.

VOYEURISM

It is true that mirrors on the wall are associated with a desire to show one's-self in the act of sex, but they are often more profoundly linked with a desire to watch what is going on. The sight of people indulging in sexual activities is for many people a stimulating one, and if the sight is of one's-self and one's love partner then we have what can be called 'autovoyeurism'.

A voyeur is someone who likes to watch others in the act of sex. Voyeurs may buy pornographic films or visit 'stag' cinemas where such things are shown. In some such sex theatres a continuous loop film will be on display, backed by a similar closed-loop sound track. You may see the face of a frantic female sucking with feigned passion on the penis of a man (usually of different skin colour) whilst unsynchronized sounds of gasping and whimpering emanate from loudspeakers. A procession of eager men enter the cinema; and a similar sequence of more subdued and satisfied clients leave at about the same rate.

Others see films made for the purpose of attracting a voyeuristic audience. *Deep Throat*, a blue movie with a severely over-stretched theme (the star character found that her clitoris had become misplaced from its normal site to an attachment low down in the gullet, and could only reach satisfaction by gulping down almost the entire shaft of an erect phallus) came close to giving respectability to such productions and was discussed at length in the quality press. But most such films are distinguished by their archness and unsubtlety (a fault so apparent in *Deep Throat* that it would certainly have been condemned as uninteresting and naïve had it been on any other subject). An example – just a quote at random from the output in recent years of the US West Coast – is a scene in which the woman 'star' is being mounted from beneath and from behind simultaneously, by two men distinguished by the almost routine look of contrived machismo superimposed on a blend of granite detachment and chronic embarrassment; we see a close-up of her pouting face as she mouths the words: 'Gee, fellers, can you feel your cocks touching inside my cunt 'n' arse?' and the audience sighs with understanding – either of the poignancy and depth of her feelings, or with the transparently contrived nature of the 'script'.

Other films feature acts of intercourse with animals, a pig being the current favourite, and there is a growing market in films of sex with children. In this case we have crossed the boundary from voyeurism into paedophilia, where it is not the fact of watching a film that is the prime stimulus, for it is only used as a substitute for sexual activity with a child. Many states are now outlawing the taking of pictures of a pornographic nature which feature children (Britain's law was passed in 1978), but child pornography has persisted as a 'growth industry' throughout the late 1970's. The repellence that one feels at the prospect is occasionally matched by the reactions of the participants: cases are on record of men who have fantasized about sex with minors, only to be disgusted with themselves when presented with an opportunity to turn the fantasy into reality.

The exploitation of voyeurism has given rise to many forms of sex display on stage, for a paying audience. The classical example is the sex night-club in some exotic capital, such as the night-clubs in the aptly-named capital Bangkok, where group sex is featured and – more often – when gyrating women dancing to Western pop music simulate masturbation, either manually or with a substitute penis or some outrageous alternative, like a plastic bust of a political figure in one extreme case. In California, sex night-clubs underwent a sudden proliferation in the late 1960's and early 1970's, when shows were featured on stage and it was difficult to ascertain whether the shows were simulated or live. In Britain there have been some prosecutions for similar offences, and the argument as to whether the copulation was real or faked has caused more than a few moments of mirth in court. I recall one such episode when, failing to get an obscenity charge to stick, it was decided to prosecute for an infringement of the hygiene regulations because of reports that topless waitresses used to dip their breasts into customers' glasses of beer.

'At no time did any part of my anatomy enter the beer,' said a defendant during that trial, an interesting comment on the ludicrous extent to which the law seems to become ensnared with definitions when dealing with such fringe areas as these.

Elsewhere in Europe the tastes of voyeurs are met by sex-show clubs, in cities such as Amsterdam and Hamburg, featuring, as one example proclaims, *Real Fucky-Fucky* every hour on the hour, like a chiming clock. Not everyone who goes is clinically voyeuristic, there being a steady stream of married people – often going together to watch – and the opinion of many of the proprietors of such palaces of fun and frolic is that middle-aged couples go to learn new tricks, and to find unexpected possibilities that might enrich their own sex lives later on. Here too, then, the clearly deviant activity of replacing normal heterosex with the voyeur's view of someone else doing it, merges into the realm of normal marital experience.

FROTTEURISM

The frotteur is one who wishes to rub himself, often against a part of the body of a love-object usually of the opposite sex. In its milder forms, frotteurism (also known as frottage) is expressed by rubbing against people in a crowded subway or a bus, the breasts and buttocks being favourite targets for men in crowds. The grabbing of a woman's behind is not uncommon in the Mediterranean countries in crowded public places, and the intimate dancing of what was once called the 'cheek to cheek' variety gives many people an opportunity to arouse themselves through frotteurism. At this level the phenomenon is socially acceptable, and dancing of the traditional intimate kind – on a dance-floor, with others looking on – is a form of mild sexuality which allows many individuals to enact a watered-down version of a fantasized love-life, the boss with his secretary, for example, or the office-boy with the seductive head of personnel.

The phenomenon merges into cushion masturbation in women at one end of the scale, and into partialism at the other. Some married men like to rub the tip of the glans backwards and forwards against the thigh or buttocks of their wives and in some cases this can take the place of normal intercourse, the individual finding himself unable to achieve orgasm through any other means than his frotteurism. Of course, we have overlapping here too: masturbation itself may involve rubbing of the same kind, notably in women, and loving caresses fit into the same general category too. Indeed it could be argued that it is the sensual caress of a mother (or father) on a child's skin that teaches him to select this option as a source of sexual pleasure as an adult – a convenient explanation for the origins of frotteurism which says nothing about why some people do develop the behaviour into an adult form, whereas others do not.

DEVIANT SEXUAL CONTACT

This is a difficult group of deviations to categorize; many forms of sexual activity could be put under such a heading. But there are three specific activities which can act as intercourse substitutes, by replacing normal genital contact with mouth or anal stimulation. They are the use of the anus as a substitute vagina, the mouth as a substitute vagina, or the tongue as a surrogate penis. These three – buggery, fellatio and cunnilingus respectively – have too much in common to be separated under section headings, and that is why they appear here under a single none-too-satisfactory sub-title.

i) Buggery

This term refers to anal intercourse, i.e. the copulation of a man with a sexual partner of either sex through the anus itself rather than through a vagina. The rectum becomes a vaginal substitute. The term itself derives from the French *bougre*, (from mediaeval Latin *Bulgarus*, an 11th century heretic reputedly given to the practice, who came from that part of Eastern Europe which since became known as Bulgaria), and is also referred to as sodomy – incorrectly, as it happens. The latter term (named after the depraved town of Sodom, see Genesis, xviii, xix) actually covers anal intercourse between males, and specifically excludes buggery of a woman, whilst it also includes intercourse between a human and an animal which is described later under the section heading *Bestiality*.

Buggery is common amongst male homosexuals, where there is also an element of sadomasochism and coprophilia. But it is not confined to homosexual intercourse. Many of the neurotic wives who seek advice from marriage guidance counsellors complain of incessant demands for buggery from their husbands, and a man who insists on this is revealing poorly-controlled homosexual impulses. To a woman geared up to heterosex, buggery is an uncomfortable and unsatisfying form of copulation as well as being illegal in many countries.

Some men prefer buggery when the vaginal musculature of their partner is lax, the anal sphincter muscles providing a tight and gripping ring of tissue. But it is fair to add that some women prefer intercourse this way, considering it satisfying from sadomasochistic impulses, *q.v.*, and often claiming that it has strong contraceptive benefits as some form of justification for what is perceived as being an unnatural (and therefore guiltily-expressed) desire.

In adult passive homosexual men, the anus may become dilated with repeated penetration, resulting in soiled underwear and a certain degree of hardening of the normally delicate skin of the anus itself. Similar changes are seen in women participants, of course; and primary lesions from syphilis at this site are known by doctors to be associated with buggery. Such cases – even when they are strictly illegal – are not, of course, reported to the authorities for prosecution! In this sense, the judgement of society is far ahead of the intolerant and absurdly restrictive nature of the law on the point. No-one suspecting VD should delay in reporting it for an instant, merely because of the possibility that habitual buggery might come to light as a result.

There is a third term often used as a synonym for buggery, and it appears as an equivalent for that term in many authoritative textbooks. This is pederasty (Greek *pais, paidos*, boy + *erastés*, lover), and as its derivation makes unambiguously clear, this term applies to the use of a boy as a lover. He can be sexually seduced by a man indulging in buggery, of course, but this is not necessary and indeed the seducer may be a woman. Pederasty (or *paederasty*, as it was until recently spelled) is therefore a synonym not for buggery, but for paedophilia, which is described later.

The only term for anal intercourse, then, is buggery; the use of pederasty or sodomy as exact equivalents is incorrect though the misuse of these terms is now very widespread.

ii) *Fellatio*

The stimulation of an erect penis by mouth is a common practice and occurs in many marriages as an adjunct to foreplay (the exact incidence being around 40-45%, according to estimates, though I do not doubt that in an era where oral sex seems to be a new fashion, the percentage is very likely increasing). There are several different means available. The penis is often kissed in a fulsome manner, suction being applied to the sensitive area around the foreskin and beneath the glans. Much direct stimulation can be applied by gentle licking from the root of the penis towards its apex, whilst the ultimate in fellatio (or 'gobbling' as the vernacular has it) is always believed to be the taking of the whole end of the glans into the mouth rather than the vagina – the *Deep Throat* situation, as it might be dubbed. The flickering action of a tongue around the head of the penis in this way produces considerable pleasure, and some men find the ultimate ecstasy in this form of communion. When that is the case it could be described as a deviation – i.e., where it replaces heterosexual copulation.

Prostitutes offer this service, and it is popular amongst male homosexuals. But many men say that the reality of fellatio does not match the excitement of fantasizing about something which is essentially 'all in the mind', a well known form of sexual self-titillation.

Many women like to perform the act, even desire it intensely. Here it is a manifestation of masochism, and the possibility of ejaculation into the mouth is typically described by both partners as being associated in their minds with defilement. When this takes the place of intercourse, we certainly have a form of deviation which many people would find disgusting and repugnant even to think about. That fact alone makes it seem all the more desirable to those who are kinky for it.

iii) Cunnilingus

I have said that something less than half of marriages feature fellatio during normal love-making; but it seems that men are a little more 'adventurous' than women – some 60% of men practise oral stimulation (cunnilingus) on their wives.

Often this is nothing more than kissing or licking of the areas around the genitalia, the erogenous zones on the thighs and around the perianal skin. But usually the tongue enters the soft area of tissue between the labia; gently parted by the tongue, the inner lips (*labia minora*) become accessible, the clitoris itself can be sought out and stimulated, and the tongue can (in the manner of a substitute penis) flicker into the vagina itself.

For some people this is a particularly exquisite form of connection; for most, however, it is a prelude to intercourse. Once again the fantasy is often better than the reality – women may say that they like to imagine passionate body kisses extending to the genitals, but find it somewhat coarse or unsubtle when they do.

Quite what we are to make of this fixation on fantasized versions of love-making as something idealized and special I am none too sure. Certainly a subtle, feather-soft, fleeting approach is more likely to entrance a lover than a too-direct and clumsy approach; the majority of women seem to agree with that!

Simultaneous fellatio and cunnilingus are known in sexual code as position 69 (or *soixante-neuf*) and the practice is much sought after by the young these days. Sexual veterans will say that the practice (known in prostitutes' circles as 'frenching') is a poor substitute for conventional copulation, though a first-class prelude to it. And of course it is only when the habit persists to the exclusion of copulatory heterosex that we can begin to consider it as a deviant activity. To those couples who resort to the practice regularly I can only apologize that it has raised its head in a chapter on deviant sex, for in its context it is of course nothing of the sort.

NECROPHILIA

The idea of copulating with the dead is one that most people find repellent.

The objection is unlikely to be a moral one (the victim of a sexual assault in this case is the one category of person who cannot be harmed by the act) but is related to deep-seated fears of death itself which we nurture. Necrophilia, like rape, can only be committed by a man, for anatomical reasons – you would need an erect penis to do it – but it is difficult to imagine how intercourse with a corpse could satisfy anything but the most depraved and deviant personality. Yet the condition is known.

Clearly it is workers in morgues who would have the greatest opportunity to indulge such a fancy, though conversations with them do not reveal much in the way of evidence that the practice is common. Sexual ecstasy involving contact with a corpse is known to be associated with amateur dabblers in magic who desecrate graves and open coffins, though this is more likely to be the thrill of an association with the corpse than actual copulation with it. But it may be that the fantasy is more appealing than the reality, in this case too.

Brothels sometimes feature a prostitute's room in the form of a morgue or a tomb, the woman herself being laid on a 'marble'-like slab and made up with cosmetics to look blue and mottled, like a corpse (or at least, like the client's idea of one). The idea of association with decay and death has its roots partly in coprophilia, and partly in the sadomasochistic personality described later. But it is certainly likely that intercourse with a living person made up to look like a corpse is more common than true necrophilia.

PAEDOPHILIA

This condition involves the use of a child as a sex partner. Often the child is a boy used by a male homosexual, in which case the condition is pederasty, but young girls may also be sought and violated in a sex act. The offence is regarded by society as serious, though the seriousness is hard to demonstrate. Most children have sexual feelings and responses, and the neurotic personality of a paedophile exploits these feelings, or imagines that they are being exploited. There is little evidence that, short of wounding or physical damage, paedophilia causes undue long-term harm to children; it is a sickness of adults and our disgust comes from imagining how we would have to feel in order to do the same thing to our own children, rather than associating with the blameless and untarnished mind of a child who is coerced into an act that its young mind does not fully understand or fear.

Many of the things we do to children as a normal and everyday part of modern life are probably as harmful. The regular exposure of children to incessant acts of violence on television is certainly cumulative in its effect and is one aspect of contemporary society that I find horrifying. If we had a revulsion about all the aspects of life that can harm a child, and protected children from scenes of violence as assiduously as we like to prevent them from seeing sexual items on television, and with anything like the repulsion we feel for paedophilia, there would be more balance in our attitudes. An instance of our double-thinking is the way we refuse to sanction any form of bad language on television, just in case children are – in some unspecified way – 'harmed' by it. We are all familiar with swearing, and there is not a smidgin of evidence nor any reasonable supposition that words can warp or damage the young mind ... so our desire to protect children from unwanted forces is overdue for a shake-out and a sensible reappraisal before we single out paedophilia, and only that, for undisguised hostility.

The ways in which children can be misused sexually is astonishing. There has been a case in recent years where a prostitute soliciting for clients through 'normal' channels has actually been acting for her own children, and submitting them to deviant practices with paying clients.

Obviously there is something that attracts a certain kind of neurotic mentality to the purity or the innocence of a young person, but in this case too it is likely that the allure of fantasy transcends reality. One such case was the prosecution in July 1978 of a British viscount's son for sexually interfering with a child. The man, Richard Bigham, apparently had a penchant for child porn literature. Most of the 44-year-old Mr Bigham's literature arrived from Denmark, and contained pictures of children engaged in acts of sex with adults. He was at that time a member of a British group calling itself PIE (Paedophile Information Exchange) campaigning for the right to undertake sex with minors, and was regularly receiving pornographic magazines by mail.

Eventually he was attracted by an advertisement which introduced him to a contact in Manchester in North-West Britain. There, for a fee of £70 (about $140) he was introduced to a woman whose two daughters, aged six and ten, were then encouraged to take part in sexual activities with him. He had a series of photographs taken of the session.

In the event, he says, the pictures were never ordered. At the end of the session, Mr Bigham gave some chocolates to the children and then left. Later he said: 'I have never before had sexual experience with a minor. I became horrified at what I had done. I went to Sussex and had a bonfire in a wood with my pornographic collection [of magazines, books and 8mm films]. I resigned from the Exchange and wrote to Denmark cancelling deliveries of porn. Before, I found porn with young girls to my liking, after, I found it repulsive.'

Yet paedophilia is not usually carried to such extremes. A liking for contact with youngsters is a strong motivation behind some youth workers who become involved with physical activities with children. I know of one Sunday-school teacher who has been observed by a colleague to sit little girls on his lap and stroke their legs, producing a sexual response which in some cases seemed to involve orgasm. There is a telephone worker who is known to kiss and fondle little boys, sometimes in public. And at least one senior churchman undertakes masturbation parties with boy scouts willing to follow to the bitter end his increasingly intimate descriptions of sexual behaviour which he introduces as being part and parcel of his 'youth work and social function'.

What is disturbing is that the number of individuals in each of those categories is high (there is no way of knowing how high, but I would be interested to know how many pulse-rates went up as readers lighted on this section). Certainly the number of adults who remember some form of paedophile assault is surprisingly high. On the good side is the fact that little long-term harm seems to come of it all, at least where the children are concerned; it is not a deeply wounding experience for most of them, though it is clearly an assault for all that and certainly could have disastrous consequences. Much of the trauma derives from the way in which shocked parents react when faced with the news - that, rather than the act, may distress and upset a child.

The bad side is that these disturbed and potentially dangerous men create unrest in all youth workers when the topic comes up for discussion. The paedophile does not undertake his seduction of a child because of well-considered moral judgements; he would act the same way no matter what the consequences. Paedophiles who have a sadistic nature have not only set out to harm children sexually, but in many cases the victims have even been killed - and no-one who is aware of the horrifying details of the lust murder of a child is going to assume for an instant that there is somehow a pure and noble motivation behind less devastating versions of paedophilia. But many youth workers (very likely the great majority) have no sexual interest in their charges, and no deep-seated ulterior motive in undertaking their work. These people are guided by straightforward motives of humanity and altruism, and it is regrettable that such a career also attracts an unsavoury and sexually deviant sector of humanity.

How may you tell the difference, if you are a concerned and caring parent? There is, of course, no way. The deviant spectrum ranges in my own experience from a drunkard on the dole to a bishop. It is a sad fact of life that our increasingly neurotic and frustrating life-style is doing nothing to lower the proportion of the sexual deviants in our midst - and the paedophile (at least one of whom works to this day as a Santa Claus, snuggling little girls on his lap and dismissing the boys with a curt word and a gesture) is no longer as rare as we all might like to think.

SADOMASOCHISM

Here we step with deceptive ease into a difficult concept, one which is often nothing more than a question of degree. Sadism (from the Marquis of Sade, author of *Les Crimes de L'Amour*) is the desire to obtain sexual satisfaction from the inflicting of pain on others; masochism (after the Austrian novelist Masoch who described a case of this sort) is the desire to experience humiliation or pain inflicted by someone else as a means of sexual gratification. Both seem bizarre. The spectacle of a respectable married man pleading with a friend to hit him on the buttocks with a surf-board, for example, seems amusing; the notion of a prostitute being paid to hit a client with a whip (a version of masochism known as flagellation) seems to most people extraordinary.

Yet in all love-making there is an essence of sadomasochism. Those hard kisses and nibbles may be – out of their context – painful enough to seem sadomasochistic; indeed the overwhelming tumbling climax of sexual orgasm itself may be sufficiently 'painful' to amount to a sadomasochistic experience. Passion is not gentle. And its effects often merge into the periphery of sadomasochistic sex.

To the non-sadist, the practices of the true deviant in this category must seem astonishing. People may be bound in ropes or chains; they may be whipped or caned; sometimes images of the utmost violence are involved. At the greatest extreme we find lust murder, where a victim may be systematically sexually violated and put to death in the most degrading and cruel circumstances. It is not unknown for a killer to masturbate over his dying victim, and there have even been suggestions (from the Vietnam war, and very likely from elsewhere) of sadists seeking sexual contact with the blood and gore of a massacre victim – an extreme form of sadistic necrophilia.

There is an interesting connection here between battle and rape. The pressures of warfare often act as a stimulant in the purely sexual sense, which is why rape is so often associated with warfare. And there are certainly subliminal codes of criteria that select wounds and wounding along with rape, the vagina and a red rose (or other flower) as jointly symbolic of sexual pleasure.

The excitement of sexual ecstasy produced in a wartime attack is regarded as manly, virile and thoroughly commendable. Yet the same proclivity in peacetime gives rise to the most damaging and tragic of all sexual deviations; a strange contrast, and an intriguing example of how circumstances alter the very substance of the degree of acceptance we attach to such phenomena.

It is said (and to an extent I incline towards this viewpoint) that sadistic punishment, like the prolonged humiliation of children by their parents and the perverse taunting of pupils by their prefects – the Tom Brown syndrome – has a sexual component. In the case of petticoat discipline, in which an erring apprentice or an office junior male is made to dress up in frilly women's clothing (sometimes including sanitary towels as an added token), the sexual overlay is clearly evident.

Of course, we are all familiar with this concept in the form of a 'persecution complex'. What this is traditionally taken to mean is a state of mind in which a person feels he or she is being persecuted by outsiders, and in this sense the term describes a form of paranoia. What is being experienced is a delusion of persecution – a conviction that cruelty is being meted out when in fact it is not.

But often this term is misapplied. The persecution, for many people, is not 'imagined' at all but a genuine response to actual sadistic persecution. It is surprising that we have been so slow to recognize that many people do suffer a strong desire to persecute, and to hand out sadistic punishment, to others.

In hierarchical systems, the office sadist is not uncommon. Individuals who complain that 'their lives are being made a misery' are assumed to be suffering from a delusion of persecution until it becomes apparent that others are suffering in the same way at the hands of the same individual. The persecution complex is there, right enough; but not in the form of anyone *imagining* they were being discriminated against at all – the complex is in the mind of the persecutor, who has a persistent desire to cause difficulties and to make underlings suffer. In many cases it is the weakest, least resilient individuals who are selected for the greatest emphasis by the sadist. He or she is deliberately bullying the underdog.

Sexual sadism could certainly account for many of these episodes. They are common enough – almost certainly there are far more people who actually enjoy bullying and persecuting their inferiors than there are people who delude themselves into experiencing persecution when none has been suffered. At present the usual answer to someone whose life is being made a misery in the office is to say, 'Are you sure you're not imagining things?' I would like to think that we could become more attuned to the incidence of pathological sadism in society, so that we would be quicker to recognize the person whose main aim in striving to improve his or her lot in the professional or business world is to live out inner sadistic neuroses.

Certainly the likelihood that we are witnessing a form of deviant sexual activity (and a diagnostic feature of someone with a desire to persecute would be a repressed or deviant sex-life) could account for many of the episodes involving disturbed and unhappy employees who feel they are being 'got at'. One case that is cited as an example of sexual repression emerging as true sadism concerns a Victorian mother who made her children sit at table until she had finished her lunch, and who regularly ate so slowly that her daughter was late for registration at school and was consequently punished. Opinions vary as to whether this is a true sexual phenomenon; but this form of sadism (which seems so frustrating to the victim since no-one would ordinarily accept that it could possibly be anyone else's fault) has innumerable echoes in the world of work.

A typical modern example is the office manager who uses his rank to hire and fire indiscriminately, and whose word is accepted because of his rank. This office tyrant, scourge of so many junior staff, finds perpetual excitement in bringing unhappiness into the lives of others and the current tendency for us to assume that all feelings of persecution are delusions in the minds of the people he is persecuting does nothing but support him in his situation.

If sadism has a societal role that has gone largely unnoticed, so too does masochism. The hen-pecked husband is a well-known feature of all societies, and is a figure of sympathy as much as of derision. More often than not, however, he was well aware of his dominating wife before he married her – and he enjoys every aspect of the relationship. This version of the syndrome has strong masochistic implications. The wife enjoys her role as (sadistic) persecutor, and the husband revels in his submissive niche in true masochistic style. There is an office counterpart, too; some of the victims welcome sadistic bullying in hierarchies of employment. Indeed it can be argued that some of the schoolboys whose careers are marked by bullying from the older boys encourage the activity by subconsciously directed misdemeanour intended to attract sadistic responses.

In other fields, masochism has been wrongly identified as a religious experience. The flagellation of young nuns in convents where physical rigour was the rule produced orgasms which were interpreted as being the ecstasy of a religious enlightenment, and there is often a hint of self-humiliation in religious observance and the strictures it entails: Pope Pius XIII wore old and badly patched garments beneath his magnificent robes of office as a gesture of essential humility and unworldliness, but there is here too a masochistic element and the fact that it is occurring in someone whose office compels him to celibacy and sexual abstinence is significant. The hair-shirt, then, has a clear sexual origin and so do many of the rituals of self-debasement practised in the name of religion.

Masochism is frequently found in young people as a masturbatory stimulant. Sometimes these come to light when a youth dies, strangled by a cord as part of the masochistic apparatus he had assembled. One case, indicative of the tragic consequences of this outwardly innocuous pastime, was of a fourteen-year-old boy of a middle social class family (his father a bank official of median grade) who was found at the end of the parents' weekend holiday to have hanged himself in the attic of their home. He was dressed in female attire taken from his mother's and sister's closets, and had tightly bound his legs together with twine. He had fixed a gag over his mouth, and had kneeled down with a noose running from his neck to the rafters above. On the floor were several mildly pornographic books and magazines.

He had masturbated whilst in this position, apparently stopping as orgasm drew near in order to prolong the sensation, and had been leaning into the noose in order to increase the sense of bondage and restriction. Unfortunately the combined effect of the gag and the increasing circulatory restriction of the tightening noose caused him to lose his balance; the cords around his knees stopped him from regaining his position and he had twisted awkwardly in the noose.

Strangulation was by now inevitable as the noose tightened and – held against its knot – it remained in position as a tight ligature around his neck. The boy threshed about in vain attempts to recover his balance, disturbing some of the objects nearby as he did so, but he died of strangulation and the necropsy examination confirmed that he had not in fact reached that final orgasm at the time of his death.

The extremes of sadomasochism are those involving the ultimate assault, namely lust murder. The gratification here centres on the drawn-out, ritualistic killing of a victim with concomitant sexual celebration of the intense suffering caused. Sometimes the victim is adult, as in the ritualized murder of Sharon Tate in California; but the victims may also be children, for example in the British Moors Murders involving Ian Brady and Myra Hindley.

But can we find echoes of a sadistic attitude towards children in ordinary life? In many ways this particular sickness is one of the commonest of all perversions. A desire to induce deliberate fright in children, through the presentation to them of frightening and lurid images, is found in a host of different guises – stories of death and destruction in fairy-tales, for example; the hideous monsters of children's television and the deliberately sadistic story-lines of horror and war comics. It is said that children 'love' frightening stories and programmes, that they like to be scared out of their wits by some hideous witch who steals into their rooms at night, or threatened by images of monsters and ghouls portrayed in cartoon feature-films.

This is patent idiocy, and the fact that we fail to recognize this instills into many young minds an unnatural capacity to accept violence and unpleasantly inhuman activities which lays down sound foundations for antisocial behaviour. Telling frightening fairy-stories is nothing more than a sickness of the mind which has often been perpetrated by such deviant personalities as Hans Andersen and Lewis Carroll (Charles Dodgson) who – though they seemed to be harmless eccentrics, good at reciting tales for children – were actually sex deviants with a tendency towards paedophilia and sadism.

Far from using such examples as justification for the continuance of this dangerous and unbalanced habit of telling disturbing stories that implant images of violence and insecurity in a young mind, we should hasten to recognize it for the sickness it really represents. A future generation of children that does not have to undergo the ritual of saturation with these sadistic images will repay us, certainly with gratitude, and possibly with more liberal and gentle ideals than those we have ourselves acquired.

CHAPTER TEN

DEVIANT SEX IN THE ANIMAL WORLD

Many accounts of sexuality lay great store by the myth that man is the only sexual pervert there is. The view is that, if someone says to you 'you make love (or have sex) like an animal', it ought to be the greatest compliment of all: only making love like mankind is perverted and crude.

This isn't true. You may argue that man's level of intellectual awareness sets him apart from the other animals on our planet and so fits him uniquely to misapply his lusts and direct his urges into channels he knows to be 'wrong', but all animals acquire their own sets of criteria by which they select options, and so they all show levels of consciousness that allow them to make decisions. That is what life *is*.

Certainly there are many examples of sexual behaviour that we can see as parallel to the manifestations of human sexuality. Courtship is replaced by outright aggressive warfare in many species. The crocodile and mink are two examples from the reptile and mammal world respectively which feature marked aggression as a necessary part of foreplay. The crocodile male attacks his mate with vigour, snapping his jaws and rushing at her with mouth open in a display of loud, roaring aggression. The culmination of the fight (for that's exactly what it is) has the female lying on her back with the aroused male astride her body. Like other reptiles, crocodiles do not possess a vagina and penis in the sense humans understand. Instead they feature a cloaca, a common duct for excretion and reproduction. The male possesses a protrusion which acts like a penis, and this is plunged into the mate's cloaca at the climax of copulation. This done, he crawls weakly away and the female struggles to her feet, later to deposit her eggs.

Mink are similarly aggressive when they pair. Here too the male approaches in warlike fashion, snapping his jaws and biting at the female. She gives as good as she gets, fighting back with eagerness. To an observer the situation has the hallmarks of a full-blooded attack and it would not seem in the least likely that the two animals would be engaged in anything so enjoyable as sexual communion.

But that is what is really behind the fighting and aggressive behaviour.

After the female has been mounted (and she shows every sign of enjoying that procedure) the two become calmer by far – though the preliminaries may have lasted many hours.

There is no absolute 'need' for such behaviour in biological terms; a less aggressive form of mate selection would be perfectly in order. But the animals who fight as part and parcel of their mating ritual do so in order to heighten sexuality, to increase their sensations, and to ensure that the level of stimulus is enough to guarantee successful fertilization. However you choose to define either term, you are witnessing 'pleasure in pain', a close counterpart to sadomasochistic behaviour in humans.

Masturbation occurs in animals too. It is known from studies of caged beasts in the zoo – monkeys sometimes cause embarrassment to parties of onlookers by masturbating (a trait that does not cause as much dismay in the onlookers if they belong to a single group; thus, Grannie will be shocked if she attends with the whole family, but amused if she is there with some other older women from a social group) and it has been believed – erroneously – that the behaviour is a response to the boredom of captivity.

But many animals masturbate purely for sexual pleasure. Dolphins will do so in the open sea, for instance, as well as directing their genitals at the inward rush of circulating warm water in a dolphinarium pool as a means of pleasurable stimulation. Lions have been seen in safari parks to lie on their backs, the males then manipulating their genitalia in masturbation. They are known to do this in the wild, too.

And elephants, who have such a delightfully anthropomorphic love-life, use mutual masturbation as a normal adjunct to pair-bonding. With their trunks they will fondle and stimulate each other's genitals, sometimes heterosexually, but occasionally in acts of lesbianism. Male elephants prefer to use their own trunk for masturbation (but the female's trunk does not reach to her clitoris as easily as the male's extends to embrace his penis).

It is interesting to see how deer males masturbate, for here the sensitive area is the velvet that covers the antlers. Adult deer will rub their antlers against vegetation and produce ejaculation shortly after commencing to masturbate. This explains how the size of those antlers corresponds to sexual prowess in some way, so that they are there for purposes of advertisement, not attack. Much of the display between males is of a symbolic nature, anyway, and is not intended to inflict real damage on an opponent (other than temporary wounding to the ego, that is). But what the deer do reveal is frotteurism in animals, which is itself interesting.

Other species use physical aids for self-stimulation. The porcupine female spends some time in a state of increasing sexual excitement, and will adopt a branch as a stimulant. Propping it between her hind legs, it becomes a surrogate mate for her and by rubbing it against the clitoris and the mouth of the vagina she produces a strong sexual stimulation for herself. Males too, finding a stick that has been ridden by a female, will stand astride it and use it as a prosthesis in a similar fashion, thrusting and rubbing against it in typical sexual movements.

Homosexual mating in birds is an equally well-documented phenomenon. Ravens, being scarce and tending to live in well-scattered communities, will pair up if two females are unable to find a male as mate. Then one will adopt a submissive role, the partner becoming dominant and masculinized in behaviour. The two lesbian crows will show all the courtesies and loving gestures that are normally expressed between heterosexual partners, and will even make a nest and lay (sterile) eggs in it.

Things become interesting when a male turns up and takes a fancy to one of the females. They may well court and mate – but in a case like this it is quite common for the rejected female to refuse to relinquish the earlier relationship and insist on staying on. The loss of lesbian affection does not deter her at all, and more often than not the male will also breed with her in a typical *ménage à trois*.

Though homosexuality in animals is associated with overcrowding and with what could be described as 'neurosis-inducing circumstances', it does have a clear functional role in some situations. The ravens, for instance, are able to find expression for their sexual desires through enforced homosexuality, only to resume normal heterosexual relationships when conditions are suitable.

But among fish, the ten-spined stickleback supplies an interesting example of a sex change, which enables males to find mates among their own sex if there are not enough females to go round. If a tank of males is kept apart during the springtime mating season, a proportion of the males will adopt the mottled coloration of a sexually stimulated female and will show all the movements typical of females. They will even simulate egg-laying movements in the gravel at the bottom of the tank.

A parallel situation will be found in a tank of females. Here, occasional individuals will take on male behaviour and will go through the sexual dance of males and even set about making nests (usually an exclusively masculine duty). The aberrant behaviour in either sex disappears rapidly if the populations are once again mixed.

Unisexual groups are found in some animals, of which the red deer is an excellent example. As the mating season approaches, the males begin to round up harems of females, the stag becoming selected by virtue of his aggressive and dominant behaviour and also through the size of his spread of antlers – stags from whom the antlers were experimentally removed show a far less successful record of harem-collecting.

After the rutting season is over, the males tend to disperse, whilst the females remain together in a formal, hierarchical 'family' unit. The order of dominance is maintained by gentle chastisement and the group is led by an essentially benevolent senior doe.

But this is not a homosexual group, of course. The deer adopt this form of societal structuring because it suits them; it is a form of community which is taught to younger members, and becomes perpetrated as a dependable orthodoxy that reflects the life-style of the species. The females live in unisexual communities, then; but they are not homosexually motivated.

The intensity of sex drive in animals leads them to persist in copulation under the most exacting circumstances. Thus, once a male frog has attached himself to his mate the embrace persists until the act of copulation is completed. It has been shown that if the body of a copulating male frog is severed at the level of the armpit, as it were, the head and forelimbs remain firmly and determinedly attached as though nothing had happened.

Copulation in the praying mantis features behaviour that seems to be the ultimate in animal sadism, for not only does she consume her mate as a rule (this is found in other species, some spiders and scorpions being among them) but this act of heterosexual cannibalism starts before mating is complete.

At the commencement of copulation, the male approaches the female from behind and what happens then has all the hallmarks of lust murder – the female is likely to turn sharply round and sever her mate's head with her jaws. This does not kill the male outright (why should it? The loss of the brain and main organs of sense does not make any immediate difference to the cell communities that make up the rest of the body) and he continues to inseminate his partner.

The cannibalistic behaviour of the mantis was first detailed by J. H. Fabre shortly before the First World War. He showed then how a laboratory community of the insects could be successfully maintained on a diet of crickets which were renewed twice daily. A colony of female mantids adapted well to the situation, and Fabre watched them mature and grow fat on their diet as the breeding season approached.

It was then that he observed a change in the behaviour of the insects. They seemed to be 'inflamed' and to react to the visible signs of swelling on the abdomen that indicated that the ovaries were ripe. Fabre says that: 'the swelling of the ovaries perverted my colony (of mantids) and they were infected with an insane desire to devour each other.' He described how they began to display in front of each other, rising into the spectral position with the talon-like front claws raised in a threatening attitude and ready for attack. The insects moved their heads from side to side, ('insulting each other' as Fabre says) and then one of them flashed out a claw, as a fencer might do in a fight between humans. The adversary waited a moment before making a riposte; and so the fencing continued until one of the rivals was wounded.

At this, she retired from the battle and the victor moved away to feed and recover from the encounter. In some cases Fabre saw that the female mantids fought to the death; the victor would hold the vanquished tightly in her graceful claws and start to eat her, commencing at the back of the neck and discarding only the wings. This was not a result of jealousy, for there were no males as rival targets for the allegiance of the female mantids. It was not a consequence of hunger, either, for the colonies were kept well provided with an abundant supply of crickets for food.

During the mating season, the devouring of her mate by a mantis female appeared. Fabre says that he watched the insects pair off, the male bowing his head and raising his thorax, looking intently into the face of his chosen partner. He awaits some form of acceptance signal which he clearly has the criteria to identify (but which Fabre could not recognize) and then approaches his mate, opening his wings in an ecstatic form of tremor. Slowly and deliberately he mounts her from behind and they stay sexually united for some five hours.

At the end of that time, Fabre observed the separating insects to, as he graphically put it, 'become one flesh in a much more intimate fashion'. The female seized her mate by the back of his neck and devoured his head; then continued down the succulent body, leaving just the wings behind as inedible. Fabre assumed that this was a habit brought on by captivity, but others have reported that similar behaviour occurs in wild mantis colonies. More remarkable is the observation that the decapitation of the male by his mate may take place at the commencement of copulation. Even if it happens so early, the decapitated male continues to complete the act of sexual union and remains in position on the female until insemination is complete, then she discards him and continues to devour what remains.

There is one biological purpose behind this. It is only the brain which can decide a male to reject the female and to discontinue the courtship and mating procedure. If this is the case, then there would be a clear evolutionary advantage in removing the head at the outset, relying on the somatic mechanisms that remain to continue mating as an automatic consequence.

Other animals have similar propensities: thus if the brain of certain amphibians is destroyed experimentally, the male animal will begin to enter a ritual of mating behaviour in or out of the mating season. So, though the conscious brain plays a vital part in selecting and recognizing a mate, it is clear that the occasions when a decision is made to reject a mate – decisions reached by the brain – can be controlled by decapitation. It is a drastic remedy, and one found rarely in the animal world. There would be little benefit in evolving such a system, in the sense that (though it suits the selected female mate well enough) it would eliminate one important means of discrimination against an unwanted partner, and this selection procedure is part and parcel of maintaining breeding between acceptable and wholesome pairs.

These courtship selection procedures are a mainstay of animal and human societies, and a strong force behind evolutionary progress, and maintaining the strength of the germ line. They often feature non-copulatory sex, paraphilias as they are known, and apart from the specific instances of masturbation, sadomasochism, *ménage* situations (pluralism) and what can only be construed as lust murder, which I have mentioned, the foreplay that dogs indulge in covers most of the ground in parallel with human activities – from coprophilia (some dogs love to roll in dung) and cunnilingus, to sadism (a minority of dogs are inborn bullies, and bully for the sake of it) and fellatio.

Man is not alone in deviant sex. What is true, however, is that man has a unique proclivity for electing to prefer non-copulatory sex in some situations to the exclusion of the normal climax of love-making. Animals seem less given to neuroses, and to psychological wounding, than mankind; and if homosexuality is to be construed as a necessary defence mechanism for our species against erroneous upbringing regimes we can safely argue that parental responsibilities are better performed by animal species that do not sophisticate their life-styles through ill-thought-out and premature changes consciously imposed on societal orthodoxies that exist for a biological purpose. Man is hampered by a spurious sense of wisdom that is more highly pronounced than his insight, and in that he is unique.

The courtship rituals maintain a level of courtesy and consideration in animal communities, too. Thus if you observe a community of rats, you will see the whole range of biological imperatives: mate selection, courtship, nest-building, the rearing of the young and a number of similar behavioural conventions designed to maintain the structure of rat society. Territories are respected. Pair-bonds are maintained. Families respond to a hierarchy which gives coherence to the whole.

There is one factor which can undermine all of this, and that is overcrowding. If colonies of rats are artificially maintained until they become overpopulated, the codes begin to break down. Young rats will invade neighbouring adults' territories and drive them out. Food will be stolen in a way that is rarely observed in normal circumstances. The hierarchies collapse, unwilling females are made to submit to the unwanted advances of males in a clear parallel to human rape. There are minor squabbles and outright fights, until the breakdown of the community causes unequal food distribution and the death from neglect or from wounding of many of the rats.

The phenomenon is a form of societal disintegration accompanied by 'civil war', and it arose from nothing more insidious than overcrowding. The analogy to human society at the breaking-point in overcrowded urban settlements is painfully obvious. And it is not sensible to argue that we are witnessing the disintegration of biological imperatives, either, since if that was the case we would see a lessening of activity as overcrowding caused less free space and led to a more circumscribed life-style for any individual rat. This is not what happens at all – the upsurge of activity is certainly a pre-programmed device that fits an overcrowded society to resist its own momentum towards high-density proliferation

I believe we must understand that a whole range of these hidden impulses have evolved in our subconscious. At present the rush towards societal discontent and the growth in subversive activity is no sinister political plot (or rather, it was not caused by any political movement), but is a manifestation of traits unleashed by the inhuman density towards which many people are forced to move. War is a form of mass suicide perpetrated by mankind as a means of emergency population control, and the breakdown we see today is nothing in the least new. Rape, pillage, mugging and murder flourished in overcrowded streets centuries ago as they occur today in a rat colony that is artificially overcrowded.

There are other clues from the world of mammals that may reveal unexpected and severely restricting effects on our sexuality from the pressures of an over-developed society. Rodents kept in experimental conditions of overcrowding are known to develop a series of responses that affect their sexuality. Sexual maturation may be altered. There may be a decline in the weight and size of accessory sex organs. Rates of ovulation have been observed to drop, as have rates at which fertilized egg-cells become implanted in the uterus. There is often an increase in the rate of foetuses failing to survive full term, and being miscarried. Furthermore, even when the young have been produced there is a raised incidence of cannibalism, and the mothers sometimes eat their litter of young, or part of it; the production of mother's milk can decrease to such an extent that the young do not thrive and may even become stunted, to die of malnutrition. In an extreme case, reproduction simply fails for a combination of these and other reasons.

We do not have to look far to discover parallels that are already appearing in our own society.

The birth-rate in many Western countries is already falling. In Britain it has reached a near zero-growth level. Against all predictions, there has been an emphasis on sexlessness in many different ways. Fashions have encouraged men and women to dress more and more like each other, in 'unisex' fashions. There has been a reduced emphasis on the secondary sexual characteristics, which produces a blending of gender roles – thus, the breasts themselves have been out of fashion, disguised by the cut of women's clothing and for some years no longer an attribute admired in contemporary film-stars. There is a rare degree of acceptance of intersexuality, and some pop-singers and culture heroes have increased their support by claiming to be bisexual. There has been a subtle change of terminology, so that the responsibilities and joys of family life have been described instead as being the 'chore' of housework that results from being 'stuck' at home with the children.

The trend in sex education has been distinctly unhealthy, saying nothing on the subject of romantic association and the courtship of pair-bond establishment, but dwelling as we have seen on the mechanisms of intercourse in isolation. There is an all-pervading desensitization of sexual relationships, which are centred increasingly on orgasm-attainment, and only that, to the detriment of foreplay and heightened response through sexual differentiation and sensuous stimulation.

The stress pressures on Western mankind have begun to result in a progressive reorientation of our attitudes away from the celebration of clearly marked sexuality into a watered-down physical form of short-term contact, based on fleeting and timed orgasms and a rejection of child-rearing at a subconscious level.

And let us be clear about this – there is no conspiratorial move to take some of the joy out of life, no politically inspired subversion that seeks to dampen down the rates of reproduction in Western society as a means of world domination by some other group. Far from it: I believe we are witnessing the far more sinister intervention of biological imperatives that will always step in when species over-reach themselves, when they impose stresses on their members which exceed their capacity to adapt. We are going to witness the progressive reduction of gender role learning, and if this continues, women will become increasingly unfeminine, with progressively smaller breasts, scantier periods, greater amounts of hair growth; and men will surely begin to become effeminate, with finer beards and a lessened sense of masculinity. There are already some reports (principally from the United States) that these changes are becoming detectable.

This is a prediction of the inevitability of gender blurring which follows a mismanaged society. It should not be construed as a call for a return to ill-considered Victorian values, or a desire to set the clock back. I have no such high-minded, or absurd, aim in view. What I wish to do is to point to an effect that we are actually witnessing, a form of social evolution that results from biological imperatives unleashed by our own behaviour. Whether it is good or bad is not the issue – it is simply a matter of being aware of what is happening to us, to our sexuality, and to our future.

SELECTED
BIBLIOGRAPHY

In order of reference

Swanson, H. D. (1974) *Human Reproduction: Biology and Social Change*, Oxford University Press, New York.

Winch, R. F. (1971) *The Modern Family*, Holt, Rinehart and Winston Inc., New York.

Ford, Brian J. (1970) Man as Microbe, in *Microbiology and Food*, 23-25, Northwood, London.

———————— (1976) criteria and feeding, in Food from the Microbe, *Microbe Power, Tomorrow's Revolution*, pp 60 *et seq*, Macdonald and Jane's, London; Stein and Day, NY.

———————— (1969) *Criteria for Selection* (lecture) reported in *Mensa Bulletin*, 39, 2, 1 December.

———————— (1977) *Areas of Ignorance*, Opening Address to Inter-Micro 77, King's College, Cambridge; BBC transcript broadcast 6 November.

———————— (1975) Microscopic Blind Spots, *Nature*, 258, 469, 11 December.

Kärrby, G. (1971) *Child Rearing and the Development of Moral Structure*, Almqvist & Wiksell, Stockholm.

Lieberman, B. (1971) *Human Sexual Behaviour - a book of readings*, Wiley and Sons Inc., New York.

Scholfield, M. (1973) *The Sexual Behaviour of Young Adults*, Allen Lane, London.

Ford, Brian J. (1974) *Period of Unrest* (transcript) in *The Listener*, 303-304, 7 March.
———————— (1978) Intelligence Quotient or Intelligence Type? *Nature*, 271 (5640) 7, 5 January.

Metz, C. W. (1959) Chromosome behaviour and cell-lineage in triploid and mosaic salivary glands of species hybrids in Sciara. *Chromosoma*, 10, 515, (and earlier papers by same author).

McClung, C. E. (1901) Notes on the accessory chromosome, *Anatomischer Anzeiger*, 20, 220-226.

Crew, F. A. E. (1965) *Sex-determination*, Methuen, London.

Ford, Brian J. (1973) The Lost Century, in *The Revealing Lens, Mankind and the Microscope*, Harrap, London, 68–90.

Hofacker (1828) *Über die Eigenschaften welche sich bei Menschen und Tieren auf die Nachkommenschaft vererben mit besonderer Rücksicht auf die Pferdezucht*, Tubingen.

Salder (1830) *The Law of Population*, London, in Crew, F. A. E., *q.v.*

Starkweather (1883) *The Law of Sex*, London, in Crew, F. A. E., *q.v.*

Seiler, J. (1929) Geschlechtschromosomen Untersuchungen an Psychiden, *Archive Zellforschungs*, 15, 249.

Goodrich, H. B. (1916) The germ-cells in *Ascaris incurvata, Journal of Experimental Zoology*, 21, 61.

White, M. J. D. (1962) A unique type of sex-chromosome mechanism in an Australian mantid. *Evolution*, 16, 75.

Arnold, J. (1879) Beobachtungen über Kernteilungen in den Zellen der Geschwülste, in Crew, F. A. E., *q.v.*

Painter, T. S. (1921) The Y–chromosome in mammals. *Science*, 53, 503.

Hsu, T. C. (1952) Mammalian chromosomes (I): the karyotype of man. *Journal of Heredity*, 43, 167.

Tijo, J. H. and Levan, A. (1956) The chromosome number of man. *Hereditas*, 42, 1.

Barr, M. L. and Bertram, E. G. (1949) A morphological distinction between the neurones of the male and female and the behaviour of the nucleolar satellite during accelerated nucleoprotein synthesis. *Nature*, 163, 676.

Barr, M. L. (1959) Sex-chromatin and phenotype in man. *Science*, 130, 679.

Piquet, J. (1930) Determination du sexes chez les batraciens: une fonction de la temperature. *Revue Suisse Biologique*, 37, 173.

Ammons, M., (1978) reported in Beam, R., *Daily Mirror*, London, 14 April, pp 16-17.

Lee, E. Y. C. (1964) reported in 'Baby Boy's abdominal cavity contained three foetuses', *Medical News*, London, 12 June 1964.
———————— (1965) reported in *Archives of Diseases in Childhood*, discussed by Dr Alfred Byrne in *Sunday Times*, London, 19 December 1965.

Suomalainen, E. (1950) Parthenogenesis in animals. *Advances in Genetics*, 3, 193.

Morgan, T. H. (1909) Sex-determination and parthenogenesis in Phylloxerans and Aphids. *Science*, 29, 234.
———————— (1915) The predetermination of sex in Phylloxerans and Aphids. *Journal of Experimental Zoology*, 19, 285.

Sprackling, L. S. (1960) The chromosome complement of the developing eggs produced by *Drosophila parthenogenetica. Genetics*, 45, 243.

Olsen, M. W. (1960) Nine-year summary of parthenogenesis in turkeys. *Proceedings of the Society for Experimental Biology*, 105, 279.

Yao, T. S. and Olsen, M. W. (1955) Microscopic observations of parthenogenetic embryonic tissues from virgin turkeys. *Journal of Heredity*, 46, 133.

Reimann, S. P. and Miller, B. J. (1939) Studies of Human Ova (I): Description of artificially induced parthenogenetic activities in one. *Archives of Pathology*, 27, 412-418.

Balfour-Lynn, S. (1956) Parthenogenesis in human beings. *The Lancet*, ii, 1071-1072.

Anon (1955) Parthenogenesis in mammals? (leader) *Lancet*, ii, 967-968.

Kaufman, M. H. (1973) Parthenogenesis in the Mouse, *Nature*, 242, 475-476.

Anon (1955) Virgin Births, front page report, *Sunday Pictorial*, 6 November 1955.

Klinefelter, H. F. Jr., Reifenstein, E. C., and Allbright, F. (1942) A syndrome characterised by gynecomastia, aspermatogenesis without ameydigism, and increased excretion of follicle stimulating hormone. *Journal of Clinical Endocrinology and Metabolism*, 2, 615-627.

Turner, H. H. (1938) A syndrome of infantilism, congenital webbed neck and *cubitus valgus. Endocrinology*, 23, 566-574.

Moore, K. L. (1959) Sex reversal in new-born babies. *Lancet*, i, 217.

Moore, N. W. and Rowson, L. E. A., (1958) Freemartins in the sheep. *Nature*, 182, 1754.

Mittwoch, U. (1973) *Genetics of Sex Differentiation*, Academic Press, London.

Ford, E. H. R., (1973) Abnormalities of the sex chromosomes, in *Human Chromosomes*, Academic Press, London.

Overzier, C. (1961) *Die Intersexualität*, Georg Theime Verlag, Stuttgart.

Kinsey, A. C., Pomeroy, W. B., Martin, C. E., and Gebhard, P. H. (1953) *Sexual Behaviour in the Human Female*, W. B. Saunders Co., Philadelphia.

Wallace, K. and Odell, E. *Love is more than Luck, an Experiment with Scientific Matchmaking*, Funk, New York.

Anon, *Daily Express* report on Bigham case, 11 July 1978, p 6.

Goldschmidt, R. B. (1923) *The mechanism and physiology of sex-determination*, Dakin, W. J., London.

Domm, L. V. (1927) New experiments on ovariotomy and the problem of sex inversion in the fowl. *Journal of Experimental Zoology*, 48, 31.

Chu, E. H. Y., Grumbach, M. M., and Morishima, A. (1960) Karyotypic analysis of a male pseudo-hermaphrodite with the syndrome of feminizing testes. *Journal of Clinical Endocrinology*, 20, 1608.

Jacobs, P. A., Harnden, D. G., Court Brown, W. M., Goldstein, J., Close, H. G., MacGregor, T. N., Maclean, N., and Strong, J. A. (1960) Abnormalities involving the X-chromosome in women, *Lancet*, i, 1213.

Jacobs, P. A., Baikie, A. G., Court Brown, W. M., Forrest, H., Roy, J. R., Stewart, J. S. S. and Lennox, B. (1959) Chromosomal sex in the syndrome of testicular feminization. *Lancet*, ii, 591.

Ashley, D. J. B. (1962) *Human Intersex*, London.

Crew, F. A. E. (1965) Intersexuality: sex-reversal, in *Sex-Determination*, Methuen, London, 55-75.

Altman, D. (1971) *Homosexual Oppression and Liberation*, Outerbridge and Dienstfrey, USA (Angus & Robertson, Australia).

Randell, J. (1973) *Sexual Variations*, Priory Press Ltd, London.

Caprio, F. S. (1957, 6th impression 1966) *Variations in Sexual Behaviour*, John Calder, London.

Allen, C. (1943) *The Treatment of Sexual Abnormalities*, Medical Press, London, 210: 23-25.

Ellis, A. (1955) *Are Homosexuals Necessarily Neurotic?* 'One' Magazine, iii, 4 (April issue).

McCary, J. L. (1971) *Sexual Myths and Fallacies*, Van Nostrand Reinhold, USA.

Fabre, J. H. (1937, 1st edn. 1911) *Social Life in the Insect World*, Penguin, Harmondsworth, England.

Ford, Brian J., (1977) Obscene language and violence on television, *The Listener*, 782, 15 December.

INDEX